Mariners Magical Season

The 2001 Seattle Mariners

MERRIL PRESS

Mariners Magical Season

The 2001 Seattle Mariners
by
Stan Emert and Mike Siegel

MERRIL PRESS

Bellevue, Washington

Mariner Magical Season: The 2001 Seattle Mariners

First Edition
Published by Merril Press
January 2002

Merril Press
Merril Mail Marketing, Inc.
P.O. Box 1682
Bellevue, Washington 98005
425-454-7009
Visit our website for additional copies ($12.00 each) of this title and others at www.merrilpress.com.

Cover Photo: AP/Wide World Photos

ISBN 0-936783-33-8

Library of Congress Card Catalog Card Number 2001098277

PRINTED IN THE UNITED STATES OF AMERICA

Dedication

The baseball season of 2001 was one where we waited with anticipation for every pitch of every game.

If we couldn't go in person we watched on television. If we were at work, we had a radio earpiece permanently implanted. But the boss didn't care because he had one too.

If we were on vacation, we scheduled our activities around watching the Mariner games.

If there was no TV and no radio, we went to the internet and found the score.

We're just fans and we dedicate this book out of appreciation to every member of the 2001 Seattle Mariners.

We thank you for your skill. We thank you for your hard work. But mostly, we thank you for your effort - it was always 100%, and that's what made the 2001 season of OUR Seattle Mariners, so magical.

Stan Emert
and
Mike Siegel

ps. A big huge heartfelt thanks to Monica Tracey for being the best Mariner fan, and making sure the book underscored the lifetime memories of this tremendous Seattle Mariner season.

TABLE OF CONTENTS

Records left wanting

"For of all sad words of tongue or pen, the saddest are these:
'It might have been!'"
*-- **John Greenleaf Whittier** (1807-1892)*

The Seattle Mariners in 2001 had one of the best records in the history of baseball. Only the 1906 Chicago Cubs won as many games in a season – 116. True, the Cubs did it in only 154 games, while the Mariners had 162. But the Cubs got to go to the World Series. The Mariners had a division championship series and a league championship series to face. Baseball competition was fierce in 1906, but it's even more rigorous today.

The M's broke records of all kinds, and had a tremendous fan base of support. Seattle led all of baseball in average attendance, drawing over 3.5 million fans to SAFECO Field. The turnstiles hummed as this year's Mariners broke franchise sellout records by several fold.

The remarkable 2001 Mariners led the American League in team batting average and the major leagues in runs scored. Only the Colorado Rockies had more hits. But we all know that pitching and defense wins games, right? The 2001 Seattle Mariners led baseball with a 3.54 ERA and tied the New York Mets for the most shutouts. The Mariners allowed the fewest hits and only the Mets and Arizona Diamondbacks permitted fewer walks. The Mariners also led the majors in fewest errors.

There were individual leaders, too. Ichiro Suzuki led the majors in batting at .350. He also led in hits with 242, breaking Shoeless Joe Jackson's seven-decade-old rookie record. Ichiro also led the majors in at bats and stolen bases. He was second in the American League to Alex Rodriguez in runs scored. Bret Boone was third. Boone led the American League in RBIs and was second in Total Bases.

Edgar Martinez was second in the American League in On Base

Percentage. Edgar and John Olerud were in the top ten in bases on balls. Mark McLemore, who didn't even have his own position on the field, and Mark Cameron made the American League top ten list in stolen bases.

Freddy Garcia led the American League in ERA. Jamie Moyer was sixth. There were only two 20-game winners in the American League. Moyer was one of them with a 20-6 record. Arthur Rhodes led the majors in being the stingiest to allow hitters on base. Kazu Sasaki was second. Jeff Nelson led the majors in holding batters to the lowest average. Garcia was second in the American League in innings per start. Sasaki was second in the league in Saves.

Several M's had outstanding won-loss records. Moyer, as noted, was 20-6; Garcia - 18-6; Paul Abbott - 17-4; and Aaron Sele - 15-5. Reliever Arthur Rhodes - 8-0. Rookie Joel Pineiro saw limited, but effective action with a 6-2 record, a 2.03 ERA, and he went through 52 right handed hitters before any of them got a hit against him.

Edgar Martinez set Mariner franchise records for hits and RBIs. Bret Boone had a career year in just about every offensive category, and played a Gold Glove second base. Mark McLemore was more versatile than Play-doh, and successful at . . . everything.

As overwhelming as these statistical accomplishments were, the sheer fun at SAFECO Field made it all even better. Certainly one of the best parks in baseball, the entire Seattle area was proud of the 2001 All Star Extravaganza. The Chamber of Commerce pleaded for sunny skies, and sunny it was. Now the entire nation understands that the bluest skies you've ever seen really *are* in Seattle.

The international theme of the 2001 All Star game was never more apparent than on the Mariners. For the first time, a Japanese position player was big in the majors. But he wasn't just impactful, he was a phenomenon. Ichiro Suzuki was simply tremendous. In addition to being a leader in many hitting and baserunning categories, Ichiro proved he was the best in right field in the game. Always stretching, Ichiro is a pioneer who blazed new trails and opened doors for more Japanese players to make the trek to the Americas.

Team chemistry of the 2001 Mariners was outstanding. The players got along with the fans and with each other. There weren't fights in the locker room – at least none that were reported. There didn't seem to be any player with a giant ego overshadowing his talent on the field. The manager didn't throw bases and the hitting and pitching coaches seemed to work as hard as the players.

It was a magical season, but there was a dark cloud. The Mariners failed to win the World Series. In fact, they didn't even get that far. In the postseason, the hitters didn't hit, and the pitchers didn't make the pitches at crunch time. Of the eight teams that made it to postseason play, only one team wins its last game, and it seemed fitting that Seattle would be that team. But "fitting" isn't baseball.

The players and fans are disappointed that the season ended in the American League Championship series. They should be. This was a great team, and it will be another 162 regular season games before the Mariners get a chance again.

But a season such as the one the Seattle Mariners had in 2001 should be savored. The frustration in the postseason can't sweep away the magic of the regular season. It was so much pure fun. Whether it was Dave Niehaus saying "My oh My!" or the "Did you see that catch?" from the crowd as Mike Cameron or Stan Javier robbed some poor opposing batter of a hit. The 32 players who donned the Mariner uniform provided memories that will stay with us for a lifetime.

To forever detail that wonderful season, we bring you *Mariners Magical Season: The 2001 Seattle Mariners.*

The Voices of the Mariners

Dave Niehaus

Ron Fairly

Rick Rizz

The Seattle Mariners are blessed with one of the finest broadcast teams in all of sports. **Dave Niehaus** is the dean of the staff, and has been with Seattle baseball since the beginning in 1977. Known for his ability to make even the mundane exciting, Niehaus is among the top two or three sportscasters in the world.

Rick Rizz is back for his second tour of duty with the Mariners, having been with Seattle from 1983 to 1991, and spent 1992-1994 with the Detroit Tigers. His unyielding loyalty brought him home to the blue skies of Seattle in 1995 where he has been a Mariner voice since then.

Ron Fairly is the baseball expert of the group. He was a a Los Angeles Dodger bonus baby and major league player from 1958 to 1978. Known for his witticisms, Fairly gives Seattle's broadcast team an all star at every position.

Chapter One

2000 - a Warmup for 2001

"Experience is a hard teacher because she gives the test first, and the lesson afterwards."
– Vern Law, Pittsburgh Pirates pitcher (1950-1967)

The 2000 Mariners were the most successful in the 31 year history of major league baseball in Seattle. A 91-71 regular season; second place in the American League West; and a wild-card playoff berth showed that the loss of the biggest star the franchise had ever had, Ken Griffey, Jr., the past year and the loss of Randy Johnson the year before couldn't keep the team down.

After a sweep of the Chicago White Sox in the AL Division series, the M's faced the dreaded Yankees. Seattle gave a gallant effort in the league championship series, but the reigning World Series kings from the year before and the year before proved they were the best team in baseball . . . again.

Despite the successes of the 2000 season, Seattle's year was filled with the ominous veil of baseball's best player leaving the team for the second year in a row. Arguably, Griffey was the best of the best in 1999. And arguably, the Mariners' Alex Rodriguez earned the title of "the best in the game" in 2000.

Griffey's tumultuous exit left a bad taste in the mouths of Mariner fans. Not a day went by in the 2000 season that fans didn't fear a Griffey replay with A-Rod.

Regardless of all the backroom concerns, the first full season of SAFECO Field, and the first full season of Pat Gillick as General Manager was ready to be played.

Fitting the team to SAFECO
After trading Junior to Cincinnati, GM Pat Gillick went for pitching

during the off-season. He landed some big catches. Perennial double-digit winner, Aaron Sele, a Puget Sound native, chose Seattle after Baltimore's muff in a free agent deal. The hope was that Sele would give the M's innings deep into nearly each game.

To bolster the bullpen, Gillick picked up flame throwing lefty, Arthur Rhodes. And to round out the relief corps, the Mariners added Japanese All Star Kazuhiro Sasaki. At 6'4" 220 lbs., the 32 year-old Sasaki, with over 200 saves in Japan, was determined to prove he belonged in Major League Baseball.

Trying to get more pop from first base, Gillick landed hometown hero and former Interlake High School (Bellevue, WA) standout John Olerud. This nearly $6 million man carried his own gold glove and was a career .300 hitter.

There was a huge question lurking about Edgar Martinez. The man who wrote the book on how-to-be-a-designated hitter had shown signs of slowing down as 1999 came to an end. Would he be able to see enough good pitches without Junior in the lineup? Could he still handle those pitches? Had his bat and legs slowed with age so that 2000 would be Edgar's farewell tour? Only time would tell.

The new patrol officer in centerfield for the Mariners would be Mike Cameron. Mike Who? Centerfield had been a position owned by Number 24, the Kid. It was a position where the Mariners owned gold gloves and captured an annual All Star spot. Would the Mariner fans ever accept someone else playing the middle of the outfield? That question would be answered soon enough.

The 2000 regular season
It was a cold Friday night at SAFECO; April 7, 2000, and the unwelcome Yankees were in town. Seattle clung to a 6-3 lead when Derek Jeter came to bat. Already with one homer in the game, Jeter sent a screaming line drive to the deepest part of the park. For the past decade the fleet-footed Ken Griffey, Jr. would nonchalantly chase down just about everything hit near or far. But now that position belonged to the unknown Mike Cameron.

The near capacity crowd watched Jeter's drive flying out of the stands only to see Cameron make a flying leap, reaching his outstretched glove over the top of the fence and snatch the would-be home-run. Go back to the bench, Jeter. Cameron made the play!

The fans went wild. They gave Cameron a standing ovation. Then he got another standing ovation when he came up to bat the next inning. Then he got yet another standing ovation after he struck out. Lou Piniella said "I don't think I've ever seen anyone get an ovation for striking out." The fans welcomed Mike Cameron, their new center-fielder well on his way to filling the giant shoes he'd inherited as he became a hometown favorite.

Other matters were established early in that season. Kazuhiro Sasaki showed he could really pitch! There was no question as to who would be the closer. Jose Mesa would become a set-up man for Kazu.

As the season progressed, and the Mariners crept to the top of the standings, the influence of new hitting coach Gerald Perry was apparent. Mariner batters exhibited a new patience – a new focus on making opposing pitcher throw good pitches. The 2000 team would break the franchise record for bases on balls, and won three of every four games when they drew more walks than strikeouts.

Seattle was on the lookout for speed and found it in all-time base-stealing king, Rickey Henderson. Though his skills had deteriorated somewhat, the 41 year-old still had the savvy to create havoc for opposing pitchers, even if he was a bit of an adventure in the outfield. But SAFECO Field requires good outfielders because the Mariners' pitching staff was built around making hitters swing. Rickey's fielding, and his failing bat, led to his release at the end of the season.

Young pitchers John Halama and Gil Meche showed promise in 2000. Halama was 4-0 in May alone. Gil Meche was throwing hard and looked like the next Bob Gibson at times. But Halama lost his control and Meche hurt his shoulder. Halama even saw some AAA action in 2001. Meche didn't see any action at all due to his injury.

The July 31, 2000, trading deadline was an act of futility for General Manager Pat Gillick. Team management had made the early season decision that Alex Rodriguez would stay a Mariner throughout the year. The team was the division leader but needed more hitting, especially after July 14, when A-Rod sprained his right knee which would hamper the All Star shortstop the rest of the season.

The Rodriguez injury made Pat Gillick's search for more hitting even more important. First baseman John Olerud offered to go to the outfield, allowing Edgar to take over at first base. This would allow the Mariners to search for a hitter regardless of position. Piniella didn't like that idea, though, remembering that past adventures by Edgar with a glove led to the disabled list.

The big catch the Mariners wanted was Kansas City outfielder Johnny Damon. The Royals replied to Gillick that Damon was not going to be traded. Other potent bats, such as Juan Gonzalez, John Vander Wal, Ricky Ledee, Richie Sexson, David Segui and Rondell White whetted Seattle's appetite.

The prime bait being cast was Brett Tomko and John Halama, but the pitchers most teams wanted were Ryan Anderson and Joel Pineiro. Tomko was relieved at remaining a Mariner and said "I'm in the clear. I don't really have to think about it anymore."

Ultimately, the Mariners acquired left-handed hitting outfielder Al Martin in exchange for utility player John Mabry and minor league pitcher Tom Davey.

In a pivotal game at Yankee stadium on August 29th, a slumping Seattle had won only two of its previous 15 games. Andy Pettitte, 16-7, started for New York. Jamie Moyer, 0-5 with a 10.40 ERA in his previous six games, started for the M's.

After surviving early game wildness, Moyer settled down, but left the game trailing 3-0. Meanwhile, Pettitte was churning Mariner hitters like a meat grinder. He carried a no-hitter into the 6th inning, and had given up only three hits until the 8th when he seemed to tire. It took four consecutive one-out singles for the M's to score their first run and load the bases for Alex Rodriguez. The Yankees'6'8" reliever, Jeff Nelson, entered and promptly struck out A-Rod.

Edgar Martinez came to the plate, as the Mariners looked like they were going to lose their 14th of the last 16 games. On a 2-0 count, though, Edgar hit a drive toward right field. In Dave Niehaus's words "Get out the rye bread and mustard, Grandma. It's grand salami time!" Martinez' home run was his 32nd and he was leading the majors with 127 RBIs. Edgar called this hit one of the biggest of his career, and Manager Lou Piniella said this game was the team's biggest win of the season.

Seattle rebounded from its August slump, but Oakland caught fire and won the division with a 91-70 record. The Mariners finished 91-71, with the difference being an Athletics' game with Tampa Bay that was called off due to Hurricane Gordon. Oakland didn't have to play the game because even if they had lost, the A's would still be division champs due to head-to-head competition with the M's. Oakland had won the season series with Mariners, 9 games to 4.

The playoffs were set with Oakland versus the Yankees, and Seattle versus the White Sox.

American League Division Series Mariners vs. White Sox
Seattle beat the White Sox as fast as you drive through a town with no traffic lights. It was almost as if there was a destiny that the Mariners were going to ascend to the next level. Even though the White Sox had won their division with an excellent 95-67 record, four games better than the Mariners, the White Sox pitching was too poor to compete with Seattle.

In Game 1, the game went to the 10th tied at 4. Mike Cameron led off the M's half with a single. Lou Piniella then called time and slowly ambled to first base to talk with the Mariners' centerfielder. Piniella claims he talked about the stock market. Cameron said they talked about drinks after the game.

Regardless, Edgar Martinez stepped to the plate and hit a homer to put the Mariners ahead to stay.

In Game 2, Paul Abbott gave the M's a strong five innings, and yielded to Rhodes, Mesa and Sasaki who preserved a 5-2 win. Jay Buhner homered for the M's.

In Game 3, the first playoff game at SAFECO Field, in front of over 48,000 fans, the Mariners completed the sweep of the White Sox. Great pitching by Aaron Sele and the Mariner bullpen limited the hard-hitting White Sox to one run, but Seattle could fare no better until the bottom of the 9th.

John Olerud led off the 9th with a vicious line drive hitting off the pitcher. Scrambling to recover, White Sox reliever Kelly Wunsch threw the ball past first base enabling Olerud to take second. Rickey Henderson came in to pinch run for Olerud.

Stan Javier then bunted Henderson to third. The White Sox pitched carefully to David Bell, who ended with a walk. Then, clutch hitting catcher Joe Oliver was due up, but Piniella sent Carlos Guillen to the plate instead. This was Guillen's first appearance of the playoffs.

As Steve Kelly, noted sports columnist wrote:
"The instructions [to Guillen] were simple. The play was diaboli -
cally hard. Push the ball to the right side. Force Chicago first
baseman Frank Thomas to make a play at the plate on Rickey
Henderson, probably the best base runner in the game's history."
(Seattle Times, October 7, 2000)

Guillen followed the instructions perfectly. Henderson scored standing up, and the Mariners extinguished Chicago, 1-2-3.

American League Championship Series – Seattle vs. Yankees
As Seattle was disposing of the White Sox, many expected the
Yankees to sweep Oakland. But Oakland wasn't as cooperative as
New York hoped, and it took all five games. The Yankees barely
hung on to get into the championship series.

Seattle flew to the Big Apple to meet New York. In Game 1 at Yankee
Stadium, Freddy Garcia pitched a gem for 6 2/3 innings. On the other
side of the field, Denny Neagle was matching him, giving up only
two runs, including an A-Rod solo shot. But the Mariners' relievers
– Rhodes, Paniagua and Sasaki threw 2 1/3 innings of nearly perfect
baseball to preserve the victory for the M's.

Game 2, again at Yankee Stadium, was progressing the same way as
the first game. Good pitching; no hitting from both teams. The
Yankees sent Orlando "El Duque" Hernandez to the mound and the
M's pitched Brooklynite John Halama.

The Mariners had managed to ooze out one run against Hernandez,
and the score stood at 1-0 Mariners going into the bottom of the 8th.
Halama had pitched the first six innings, and Jose Paniagua got New
York out in the 7th. A combination of playoff-savvy hitting by the
Yankees and the Mariners' poor pitching and fielding miscues,
opened the floodgates. The defending champions crossed the plate
seven times, and finished with a 7-1 victory.

To many fans, Game 2 seemed to seal the Mariners' fate. After all,
Seattle had only scored three runs against New York's number 3 and
4 starters. How would they do against Clemens and Pettitte?

In Game 3, at SAFECO, Andy Pettitte and Aaron Sele were ready for
battle. The Yankees brought their bats. The Mariners didn't. Game
over. Yanks won 8-2.

In Game 4, the Mariners sent Abbott to face Clemens. Clemens pitched an absolute masterpiece. At age 38, the artful Roger struck out 15 batters, allowed only one hit (and that in the 7th inning), and permitted a mere three baserunners. After the game, Edgar Martinez said he had never seen Clemens pitch better.

There was a typical event for a Clemens' pitching performance. An earbuzzer from Clemens to the M's' Alex Rodriguez in the 1st inning brought a swift response. The Yankees' Jorge Posada was sent to the ground by Paul Abbott in the second, nearly prompting a brawl by the two teams. Instead, Yankee manager Joe Torre and Seattle manager Lou Piniella just yelled at each other, and seemed satisfied that each pitcher and each team had spoken with high and tight fastballs.

In Game 5, there was another sellout crowd at SAFECO to see a rematch of game 1 - Freddy Garcia against Denny Neagle. The feeling at the game was one of almost admission that the Yankees were the better team, but the Mariners were going to give it one more shot.

Garcia was clearly up to the task, and so was the bullpen. And the Mariners' bats came alive. A-Rod hit a two-run single in the 5th and Edgar and Olerud hit back-to-back dingers.

The Mariners closed the series gap to 3-2, Yankees lead, with the remaining games to be played in New York.

Game 6 ended the season for the Mariners, but not without putting a scare into the Yankees. The pitching duel was John Halama against Orlando Hernandez, and the Mariners scored two runs in the first on back-to-back doubles by A-Rod and Edgar. The M's added two more in the 4th on a homer by Carlos Guillen.

But in the Yankees' half of the 4th, the home team quickly scored three runs before Brett Tomko could be brought in to calm the storm. A Mariners' rally in the 6th was snuffed by a superb defensive play by Yankees shortstop Derek Jeter.

The game stayed at Mariners 4, Yankees 3, until the 7th, when Jose Paniagua started the inning for Seattle. Two of the first three batters reached base, and David Justice came up to the plate. Arthur Rhodes relieved Paniagua – a good percentage matchup for Seattle. But Justice, known for hitting lefthanders, parked a 95-mile an hour fastball from Rhodes into the upper deck in right field giving the Yankees a lead they wouldn't relinquish.

The game was over. The Mariners'best season - the season of 2000 - was history. Most of the questions from early in the season had been answered, except for the A-Rod question.

After the final game, Rodriguez and Piniella reminisced in the clubhouse. "I hugged him and told him I gave it everything I had. And that just wasn't enough," said the Mariners' hard-hitting shortstop. There were hugs and tears, and "see you in Arizona," but for Pat Gillick, the 2001 season had already begun.

Chapter Two

Over the Winter:
Restocking the Shelves

*"Every winter, baseball holds an auction. Every year, it operates
on the 'greater fool' theory. The biggest fool sets the market."*

-- Thomas Boswell, Washington Post, December 12, 2000

The playoffs of 2000 weren't even over before the discussions
for 2001 had already begun. During the two preceding years,
the Mariners had lost one of baseball's best pitchers, Randy
Johnson, and one of baseball's best players, Ken Griffey, Jr. Both of
these superstars left Seattle under less-than-friendly circumstances
which soured many Puget Sound fans on baseball.

The cloud of "Stay-Rod" hung over the Mariners all season. If it
weren't for Alex Rodriguez and Mariner management agreeing to
play ball first and discuss contracts later, it is likely that the entire
season of 2000 would have been littered with negotiations, not baseball. But with the Yankees' victory in the ALCS, A-Rod had to begin
answering the question he refused to answer all season long.

Rodriguez was a superstar in every definition of the word. In five full
seasons with the Mariners, he averaged 37 homers, 115 RBIs, 122
runs, while hitting .315. He was one of the best fielding shortstops in
baseball. Further, his personal charisma made Alex one of the most
desired spokespersons in the game. His agent, Scott Boras, had the
sole job of securing the best deal for his client. How "best" was
defined for A-Rod was yet to be determined.

But first, Lou
Even before dealing with how to re-sign Alex, the Mariners had to
consider the possibility of losing manager Lou Piniella. The world

champion manager in 1990, and the Mariners' all time winningest manager was a free agent. Lou's home is in Tampa and he was hot property for general managers in search of a field general. The GM most aggressively seeking Piniella was Cincinnati's Jim Bowden.

The Mariners reportedly had offered Piniella a three year deal worth $6.5 million but he sought permission to talk with the Reds. The Mariners said "OK," but nervously wished Bowden couldn't pry the dollars loose from the iron-fisted Cincinnati ownership.

By the end of October, the attractiveness of Cincinnati was apparent. It was the place where Lou got his World Series ring and it was where Griffey went. Some may say that wasn't a positive because of Junior's childish and potentially team-destructive behavior. But Piniella was one person who knew how to harness Griffey's immense talent and win with him on the team.

On October 31, Piniella and his agent, Alan Nero, gave the Reds 24 hours to issue an offer. Cincinnati knew of the millions the Mariners dangled to keep their popular skipper. The Reds, according to Piniella, chose not to make an offer. Lou was happy to stay in Seattle.

The retention of superstar manager Piniella was considered by many to be the best hope to keep superstar shortstop Alex Rodriguez. After all, it was expected that several teams, including the Mariners, were going to be able to meet Boras's financial demands. It would be the intangibles that would sway A-Rod's decision, or so the fans thought.

Shortly before the playoffs with the White Sox, Boras complimented Seattle on the conduct of the season. "They've handled this year absolutely perfectly." He added that the M's acquisition of first baseman John Olerud, and pitchers Arthur Rhodes, Kazu Sasaki, and Aaron Sele was part of the Mariners' perfection. Boras had previously stated that Piniella was one of the top managers in the game.

Having said all the niceties, Boras indicated that Rodriguez's "confidence level in the Seattle organization is there."

A-Rod's agent then set the tone for what the negotiations would be about: "We don't want clubs to spend a lot of money on Alex and then not have it to spend on other needs." He added that Rodriguez was looking for a long term deal with a team that had the ability to win every game. "For one thing, we have to make sure the club Alex signs with remains competitive."

Summing it all up, Boras said the three aspects of the decision would be money, ability to win, and intangibles. "Alex has been happy in Seattle, and my basic interest is to see he remains happy."

As the postseason progressed, speculation about A-Rod became almost as big a story as the playoff games themselves. Sports columnist Steve Kelly, wrote:

"He wants to win. He wants the rings his Yankee friend, Derek Jeter, already has. He wants to play a major part in every October. . . . And if Rodriguez stays, they are guaranteed to remain contenders. He's playing for a franchise that is rich with pitching prospects; a franchise that has one of the best farm systems in the game. If all he wants is the fences moved in, say 7 feet, the Mariners should be accommodating. If he wants the roof closed a few more days every season so the ball will carry better, close the roof. Is he stays, Rodriguez can have all the money, the fame, even the chances at the rings, he could have anyplace else."

[Seattle Times, October 13, 2000]

Then the reports started as to who would be the top contenders for A-Rod's services. Both the Mets and the Yankees were considered, but Mel Antonen of *USA Today* said that the top three were: Seattle, Anaheim and the Chicago White Sox. Antonen added *"Money is a low priority for A-Rod. He wants to take a new team to a World Series championship." [USA Today, November 10, 2000]*

Antonen reasoned that the Angels had strong pitching. If Mo Vaughn were traded, there would be cash available for A-Rod. The White Sox were rising stars and Chicago was a market that treated superstars well.

Finally Antonen indicated that the Mariners might be a good place for A-Rod to remain for three more years, and then test the free agent waters. The extra years would be good ones, adding to his value.

These teams were then dismissed: Mets – they have to rebuild the pitching staff first; Yankees – Who would switch positions? Rodriguez or Jeter?; Braves – pitching is aging and will cost bundles to replace; Dodgers – directionless organization; Rockies – What pitcher would go there?; Red Sox – Nomar, No A-Rod; Blue Jays – Just spent huge dollars on Carlos Delgado, and couldn't afford that type of money again; Diamondbacks – too much money in aging free agents who would have to be replaced. The Texas Rangers were not mentioned.

Meanwhile, Scott Boras had prepared a 65 page dossier about Alex. Boras made unabashed projections that Rodriguez would end his career at age 40, having achieved nearly 4,000 hits, nearly 800 home-runs, and having stolen over 500 bases. The Boras book may have stroked the superstar's ego or may have provided a job for a Boras crony. The dossier's worth has yet to be explained.

In the meantime, the M's re-opened the pursuit of Kansas City's Johnny Damon, and inquired about the availability of St. Louis' Ray Lankford. And in a move not widely reported, Seattle exercised its option two years early to pick up another year of the services of Kazu Sasaki. The ownership presence of Hiroshi Yamauchi, the Nintendo of Japan Chairman, greatly influenced Sasaki's decision to come to Seattle. Yamauchi was adamant about increasing the visibility and popularity of Mariner baseball in Japan.

Sasaki wanted the company of his countrymen. In November, while on a tour with other professional players in Japan, Sasaki went to din-ner with Japan's best position player, Ichiro Suzuki. The Japanese system allows players to be available for bid at certain times to American teams, and Ichiro's number was coming up soon. Yamauchi had mentioned the outfielder's name to Lincoln, but Ichiro had already been to spring training with Seattle several years before.

Bring in the fences
With Thanksgiving 2000 only a few weeks away, the rancor over A-Rod exploded caused by Rodriguez's own comments. In response to a question about the fences at Seattle's ballpark, Rodriguez said "With or without me, they [Mariners] have to bring them in substan-tially – to make the game better at SAFECO. I couldn't care less either way, but it's not good for baseball."

Rodriguez's protests were noted on the now defunct website, *www.athletesdirect.com*:
"I'd say the fences should be moved in 20 feet in the power alleys, 5-10 feet in center and 10-12 feet down the lines. We can't even hit it to the warning track, and the track is 20 feet. . . . If you hit it 430 feet, it should be a home run, not an out like it is now."

Alex had an unusual grasp of numbers, at least when referring to dis-tance. Here's the straight scoop:

Field Dimension Comparisons
SAFECO Field: 331 feet LF; 390' in left center; 405' CF; 387' in right center; and 327'RF

Ballpark at Arlington (Texas Rangers) 332 feet LF; 390'in left center; 407'CF; 381'in right center; and 325' RF.

Turner Field (Atlanta Braves): 330 feet LF; 380'in left center; 401' CF; 390'in right center; and 320'RF.

Alex's comments seemed to signal a war of words being waged with Mariner management. Upon hearing of Rodriguez's statements, Howard Lincoln, Mariner Chairman and CEO, publicly wondered which Alex Rodriguez was speaking to Seattle. Was it the Alex who privately indicated that SAFECO Field was perfect? Or was it the Alex criticizing the park, perhaps setting up Mariner management for blame if A-Rod chose to leave Seattle?

All of this notwithstanding, Boras claimed that SAFECO Field was "not a detriment" to A-Rod staying in Seattle.

Ichiro comes to America
Back in Japan, the bids for the right to negotiate with Ichiro Suzuki, known only as "Ichiro," were in, and the Mariners had won. Seattle paid $13 million to the Orix Blue Wave, Ichiro's team, just to be able to talk with Japan's best player.

A 5-foot-9, 165-pound right fielder, Ichiro won seven straight Pacific League batting titles in Japan, beginning in 1994. His last year was one of his best for the Blue Wave. He finished with an impressive .387 average, 12 home runs, 73 runs batted in and 21 stolen bases. In nine seasons in Japan, he hit .353 with 118 homers and 529 RBI.

In stark contrast to the Alex Rodriguez situation, the negotiations with Ichiro were as quick as a dash from the batter's box to first base. On November 18, 2000, Ichiro signed a three-year contract with Seattle worth about $18 million. The signing was historic in both the United States and Japan. *The East*, a publication based in Tokyo, commented about Ichiro:
> *"A Mark McGwire he's not. He would be David against the Goliath of MLB pitchers. . . . If Ichiro succeeds, others will follow. The nation's eyes will be on him. His will be a sports story worthy of the new century." [The East November/December 2000.]*

Just after the Mariners signed Ichiro, Texas surfaced publicly for the first time in the A-Rod sweepstakes. Since Carlos Delgado has signed with Toronto for $17 million a year, it was expected that Rodriguez would demand $20 million annually. Rangers' owner and media mogul Tom Hicks was one of the few owners considered willing and wealthy enough to meet A-Rod's price tag.

Nelson signs

In early December, the Mariners received a Christmas present. Jeff Nelson, a key setup reliever in the lethal Yankee bullpen for the past five years, was bringing his 95 mile-an-hour fastball to Seattle. Nelson was a Mariner from 1992-1995 and had now returned home. Signing a three-year deal worth over $3 million a season, Nelson indicated that Seattle was his number one choice. He added some advice about A-Rod. Nellie's words now seem prophetic:

> *"I'd love to see Alex come back. It doesn't take one guy to make a champion; it takes 25 guys. If he goes anywhere else, he'd be starting from scratch instead of continuing what they've done here. Hopefully he doesn't make the same mistake [Griffey] made by wanting to be traded. Hopefully he makes the smart decision by wanting to come back. . . . If Alex leaves and all of a sudden they [Seattle] win a World Series, he's going to kick himself."*

Pat Gillick proudly celebrated the signing of Nelson as proof that the Mariners would have a dominant bullpen with Jeff Nelson, Arthur Rhodes and Kazu Sasaki. As he took that information to Florida for a December 7 meeting with Rodriguez, Gillick announced that SAFECO Field's fences were remaining as they were.

The Mariners took another tactic in the A-Rod negotiations. While seeking to sign the superstar to a long term deal, Seattle offered Rodriguez arbitration for a one year contract. But there was true optimism expressed by Gillick as he mentioned that shortstop was Carlos Guillen's natural position. And Guillen, who had played third base in 2000, was ready to wear his glove at shortstop once again.

Following the December 7 meeting between Rodriguez, Scott Boras, and Pat Gillick, the Mariners released a guarded statement that Alex had expressed an interest in returning to Seattle. At the same time, it was reported that Boras's demand for A-Rod was a 12 year, $20 million/year contract, with an escalator clause to keep Rodriguez baseball's highest paid player and an escape clause if the club was not progressing to his satisfaction.

Buhner returns

Back in Seattle, the popular Jay Buhner signed a free agency deal for a substantial reduction in pay. The one year contract was laden with incentives. The oft-injured slugger had 26 homers and 82 RBI in just 112 games in 2000.

Rodriguez negotiations end

Following the Mariners/A-Rod meeting of Thursday, December 7, the White Sox, Braves and Rangers made pitches to Boras and his client over the weekend. The Mariners were expecting to meet with Alex early the following week. Although Seattle management had left Florida, they were all on call to return to complete discussions to bring Rodriguez back to the only team he had ever known.

No new meeting would ever happen, though, because the duo of Tom Hicks and Alex Rodriguez shocked baseball by signing a $252 million 10-year contract on December 11. A-Rod (a/k/a "Pay-Rod") had become a quarter-of-a-billion dollar man. A surprised Howard Lincoln called Hicks a "fool" and said the Mariners were used by Boras and Alex as a "stalking horse."

In search of a bat

In the previous two years, 85 home runs and 230 RBI per year departed the Mariners'lineup care of Griffey and A-Rod. The prime replacement so far had been the risky Ichiro, whose skills were unquestioned . . . in Japan. So, Pat Gillick needed to find a new hitter to fill the giant hole in Seattle's arsenal.

Trade rumors involving Johnny Damon persisted. Minnesota's Matt Lawton and Boston's Troy O'Leary were added to that list. Other hard hitting outfielders, Juan Gonzalez, Jeffrey Hammonds and Reggie Sanders were still available. But Gillick was having none of them. He wanted the team's new bat to be an infielder.

Phil Nevin, 3B, of the San Diego Padres, was the target. A 30 home run, 100+ RBI, .300 hitter, Nevin would round out a strong offensive infield with Olerud at first, Bell at second, and Guillen at short.

Other infield candidates in Gillick's sights included shortstop free-agent, Mike Bordick, and the Rangers' shortstop, Royce Clayton. Neither provided the offense Gillick was seeking, though. St. Louis third-baseman Fernando Tatis was also a possibility.

Another mentioned free agent infielder was the run of the mill-hitting

Bret Boone. A former Mariner, the 31 year-old second baseman was a career .255 batter and had averaged 21 homers in his previous three seasons. Rumors of past disharmony between Boone and Manager Lou Piniella were dismissed as Boone's "youthful exuberance."

In 1993, Boone and pitcher Erik Hanson had been traded from the Mariners to Cincinnati for catcher Dan Wilson and reliever Bobby Ayala. At the end of the 1998 season, Boone was traded to the Atlanta Braves. Boone's 1999 with the Braves was a good one. He posted personal bests in at-bats, stolen bases, doubles, runs scored and a hitting streak. He hit .573 in the World Series against the Yankees.

But he and Atlanta parted company after the season, and Boone found a new home in San Diego. His 2000 season as the Padres' regular second baseman was going to be Boone's best. He had 19 homers, 74 RBI, and was batting .326 when his season ended with a knee injury on August 26.

A free agent, Boone tested the waters. Despite his improving numbers over his past three seasons, his knee injury caused questions. His reputation of volatility also hung over his head, and at the age of 31, betting the farm on Bret Boone was something no team would do. Tampa Bay, though, was vying for Boone's services.

The Mariners did bet $3.25 million on Bret for one year, with an incentive for him to earn another million. Gillick called Boone a proven hitter with "a little pop" and a solid defensive player.

At the same time, just before Christmas, the M's re-signed the dependable Tom Lampkin. A local Bishop Blanchet High School graduate, Lampkin was a clutch hitter who would be one of three catchers in Spring Training.

Nervous fans as Spring Training approaches
With the new year, a poor Sonic basketball season forced Seattle sports fans to turn to the Mariners for hope. But the winter was one of discontent. Fans'complaints were getting louder that Bret Boone and Ichiro Suzuki were "nice" additions, but not likely to upgrade the team over the past playoff year. Steve Kelly of the *Seattle Times* noted that the Mariners hadn't seemed to make serious attempts to sign Johnny Damon (traded to the A's), Juan Gonzalez (signed by Indians), Manny Ramirez (signed by Red Sox), or Charles Johnson (signed by White Sox). Even the world champ Yankees improved with the addition of pitcher Mike Mussina. Kelly added that *"The*

best teams in the American got better. Every team, that is, except the Mariners." [Seattle Times, January 10, 2001]

The negotiations for Phil Nevin were not bearing fruit. Mariner salaries neared the $80 million mark, and in late January the rumor mill had it that Sammy Sosa may be coming to Seattle. Gillick was quick to show caution, though, indicating that he was interested in the long-term, and Sosa was likely a one-year fix. Moreover, club president Chuck Armstrong said that the team would not be offering "Alex" money to Sammy.

In February, just before the pitchers and catchers were due to report, to camp, GM Gillick compared the Mariners to the new super bowl champion Baltimore Ravens. Like the Ravens, the Mariners were a team without "marquee players," said Gillick.

Piniella agreed with Gillick that there was no dominant Mariner, but disagreed with what Chairman/CEO Howard Lincoln was touting. Lincoln, excited about the team's new Japanese player, stated: "If we're right on Ichiro, and I think we are, he will perform in the same way as Sasaki, and eventually we will have a legitimate superstar."

Upon hearing Lincoln's pronouncement, Lou showed a look of surprise, and said the "superstar" label was too much. "He's going to be a solid player, but a superstar is overdoing it right now."

Piniella also talked about the Mariners'lineup. The leadoff spot was looking to be either strike-out prone Mike Cameron or the disappointing Al Martin. Other possibilities were Carlos Guillen or Stan Javier, or some combination thereof. Ichiro would bat third; Edgar cleanup; followed by Olerud. The manager added he was looking for better plate appearances from Dan Wilson and David Bell.

Jamie Moyer became trade bait. The Mariners were overstocked with starting pitching: Ryan Anderson, Paul Abbott, Freddy Garcia, John Halama, Gil Meche, Moyer, Aaron Sele and Bret Tomko. A proven veteran, the Mariners had won an incredible 66% of the games Moyer had started. Although not a number one starter, the left-handed Moyer could help any club.

But the other teams coveted the young arms - Garcia, Anderson and Meche – even more. Gillick termed them all, even Meche who was likely to be out with an injury until the All-Star break, "untouchable." If the Mariners were going to land a bat, it would be with Moyer,

Tomko, Halama or Jose Paniagua.

Trade talks halted for the time being. The winter was gone and all the clubs were preparing for pitchers and catchers to report. No Mariner trade for a hitter had happened. Getting that extra bat was going to be Pat Gillick's main focus as the sunshine, hot weather and Spring Training arrived.

Chapter Three

Spring Training

"People ask me what I do in winter when there's no baseball. I'll tell you what I do. I stare out the window and wait for spring."
-- Rogers (Rajah) Hornsby, Hall-of Famer pl. 1915-1937

Players invited to Spring Training are separated into several categories. One group is the returnees who the team expects to play a big role in the upcoming season, such as Freddy Garcia or Mike Cameron. Another group includes the young players, who the major league team wants to give a shot at big league pitchers or hitters, but who are not expected to go north with the team in April. Examples of these for the Mariners were Greg Wooten and Willie Bloomquist. Another group is composed normally of veterans, who are trying out with the team hoping to catch a manager's eye. Seattle had a few of these – Norm Charlton and Carlos Baerga in particular. Yet another group are the injured players who are on the roster, but protected due to their injured status. Gil Meche and Chris Widger were two players on this list who never saw an inning on the field in 2001 either in Spring Training, during the regular season or the playoffs. Their chance won't come again until 2002.

Seattle Mariners Spring Training Roster 2001
* 40 man roster ^ non-roster invitee

Abbott, Paul (P) *	Halama, John (P) *	Pineiro, Joel (P) *
Alexander, Chad (OF) ^	Grabowski, Jason (3B) *	Podsednik, Scott (OF) ^
Alexander, Manny (IF) ^	Guillen, Carlos (SS) *	Ramsay, Robert (P) *
Anderson, Ryan (P) ^	Hodges, Kevin (P) *	Rhodes, Arthur (P) *
Baerga, Carlos (IF) ^	Horner, Jim (C) ^	Sanders, Anthony (OF) *
Barthol, Blake (C) ^	Javier, Stan (OF) *	Sasaki, Kazu (P) *
Bell, David (IF) *	Kaye, Justin (P) *	Sele, Aaron (P) *
Bloomquist, Willie (IN) ^	Lampkin, Tom (C) *	Soriano, Rafael (P) *
Boone, Bret (2B) *	Martin, Al (OF) *	Stark, Denny (P) *
Buhner, Jay (LF/1B) *	Martinez, Edgar (DH) *	Suzuki, Ichiro (RF) *
Cameron, Mike (CF) *	McLemore, Mark (IF) *	Tomko, Bret (P) *
Charlton, Norm (P) ^	Meche, Gil (P) *	Vasquez, Ramon (IF) ^
Christianson, Ryan (C) ^	Meyer, Jake (P) *	Watson, Mark (P) *
Falkenborg, Brian (P) ^	Moreta, Ramon (OF) ^	Widger, Chris (C) *
Franklin, Ryan (P) *	Moyer, Jamie (P) *	Wilson, Dan (C) *
Fruto, Emiliano (P) ^	Nelson, Jeff (P) *	Wooten, Greg (P) *
Fuentes, Brian (P) *	Olerud, John (1B) *	Zimmerman, Jordan (P) *
Garcia, Freddy (P) *	Paniagua, Jose (P) *	
Gipson, Charles (OF) *	Perez, Antonio (IF) ^	

February 20 was the big day for Mariner pitchers and catchers to find the rays of the hot Arizona sun. The big news in camp was about a lefty reliever coming out of retirement, asking for the chance to pitch again. When Seattle took over the farm team in his hometown of San Antonio, Norm "The Sheriff" Charlton called the M's and said he wanted to play. As long as he could still get people out, the Mariners would be happy to have another lefthander in the bullpen. Besides, Lou Piniella had managed Charlton at Cincinnati and in Seattle when both those teams went to the postseason. The Sheriff would be given every chance to make the team.

Charlton reported that first day of camp in the best shape he had been in years. Pitching Coach Bryan Price was impressed and commented he could tell Charlton had the mechanics of a power pitcher.

The Sheriff also brought his twisted wit to the team. Upon seeing Edgar Martinez and Jay Buhner running in the outfield, Charlton commented it was the first time he had ever seen "fossils move."

As Norm Charlton was trying to just make the team, Bret Tomko was trying to gain a spot in Seattle's starting rotation. But the trade rumors of the winter became the trade rumors of the spring. The latest gossip had Tomko going to San Diego as part of a Phil Nevin deal. Tomko's parents live in San Diego, and the righthander expressed a willingness to go: "It was hard not to hear all the trade possibilities. You would think that if a number of teams have asked for me, the Mariners would think I have some ability, too. It doesn't matter. Wherever I am, I want to pitch."

Another lefthander who was getting a look in Peoria, Arizona (the Mariners' spring home) was Brian Fuentes. The 24 year-old was impressive, and fighting Charlton for a spot on the big league roster.

But not all the news was good in the early days of Spring Training. Ryan Anderson, 6'10" lefthander, nicknamed "Little Unit" due to his physical similarities with Randy Johnson, was found to have a tear in his left shoulder. Rather than risk further injury, the Mariner's announced that Anderson would be out for the season. Anderson expressed anger and frustration at his injury, indicating that he hadn't been examined properly in 2000. Anderson felt he was ready for the big leagues. In fact, a Minnesota scout stated that Anderson and Gil Meche, who was due to be out for the first four months of the 2001 season, would both have been in the Twins' starting rotation in 2000. The only good news about Anderson's and Meche's injuries is that the return success rate is high.

All players had arrived in camp by the time of the Anderson announcement, including former All-Star Carlos Baerga. The 32 year-old .291 career hitter had signed a minor league contract after having seen little action anywhere in the previous two seasons.

The departures from the highly successful 2000 team, in addition to Alex Rodriguez, were Jose Mesa (released), Rickey Henderson (released), Joe Oliver (free agent), Frankie Rodriguez (released) and Raul Ibanez (free agent).

Spring games begin
The M's began the Cactus League at 0-4 by losing two straight split-squad matches on the first two days. Hitting deficiencies clearly had Piniella worried. "We expect the pitching to resolve itself, but the offense is another story. We really need one more bat."

Now that Ryan Anderson and Gil Meche were both on the injured list, the trade prospects for a hitter dimmed. "We're limited now in what we can do. We just don't have the pitching depth we had to trade from," said GM Pat Gillick. Still the prime target remained Phil Nevin at 3B. In addition to being a good hitter, he was significantly underpaid for the market at "only" $1.625 million.

On the field, there were the start of rumblings from Japanese import Ichiro. He had been a leadoff hitter most of his career, but was being asked to hit third for the M's. Ichiro, via translator, said that the approach to hitting is different in the two lineup positions. Piniella expressed the preference that Ichiro hit third so that Edgar Martinez and John Olerud could remain in the cleanup and fifth positions.

The six starters vying for the five pitching spots were Garcia, Moyer, Sele, Abbott, Tomko and Halama. Greg Wooten and Joel Pineiro were also expected to see more action in Spring Training with the absence of Anderson and Meche. Pineiro would become a force for the Mariners late in the season. Wooten was a dependable pitcher all year for the AAA Tacoma Rainiers.

The Mariners were also in search of another lefty reliever to support Arthur Rhodes. The early candidates were Charlton, Ramsay, Fuentes, Watson and Zimmerman.

In Los Angeles, excellent batsman, below average fielder, and high maintenance, high salaried left fielder Gary Sheffield demanded to be traded. The Dodgers reportedly offered Sheffield to Seattle in an even trade for Ichiro. Mariners' chairman Howard Lincoln made quick work of that proposal:

"Why would you want to trade a man whose highest ambition in life is to play for the Mariners [Ichiro] for a mean-spirited man who has trouble understanding contractual obligation [Sheffield]? I like the idea that people want to play for us in SAFECO Field and connect with the fans. Mike Cameron is the perfect example of what I'm talking about – a decent person and an extraordinary player. To bring in some petulant superstar who complains he is underpaid is a giant turnoff to the fans."

Sheffield ultimately righted himself and had a very productive season. Ichiro, on the other hand, is quite another story.

Lincoln added that superstar status is unnecessary to a team's success. "The more I see, the more I am convinced there isn't a connection between superstars and winning." Lincoln's excellent perception got progressively more prophetic throughout the season.

Superstars or not, Seattle had the eleventh highest payroll in baseball in 2001, and to add a Gary Sheffield or Sammy Sosa, or to have paid A-Rod, would have taken that figure close to $100 million. While Seattle is not a small market, it is not a Los Angeles, New York or Chicago that can support such a huge expenditure.

Caution: Mariner Offense Missing
After the first 10 games of spring baseball, manager Lou Piniella was becoming monotonous. "We haven't hit with any consistency. I would say the offense is throwing up a caution flag," said the skipper. Throughout that period, the Mariners were driving in less than one of every four runners in scoring position.

In the meantime, Gillick was scouring both Florida's Grapefruit League and the Cactus circuit for hitting. Agrowing concern was Jay Buhner, who had not yet played in the first ten games. Soreness in his left arch had banished Buhner to the weight room. "It's real unfortunate. I'm in the best shape in years," said Bone.

Within a week after Gillick's trip around the spring leagues, the GM announced that there were no deals to be made at that time. In the previous two spring games, the Mariners had managed only 11 hits, all but two of them singles. A younger Lou Piniella may have been throwing bats by this time, but chose to lash out with words instead: "We're not hitting the ball for any power; that's obvious, and when we do get a man on base, we don't seem to get him in. We've played OK baseball. We have a chance to win every game, but we just don't get the hits when we need them."

The Sheffield deal surfaced again, this time without a Dodger demand for Ichiro. Gillick, once again, nixed the idea. "I don't think he fits into our group," said Gillick. The triumvirate of Howard Lincoln, Pat Gillick and Lou Piniella had a clearly unique view for professional sports regarding the type of person who would don a major league uniform in Seattle. Team chemistry was more important than raw talent. Though hitting was a problem, the lineup did begin to take shape. The experiment at moving Ichiro to hit third in the lineup was over. He was installed as leadoff man, and the search was on for someone to bat third in front of Edgar and Olerud.

The M's had made some roster moves by the middle of March, sending down the following: Anderson, (Chad) Alexander, Falkenborg, Christianson, Grabowski, Kaye, Meyer, Soriano, Moreta, Vazquez, Watson and Wooten.

More settling on the lineup took place in the third week of March. It appeared that the first five would be Ichiro, Cameron, Olerud, Martinez and Boone. Piniella expressed worry about left field. Since Buhner had not yet played, the bat of the hometown favorite and long time slugger hadn't even been tested.

Piniella also commented about the throngs of Japanese media about Ichiro. To date in the spring, Ichiro had few hits, and those were not with any authority. But his seven straight batting titles in Japan didn't come by accident. The manager warned: "He needs to be left alone. Players who have had this much success will make the necessary adjustments. If he can hit around .300; steal a few bases; score some runs; I'll be pleased." It was later reported that Ichiro indicated to Piniella in spring training that he was merely "setting up" the opposing pitchers. He was drawing in the defense while letting it get around the league that he couldn't handle American League fastballs.

Could anyone be that cunning?

Though the hitting was a concern, the bullpen dominance Gillick talked about over the winter was starting to show. The trio of Nelson and Sasaki from the right side and Rhodes from the left, meant that any Mariner lead going into the seventh inning would be difficult for the opponent to overcome.

By March 26, the Mariners had made more cuts, sending down (Manny) Alexander, Barthol, Bloomquist, Fuentes, Horner, Hodges, Perez, Pineiro, Podsednik, Ramsay, Sanders, Stark, and Zimmerman.

The Mariners solidified their starting four in the rotation with Garcia, Moyer, Sele and Halama. The fifth spot was still not settled, but Paul Abbott appeared to have a strong lead. That left the long reliever's job up for grabs to Tomko, Ramsay and Ryan Franklin.

The leader for the second lefthander in the bullpen was Norm Charlton. Ramsay and Fuentes had pitched well, but didn't have as good an "out" pitch as The Sheriff's which would be needed in pressure situations.

Jay Buhner had his first - and last - at-bat of the spring. He reinjured his foot in his first plate appearance. A frustrated Buhner indicated that he may retire. In the meantime, with one more bat gone from the Mariners and the prospects for a trade dimming more every day, Seattle's offensive worries continued.

Opening Day was about a week away and with the weak Mariner offensive attack so obvious, the attention turned to pitching. Seattle still had 13 pitchers, four catchers, six outfielders and eight infielders on the roster. It was likely that at least three Mariners were going to start the season on the disabled list – Buhner, Meche and Widger, who had injured his shoulder. That left another three Mariners to be dropped before the team headed north.

One of the cuts made was Carlos Baerga. At 5'11", Baerga didn't fare well in camp due to the near 230 pounds he was carrying. He later played with the Long Island Ducks of the Independent League who sold his contract to a team in the Korean Baseball League.

Edgar Martinez, Baerga's friend, was sorry to see him go, but commented on his and the Mariners' future: "One of the big reasons I came back [having considered retirement last year] is that Lou came back. We'll miss Alex but as long as we have Lou we have a chance."

Chris Widger was placed on the disabled list due to his shoulder injury. That left the 25th spot on the roster to be between Norm Charlton and Ryan Franklin.

On Sunday, April 1, the 2001 version of the Seattle Mariners played an exhibition game at home against the St. Louis Cardinals. Young and wild lefthander, Rick Ankiel was on the mound for the Cardinals. Mariner manager Lou Piniella, who chose to keep Ichiro on the bench, caught the wrath of the Japanese reporters who had traveled thousands of miles to record Ichiro's early moments at SAFECO Field. "I wasn't going to risk getting Ichiro hurt," said the skipper.

At the same time, trade talks with the Red Sox were a last ditch effort by GM Gillick to get another bat in Seattle. It was known that the Sox liked Bret Tomko. The Mariners wanted an infielder, but with the season on the brink of getting under way, would have settled for an outfielder.

But the Sox had lost Nomar Garciaparra for an indefinite amount of time. Any loss of power in the Bosox lineup would hinder their attempt to overcome the rival Yankees. So, with that last effort, the Mariners gave up on getting the Red Sox hard hitting, but troubled outfielder, Carl Everett.

Back to the decision as to who to keep: Ryan Franklin or Norm Charlton. Paul Abbott's pulled a muscle in his shoulder in his last start. That gave the Mariners an out. Abbott wasn't expected to start for at least two weeks because of early season gaps in the schedule. Abbott's injury gave Seattle the opportunity to start manipulating the roster from the beginning of the season. Paul Abbott went on the 15 day disabled list. Ryan Franklin stayed in the big leagues. Norm Charlton made the Mariners for the third time in his eleven year major league career.

The 2001 Mariners started setting records in Spring Training. The team lost the most preseason games ever in franchise history. But a different win-loss record would be set before September.

Preseason Predictions

CNN Sports Illustrated:
"The Mariners may not be on the same level of the Yankees, Indians or White Sox, but pitching will keep Seattle in the hunt for a wild-card berth. Sweet Lou is one of the best managers in baseball at drawing every possible ounce of effort out of his players, and if GM Pat Gillick can swing a deal for a slugger, the M's could contend with Oakland for the West title." -- Jimmy Traina, CNNSI.com.

Baseball Weekly's writer Steve DiMeglio gave this rundown of the Mariners:

Strengths: *Talent and depth in starting and relief pitching, the managing of Lou Piniella, DH Edgar Martinez in the middle of the order, and a strong defense.*

Weaknesses: The lack of power is evident and scoring runs will be a challenge, especially if teams decide to pitch around Martinez.

Worried about: John Olerud doing the job as the No. 3 hitter, and someone else stepping up to fill Olerud's old No. 5 spot and pro - vide protection for Martinez.

Spring info: Jay Buhner contemplated retirement because of a sore foot that will keep him out at least six weeks. Buhner, 36, was supposed to platoon with Al Martin in left field. Injuries also impacted the starting pitching, as lefty phenom Ryan Anderson and right-hander Gil Meche broke down, which hindered the club's efforts to trade for some offense. Japanese newcomer Ichiro Suzuki earned a starting spot in right field amidst all the hoopla generated by his signing.

OUTLOOK

Best case: The Mariners excel playing a National League brand of baseball, with strong starting pitching, a great bullpen, solid defense and just enough timely hitting, and win a lot of close, low-scoring games.

Worst case: The Mariners lack timely hitting and lose a lot of close, low-scoring games.

Reality: Piniella often said during spring training that he needed a No. 3 hitter, one that could hit 30 homers and knock in 100 runs. He didn't get one. In this day and age of offense, the Mariners won't have enough to beat the A's and win the division.

DiMeglio also predicted that the Mariners would be the biggest disappointment of any team during the season. He also predicted Ken Griffey Jr. would hit 57 homers for the Reds in 2001.

The preseason **Super Power Rankings** from **ESPN** had Seattle at # 13, stating: *"Edgar Martinez swings at almost anything; he might have to."* [Even in a quick quote like the one ESPN made about the Mariners, whoever wrote it should at least try to be accurate. Edgar is well known to be one of the most patient, selective hitters in the game. - *SE*]

Lycos Sportswriter By Pete Kahle, predicted the top three finishers in the AL West:

Oakland Athletics
1st Place - 94-68

The AL West has shaped up to be the toughest division in baseball and the A's are the cream of the crop. With the addition of base - ball's premier leadoff hitter in Johnny Damon to complement 2000 MVP Jason Giambi, Eric Chavez, and superstar-in-the-mak - ing Miguel Tejada, the Athletics epitomize their nickname. And it doesn't stop with the offense. Tim Hudson, Barry Zito, and Gil Heredia rival the Yankees and Braves for the best 1-2-3 punch off the mound. Last year's Pacific Coast League MVP, Jose Ortiz (.351, 24 HR, 108 RBI, 107 R and 22 SB in AAA Sacramento) is one of the leading Rookie of the Year candidates and has already secured the starting 2B job. Oakland has the best chance of any club to dethrone the reigning champion Yankees. Get used to the colors green and gold. They'll be around for a while.

Breakout Player - Eric Chavez
On The Decline - T.J. Mathews

Texas Rangers
2nd Place - 88-74

With his mind-boggling 10 year, 252 million dollar contract, Alex Rodriguez has gone from a star in Seattle to a supernova in Texas. Plug him into a lineup boasting Andres Galarraga, Rafi Palmeiro, and a certain other guy named Rodriguez, and the Rangers have lineup with the firepower of a bazooka. Unfortunately, their pitch - ing leaves something to be desired. Helling and Rogers can hold their own, but the bottom drops out after that. Fans down in Arlington can expect to see a lot of 11-9 games with the Rangers likely to break through the 1000 run ceiling this year. When it all ends, though, the boys from Texas will fall a few games shy of the wildcard.

Breakout Player - Gabe Kapler
On The Decline - Randy Velarde

Seattle Mariners
3rd Place - 87-75

You would think that after losing Ken Griffey, Jr. and Alex Rodriguez in consecutive years, the Mariners would be languish - ing in the division cellar. Far from the truth. They've traveled across the Pacific to sign Japan's 7-time batting champ, Ichiro Suzuki. Widely regarded as the frontrunner for rookie of the year, Suzuki doesn't have much power, but can be expected to hit .325 with 110 runs and 25-30 stolen bases. In their second full season at SAFECO Field, the Mariners have adapted quickly to one of

the better pitcher's parks. Reaping the benefits of their expansive home will be Freddy Garcia, John Halama, and Aaron Sele, each of whom can be expected to exceed 15 wins. In the pen, last year's import, Kazuhiro Sasaki is one of the top 5 closers in the game, and Jeff Nelson, from New York will be a workhorse in long relief.
  Breakout Player - Ichiro Suzuki
  On The Decline - Jay Buhner ·

Bob Storch of **Worldwide Church of Baseball** predicted the AL West in this way:
  Winner: Seattle: America will learn to say, "Kazuhiro Sasaki."

The Baseball Page Staff Predictions included Oakland as the AL West champ, Seattle as the AL Wild Card and Ichiro as the Rookie of the Year.

The **Baseball Journal**'s David N. Townsend summed the AL West this way:

1. Oakland Athletics. No argument here. They won last year with great talent, and they got better this year. Pundits trying to find a weakness cite "Jason Giambi's contract status," which only tells you that this team has no weaknesses. Replacing Grieve with Damon is a gamble, in the sense that they're going for it all in one season, but that's a gamble worth taking. Hudson is obviously already an elite starter, although personally I'll wait until Zito pitches 200 major league innings before I'll anoint him a super-star, too. And Isringhausen isn't totally proven, either, but Jim Mecir may be the best setup man in the business. Anyway, when you have the kind of offense that this team has you can survive a couple of below-expectation performances from your pitching staff. It's too bad they play in Oakland, which has won far more than its share of Pennants and World Championships in the past 30 years, because this is a team, like the Indians, that a baseball fan can be proud to root for.

2. Anaheim Angels. Why the heck is everyone so disparaging of this team? Granted, they underperformed in the run-scoring department last year and now they have to live without Mo Vaughn. But this remains a deadly hitting team, that will pummel many opponents. The same resume is getting the Rangers rave reviews. The conventional wisdom is that the Angels have terri-ble, unproven pitching. Unproven, sure -- who doesn't? But ter-rible -- says who? Ramon Ortiz looks like a legitimate Ace in the making, and both Jarrod Washburn and Scott Schoenweis can be solid major league starters. If Ismael Valdes could return to his 1997-99 form, this staff would be every bit as good as the Rangers. Plus, they've got a much more established closer in Percival, and an excellent setup man in Hasegawa. In a head-to-head matchup with Texas, I see a virtual draw, with the contrarian edge to Anaheim.

3. Texas Rangers. Adding A-Rod to I-Rod certainly gives them two of the most exciting and satisfying players of any generation. But beyond those two, the team is surprisingly suspect. They're relying on either aging veterans -- Palmeiro, Galarraga, Caminiti, Velarde -- or injury prone youngsters -- Kapler, Mateo -- and hoping that all the pieces fit together. Meanwhile, Darren Oliver is still in the rotation, the other kid pitchers have proven nothing to date, and there's no closer. They didn't finish last in '00 for no reason, and they won't rise much higher this year.

4. Seattle Mariners. The joy ride they've experienced since jettisoning both Randy Johnson and Junior Griffey will not continue following the loss of A-Rod. In the first place, they actually got decent compensation for the first two (Garcia, Guillen, Cameron), whereas the only new addition following Rodriguez's departure is Ichiro Suzuki, a glorified Triple-A hitter from Japan. Jamie Moyer is probably all done, and the pitchers who are supposed to be their salvation (Meche, Anderson) are all trapped in the doctor's office. Their best asset is their bullpen, which is ironic since in the past they won the Division with horrendous relief pitching. You can bet Piniella will find a way to screw up Nelson, Rhodes, et al. [This guy seemed to miss his prediction a bit. Heh, heh. - *SE*]

One final prediction (sort of):
Opposing scout on Ichiro: "*Has some tools, and won seven Pacific League batting titles in Japan, but in spring training major league pitchers are just knocking the bat out of his hands. He can't hit the inside pitch; he just keeps fouling balls over the third base dugout. He can really run, but right now he's really overmatched.*"

Hmmmm . . . perhaps that scout rates pitchers for the Texas Rangers.

Let the season begin!

Chapter Four

April, 2001

*"It [Baseball] is designed to break your heart. The game
begins in the spring, when everything else begins again, and
it blossoms in the summer, filling the afternoons and evenings,
and then as soon as the chilling rains come,
it stops and leaves you to face the fall alone."
-- A. Bartlett Giamatti, "The Green Fields of the Mind"*

The 2001 season contained one significant change -- the unbalanced schedule. The new format places a much stronger emphasis on games against teams in the same division with more games being played against the in-division opponents.

In the Mariners'case, the first 19 games were against teams only in their division. The wins would be more important. The losses would be more costly. Regardless, at the end of those first 19 games, all of baseball would wonder if the Mariners were the team to beat in the AL West race instead of the exalted Oakland A's.

Three game series at home vs. Oakland (M's take 2)
April 2 The season opened at SAFECO Field with a matchup of two dominating pitchers: Freddy Garcia for the Mariners against Tim Hudson for the Athletics. Both of these young righthanders had Cy Young stuff. Apacked Opening Day crowd saw Garcia and Hudson hit the showers early.

But before all else, the people noticed a smallish figure, and barely a beard covering his face which was hardly discernible under a hat.

This player positioned himself in what other teams call right field, but in Seattle it's called "Area 51." He trots out to Area 51 with a silent confidence. Every move is as if it were choreographed. Nothing is wasted, including time.

While the pitcher prepares to throw, he bends from the waist, touch - ing his toes. He sits in a squat forcing his upper thighs to graze his heels. In the on-deck circle he reaches over his right knee, touching the ground, and then reverses – reaching over his left knee, touching the ground again. What kind of being is this? Is he a gymnast in a Mariner uniform?

*Then he strides to the plate, into the batter's box. He draws his bat which looks more like a wand in the hands of a magician. The baton in his grip; his arm completely extended, he looks toward the oppos - ing pitcher before the first pitch is even thrown. His routine says it all, and with one last steely-eyed look toward the mound, these words are never spoken, but heard just the same: "**Let the battle begin.**"*

The magician – The Wizard – is Ichiro Suzuki. (SE)

Ichiro Suzuki – OF
Born: 10-22-73, Kasugai, Japan
Lives in Kobe, Japan with wife Yumiko
5'9" 160 lbs
Signed through 2003

Back to Opening Day.
Fortunately for the Mariners, the win was preserved with a strong long relief performance from Bret Tomko, and then Arthur Rhodes and Kazuhiro Sasaki came in to close the door. In another foreshadowing of the season, the Mariners had seven hits, all singles. Edgar had three and Ichiro had two. Plus, the M's had two stolen bases.

Perhaps the most poignant point of the inaugural game indicating what the rest of the season was going to be like was how the winning run was scored. Carlos Guillen drew a leadoff walk with the game tied in the bottom of the 8th. Then Ichiro bunted and flew down the first base line. Ichiro's speed caused pitcher Jim Mecir to make an errant throw to first, enabling Guillen to wind up on third.

Mike Cameron next flew out to center, but not deep enough to send Guillen. Edgar was intentionally walked. John Olerud then hit a deeper fly to center and Guillen trotted home for the winning run.

Doing the little things to score a run - - it would happen time after time, and often in an inning the Mariners seemed to own all season long, the 8th. M's 5, A's 4.

April 3 Barry Zito of the A's shut down Seattle, exposing the feared hitting weakness. The M's collected only six hits, including their first extra base hit, a Mark McLemore double. The Mariners' John Halama was knocked out in the 4th inning, and the relief of Ryan Franklin, Jeff Nelson and Jose Paniagua pitched one hit ball the rest of the way. A's 5, M's 1.

Edgar Martinez went into first place on Seattle's hit list with 1,743.

April 4 In the rubber game of the series, the M's Aaron Sele and the A's Gil Heredia, who would ultimately get pushed out of the Athletics' starting rotation, held opposing hitters to two runs a piece until the bottom of the 6th, when the M's exploded for seven runs behind seven hits. Edgar got three more hits, including his first extra base hit (double). He was hitting .800 after his first three games.

Sele pitched six strong innings, and Arthur Rhodes and Norm Charlton pitched three shutout innings, continuing the Mariners relief mastery. M's 10, A's 2.

Three game series at Texas (M's take 2)

The Mariners went on the road for the first time in 2001 and received their first look at former team-mate Alex Rodriguez in the Ballpark at Arlington. The series typified the Rangers' season. In the three games, Texas pitchers gave up 19 runs, including three Mariner homers in game 1.

April 6 Ichiro gathered four hits in game one, two singles, a double and his first home run. The homer in the 10th against Jeff Zimmerman proved to be the winning run. Arthur Rhodes got his second win of the young season, and Kazu Sasaki collected his second save.

> Early in the winter, a former Mariner shortstop had a visitor. Carlos Guillen and his family were invited to A-Rod's home. "I just told him," said Alex, "that he was going to be a big part of the Mariners whether I came back or not."

Mark McLemore got his first home run of the season and added two RBIs. The 36 year-old played second base in this game, the first of five positions he would play during the season. M's won 9-7.

Mark McLemore – iF/OF
Born: 10-04-64, San Diego, CA
Lives in Southlake, TX with wife Capri
and three children
5'11" 207 lbs
Signed through 2001

April 7 In game 2, Ranger pitching continued to suffer and Mariner bats benefited. The first five Mariners in the lineup (Ichiro, Cameron, Edgar, Olerud, and Boone) got 11 of the Mariners' 12 hits. All but two of the hits were singles, and the other two were doubles.

Once again, the Mariners' starting pitching needed early bullpen help. Bret Tomko lasted until the 4th, and Ryan Franklin, Jeff Nelson, and Jose Paniagua pitched 4 2/3 shutout innings. Kazu Sasaki pitched the 9th and got his third save. M's won 6-5.

April 8 The final game of the series in Texas brought Freddy Garcia to the mound for his second outing of the season. Garcia, who won 26 games over his first two years in the major leagues, was expected to be the M's number one starter.

Against Texas, Garcia, who was acquired as a prospect from Houston in the Randy Johnson deal, surrendered eight hits and five walks in six innings. This was his second unimpressive appearance of the season, prompting Piniella to warn the starters that the bullpen was getting overworked. After the first six games, the bullpen had pitched in as many innings as the starters. The Mariners lost game 3 by a score of 5-4.

Three game series at Oakland (M's sweep!)
The team nearly every expert predicted to win the AL West was the powerful Oakland Athletics. The Mariners had won their first two series. But a stern test from the Giambis and the A's strong pitching rotation faced Seattle. Oakland was hoping to extract revenge for the opening series embarassment. It would be a defining series for the Mariners and would be remembered even in September.

April 10 Seattle starter John Halama gave the bullpen a much needed break. He stopped the dangerous Athletic hitters on a mere four singles going into the 7th inning. This effort was despite getting hit on his throwing hand by a Johnny Damon line drive in the 1st inning. The Mariner's version of 1-2-3 and you're out - Jeff Nelson, Arthur Rhodes and Kazu Sasaki - allowed only one more hit preserving the 5-1 win.

The A's chose not to let Edgar Martinez beat them. Edgar, who had nine hits in eleven at-bats against Oakland at this point, walked four times.

After Mark McLemore hit his second home run in as many nights against Texas, manager Lou Piniella said: "We'll find somewhere to get him in there."

Lou kept his promise.

David Bell auditioned for the play-of-the year with a diving stop of a Johnny Damon grounder, and then throwing out the speedy Athletic while sitting on the dirt. Definitely ESPN "play of the day" material, after the out, Bell calmly got up, dusted himself off and got ready for the next play. This was yet another early-in-the-year example of the professional attitude of the Mariner team. Each member seemed to recognize his role, and did it without fanfare. M's won 5-1.

April 11 This was the kind of baseball game that was a baseball fan's delight. Two good pitchers, Aaron Sele and Oakland lefthander Mark Mulder battled pitch for pitch until the 8th inning, but it was "The Throw" that will forever mark this game.

The Mariners had gotten three runs against Athletic reliever Jim Mecir in the 8th on two singles, an infield out, an intentional walk and a Bret Boone double. Through the first seven innings, Sele had allowed only two hits and three baserunners. In the bottom of the 8th, the fleet-footed Terence Long led off with a single. After an out, Ramon Hernandez hit a ground ball single to right field. As Ichiro charged the ball, Long rounded second base.

Against all but a few right fielders there wouldn't even have been a play at third base, but this was the play that warned the rest of the American League not to run on Ichiro. Scooping up the ball on the run, Ichiro stepped and fired a frozen rope to David Bell at third base. Frantically, the A's third base coach was waving Long to get down. But by the time Long entered his slide, Ichiro's thrown was nestled in Bell's glove awaiting the tag. Anational TV audience on ESPN, a Japanese audience on NHK and 16,652 fans in the stands witnessed "The Throw."

Sasaki pitched a perfect 9th to seal the 3-0 shutout.

April 12 The M's went for the sweep with Jamie Moyer against A's ace Tim Hudson. Moyer didn't have a Halama or Sele type of game, but lasted long enough to turn it over to the Mariners' strong bullpen. Edgar Martinez hit a three-run homer in the M's five-run third. The win gave the Mariners a 7-2 start, the best in franchise history. M's won 7-3.

> "I only heard the ball as it went past my ear. When I saw Long head for third, I just said, 'You're out. Period, man, you are out.' And was he ever out."
> – Bret Boone, quoted in *Seattle Times*, April 12, 2001

Controlling Fans

Not everything was pleasant for the division leading Mariners. In Oakland, Mike Cameron had coins thrown from the stands whiz by him. Ichiro was not so lucky. He was hit in the head by a coin. Oakland promised to increase security following the incidents.

Speaking of security, the Mariners released a statement in anticipation of Alex Rodriguez's return to SAFECO Field. Urging fans to maintain a family-oriented atmosphere, Mariner management stated: ". . . the Mariners will not participate in or encourage any organized efforts by third parties to disrespect Alex or any opposing player."

Seattle sports radio station KJR-AM fielded call-after-call about A-Rod's return, and it seemed many of the callers weren't too impressed with the Mariner management statement. Neither was sports columnist, Art Thiel, who wrote:

"Most curious in the Mariners announcement was the statement that if the code is violated, 'our staff will proactively intervene.' What does that mean? When the LAPD beat Rodney King, was that a 'proactive intervention'?" [Seattle Post-Intelligencer, April 12, 2001]

But before Texas would come to Seattle, the M's had to travel to Anaheim.

Three game series at Anaheim (M's take 2)

April 13 Bret Tomko's second start of the season was the first time the Mariner bullpen had failed. Tomko pitched respectably, giving up two runs and four hits through five innings.

The game featured another first - - a Japanese pitcher, Shigetoshi Hasegawa, against a Japanese hitter, Ichiro. The two had played for the Orix Blue Wave several years before. Both figured prominently in the game.

In the bottom of the eighth, with a man on first, the Angels' Tim Salmon hit a screamer toward right field. Ichiro dove to make the catch, robbing Salmon of a potential double, and then fired to first to double-up the runner.

Ichiro's former teammate, was the winning pitcher, though, when Garrett Anderson took a low Kazu Sasaki splitter into the rightfield stands in the bottom of the ninth for the first bad outing from the Mariner bullpen. Angels won 4-3.

April 14 Seattle got back on track as Freddy Garcia and Nelson, Rhodes and Sasaki combined for a two-hit, one run, no walk, 2-1 victory over the Angels' Ismael Valdes. Garcia had taken a no-hitter into the sixth before surrendering a single to Orlando Palmeiro.

The M's collected only four hits, scoring their two runs on consecutive singles by David Bell and Ichiro. M's won 2-1.

April 15 The Mariners had won the first three series of the year, and to continue, they were going to need a second straight good game from lefty John Halama.

It was another tight pitching duel, with the Angels taking a 3-1 lead in the bottom of the seventh inning. But in the 8th, hits by Edgar Martinez, John Olerud, Bret Boone and a perfect suicide squeeze brought in six runs. M's won 7-5.

The three-city road trip was the best in team history, and the 9-3 Mariners returned home to face the Rangers.

Three game series at home vs. Texas (M's take 2)

Alex Rodriguez's first return to the city where he grew up in baseball was about to take place. Talk radio, whether sports oriented or not, was abuzz with chatter about A-Rod. How loud would the fans boo? Would Seattle fans emulate other places and hurl projectiles at their former shortstop? Just how far would people go to show their displeasure that Alex had left Seattle?

But any analysis of A-Rod's jump to Texas must consider the bottom line: Rangers owner Tom Hicks pled *non compos mentis* for offering any one person $252 million to play baseball. And Alex Rodriguez would have been even loonier not to take it. Who among us wouldn't have?

The Texas Rangers came to town with one of the major league's best hitting and worst pitching teams. Since SAFECO Field was a "pitcher's park," the hometown Mariners should have had a distinct edge.

April 16 The Mariners sent former Texas hurler Aaron Sele to the hill against the Rangers' Ryan Glynn, who owned the majors worst ERA as a starter at 6.50. Neither would last past the third inning. The M's collected six hits, seven walks and seven earned runs in the first three innings against Glynn, attaining a 5-0 lead. But Sele couldn't keep the Rangers in the stall, and surrendered seven hits, two walks and four runs in two innings.

Ryan Franklin continued to show he was *the* M's long reliever by holding the powerful Texas offense to one run over the next four innings. But the Rangers' relievers didn't fare so well. By game's end, Seattle had eleven hits and ten walks. But no Seattle pitcher, except Franklin, stopped Texas. Norm Charlton and Kazu Sasaki each gave up runs, both sporting ERAs over 5.00. For short relievers, giving up that many runs would not bring a championship home.

Ryan Franklin – P
Born: 03-05-73, Fort Smith, AR
Lives in Spiro, OK with wife and two children
6'3" 165 lbs
Signed through 2001

In the game, Rafael Palmeiro continued his career ownership of Mariners pitching by belting two home runs. M's won ugly, 9-7.

April 17 Jamie Moyer came to Seattle's rescue again, and Ichiro provided the highlights. The Mariners had a four run lead through two innings, behind Ichiro's electric triple, and Olerud and Guillen homers Moyer pitched 6 1/3 good innings and left with a lead.

Al Martin, who had opened the season batting one for twenty-three, started in left field and hit two singles. Ichiro, also the game's defensive hero, was 4-4, and Kazu Sasaki, recorded his seventh save in pitching a scoreless 9th, lowering his ERA to 5.87 in the 6-4 win.

Oh yes, to the delight of many fans at SAFECO, A-Rod graciously contributed to the Seattle victory with two errors.

At 11-3, Seattle had the best record in baseball. M's won 6-4.

April 18 Bret Tomko got another start and gave up ten hits and seven runs in five innings. The M's nearly kept pace, though, but were beaten 8-6. Ichiro extended his hitting streak to 13 games, with his second homer.

> "Rodriguez shouldn't be booed. He hit .308 here. He hit 189 home runs in Seattle. He gave this city the kind of memories only Hall of Famers give. Like Griffey and Johnson, like Edgar Martinez and Jay Buhner, he has given us many glimpses of greatness. He was part of the dramatic evolution of Seattle into a baseball town." - Steve Kelly, *Seattle Times*, 4/15/2001.

Alex Rodriguez limped back to Texas having hit just .250. By taking two of three games from the Rangers, Seattle won its fifth straight series. Rangers 8, M's 6.

Four game series at home vs. Anaheim (M's sweep!)
Seattle was playing an incapacitated Angel team. Without Mo Vaughn, the Halos were without their leader for average and power, and in the clubhouse. Vaughn's season-ending injury doomed the Angels even before the season started.

April 19 The last time Freddy Garcia of the Mariners and Ismael Valdes of the Angels pitched against each other, it was an M's 2-1 win at Anaheim. Game 1 of the home series was nearly a carbon copy, with Garcia again on top, 3-2.

The Mariners drew first blood in the bottom of the sixth after an Ichiro single, Javier walk, a double steal and consecutive singles from John Olerud and Bret Boone. The Angels got one back in the top of the seventh but could never get ahead. Arthur Rhodes and Kazu Sasaki closed out the game. M's 3, Angels 2.

Freddy Garcia – P
Born: 10-06-76, Caracas, Venezuela
Lives in Baruta, Venezuela
6'4" 235 lbs
Signed through 2001

April 20 The Mariners'starting pitching came through again. Lefty John Halama improved his record to 5-0 lifetime against the Angels by scattering six hits over seven innings. Nelson and Sasaki shut the door in the eighth and ninth. Sasaki earned his league-leading ninth save and lowered his ERAto 5.59.

Ichiro, at .378, collected two of the Mariners' six hits and extended his hitting streak to 15 games. Stan Javier got his first homer of the season. M's 4, Angels 1.

April 21 Jamie Moyer was back on the mound for game 3 of the Angels' series. With two junkballing lefthanders pitching back-to-back (Halama and Moyer), conventional wisdom had it that Anaheim would catch up with seventy mile-an-hour change-ups. But the Angels had no such luck on this Saturday afternoon. Pitching on just three days rest, Moyer gave up only three hits and one run in five innings. This time it was Franklin, Rhodes and Nelson who finished the game, giving Sasaki a much needed day of rest.

John Olerud provided most of the offensive punch with his third home run of the season and four RBIs. Ichiro's hitting streak was stopped at 15. M's 5, Angels 2.

April 22 In the last game of the rare four game set, three Mariner pitchers combined for a six-hit shutout of the division rival Angels. The dominating performance was supported by eleven Mariner hits, including Al Martin's first homer. Martin hit in the DH spot giving Edgar Martinez a rest, and raised his average to .158. Ichiro got two hits of his own, as did ninth hitting Mark McLemore, who was playing third base. McLemore raised his average to .323. The "utility player" tag on McLemore was quickly transforming into "What position will Mark play tonight?" M's 5, Angels 0.

The completion of the first round of divisional play found Seattle at

15-4; 5 1/2 games in front of second place Texas. But with a visit to the mighty New York Yankees next up for the M's, all of baseball would see if the Mariners were the real deal or merely a fluke.

> McLemore was the symbol of the ingredients that made the Mariners so special. He contributed what the team needed, not thinking of his own statistics. – MS

Three game series at Yankees (M's sweep!)

Any good team in any sport will receive its share of breaks. In game 1 at Yankee Stadium, the Mariners got a big one.

April 24 The game could have been a classic power pitchers' duel between the Yankees' Roger Clemens and the Mariners' Freddy Garcia. But neither was at his best, as both gave up five runs in seven innings.

The Mariners' good fortune came in the seventh with one on and Tom Lampkin at the plate against Clemens. The Yankees led 5-3 at the time. Lampkin sliced a Clemens' fastball toward the short left field fence. Chuck Knoblauch, the former second baseman turned left fielder, sped after the ball, but was cautious of the upcoming warning track. Knoblauch timed his leap only to deflect the ball up with his glove.

The ball careened upward and seemed to disappear from view, but was called a home run by third-base umpire Lance Barksdale. Though the hometown Yankee fans were screaming, New York manager Joe Torre didn't protest the call. "He [the umpire] was in the best spot to see the play," said Torre.

Replays showed that the ball never left the park. It rolled on top of the fence, was never touched by a fan, and then fell back onto the field. The hit should have been a ground-rule double, but, instead, the Lampkin homer tied the game.

The fans were still screaming the next time the Mariners came up in the 8th, when Edgar hit a two-out, two-bagger and Olerud drove him home to put the M's ahead to stay.

Norm Charlton struck out the side in the bottom of the 8th and Sasaki pitched another perfect ninth to preserve the 7-5 win, quieting the Yankee fans until another day.

April 25 Intent on revenge, Andy Pettitte, 19-game winner the year before, strode to the mound for the Yankees against fellow lefty John Halama. Again, neither pitcher survived as far as the 7th inning on a very chilly New York spring evening.

> The Lampkin homer against Clemens is the kind of break the Yankees have gotten over the years. It was nice to see a reversal.
> – MS

Four Mariners crossed the plate in the second inning behind Carlos Guillen's bat. Guillen's turn at the plate in the second was a tribute to hitting coach Gerald Perry.

"He's [Perry] been talking to us about patience and fouling off close pitches until we get one we can hit," said Guillen. The young shortstop did just that against Pettitte in fouling off eight pitches before hitting a bases loaded seeing-eye single.

But John Halama was no mystery to the Yanks, and gave up four runs in four innings. In the sixth, with the game tied at five, Guillen was at the plate again with two outs and drove in the winning run with another hard fought at-bat.

Franklin, Rhodes, Nelson and Sasaki combined for 3 2/3 innings of shutout relief. M's won 7-5.

April 26 Mariner big game pitcher Jamie Moyer faced perennial All-Star Mike Mussina. The game was huge for the Mariners because a win would be a sweep on the road against the world series champion for the past three years, and an even bigger statement that the Mariners could defeat the best competition.

For the third consecutive game, the M's put seven runs on the board, but the bulk of the Mariner runs didn't come until the 7th inning, though. Edgar Martinez, batting just .194 over his past seven games, had three hits and four RBIs to lead the offense.

This time Mariner pitching wasn't so giving. Moyer scattered six hits over six innings, and Paniagua, Nelson and Rhodes only gave up one run (unearned) over the final three innings to preserve the sweep. M's won 7-3.

As the Mariners boarded the flight out of town, they were sporting an 18-4 record, eight games up on the second place Rangers.

Three game series at White Sox (M's take 2)

The hottest team in baseball rolled into Chicago to take on last year's Central Division winner, the Chicago White Sox. This was the first meeting between two teams since the Mariners' sweep in the previous year's Division Championship series.

Through April 24th, the Mariners had scored nearly 40% of their runs with two outs, prompting the slogan "Two Outs . . So What?"

April 27 Aaron Sele and James Baldwin, two veteran right-handers, went to the mound for their respective teams.

Though Sele had a good career winning percentage, he is a pitcher who needs more run support than other successful pitchers. The M's gave that support in this game against the Sox. With the bases loaded and two outs in the second inning, Ichiro shot a liner off first baseman Frank Thomas' glove, driving in two runs. By the fourth inning, the Mariners had pushed the lead to 5-0, when the White Sox capable bats of Magglio Ordonez and John Valentin drove in three runs on homers. But that would be the only blemish on the Mariners. Sele pitched seven, and Franklin and Sasaki, who earned his 12th save, closed the door. M's 8, White Sox 3.

Aaron Sele – P
Born: 06-25-70, Golden Valley, MN
Lives in Buckley, WA with wife Jennifer and one child
6'5" 218
Signed through 2001

April 28 The Mariners were going for a new club record: 20 wins in a month. Paul Abbott came off the disabled list for his first start of the year and fell behind 2-1 after the first inning. By the sixth inning both Abbott and White Sox starter Rocky Biddle were gone.

Ichiro and Bret Boone had three hits each. Boone also drove in two runs, but the star of the game was a combination of players from the bullpen. Bret Tomko, Jeff Nelson, Arthur Rhodes and Kazu Sasaki pitched 4 2/3 innings of two-hit ball. It was the Mariners' ninth straight win and a club record 20th win in a month. Sasaki earned his major league record 13th save in a month. M's 8, White Sox 5.

April 29 The final game of April pitted Freddy Garcia against the young Mark Buerhle. The game, on paper, had the makings of a crushing by the hard-hitting Mariners, but both teams matched each other pitch for pitch from the top of the first until the bottom of the 14th, when the White Sox finally won.

The weather of Chicago took a huge toll on the hitters. A swirling wind and near-blinding shadows helped the batters look awkward and the pitchers look unhittable. Garcia had a four hitter through 8 1/3, and Buerhle had allowed only two hits, including a Bret Boone solo homer run.

Paniagua and Franklin held the White Sox at bay, while three Sox relievers did the same to the Mariners. In the bottom of the 14th, Paul Konerko ended the four hour contest by driving in a run against Franklin on a wicked 3-2 slider. Sometimes even the best pitches are handled by major league hitters.

White Sox pitcher Gary Glover, who entered the game with a 6.17 ERA, completely shut down the torrid Mariner offense by striking out four, and giving up only one hit in three innings of relief. White Sox won 2-1.

Jose Paniagua – P
Born: 08-20-73, San Jose de Ocoa, DR
Lives in Santo Domingo, DR with his two daughters
6'2" 195 lbs
Signed through 2001

The Mariners' win streak was over, but with a 20-5 record, the M's were the talk of baseball. The player of the month could have been Sele or Moyer, both with 4-0 records. It could have been Boone with a .344 average and 22 RBIs or Sasaki, with 13 saves. But if there had to be one player of the month of April 2001, it would be Ichiro. He was second in the league in hits, ninth in batting average, leading the league in hitting with runners in scoring position, and had established himself as an intimidating base running threat and talented defensive player. He did all of this without ever having faced all but one of the pitchers he saw, and under the intensely probing eyes of a massive number of Japanese media.

April Magical Moments (20 wins - 5 losses . . . Season 20-5)
1. Opening Day is always magical (2nd)
2. Edgar 1st on all time Mariner hit list (3rd)
3. Ichiro gets 4 hits, 1st HR (6th)
4. Bell's throw from the seat of his pants (10th)
5. Sweep of Oakland (10th-13th)
6. Ichiro's "The Throw" (11th)
7. First Japanese hitter vs. Japanese pitcher in major leagues - Ichiro vs. Nomo (13th)

Special Note:
After a month of watching Ichiro play, the most impressive elements of his game are his bat control and focus. In fact his overall game, when all is said and done, may be comparable to Ty Cobb's. Ichiro's focus is so precise that he is probably the player least affected by cheers at home or boos in the road. He is always tuned to the moment. - MS

The Home Field Advantage

In 1995, the Mariners announced they would move to another city if they didn't get a new stadium. The team was housed in a building that had outlived its usefulness. The Kingdome was never a baseball facility. Tampa wanted a team, and it looked like the team of Randy Johnson, Ken Griffey, Jr., Edgar Martinez, and a young Alex Rodriguez would have a new home in Florida.

To some, that would be blackmailing a city. But to others, and I among them, a new stadium could be a unifying factor for an entire community. New baseball parks around the nation were a part of urban revitalization, and the architecture could make the area citizens proud.

I was a local talk radio host doing mostly current events issues in Seattle at the time, and convinced station management that the issue of a new stadium should be covered. I hosted radio programs from Coors Field in Denver and Jacobs Field in Cleveland to show the people of Seattle the financial success stories of these new ball parks. Could this do the same for Seattle?

But, for me, there was an overriding reason for building a new stadium. As a child in Brooklyn during the 1950's, the Dodgers were my passion. I never missed a game if I could help it. And, the players became heroes to me. There was one special player.

Edwin Donald "Duke" Snider, Dodger center fielder, was my ultimate hero. I would literally count the number of Dodger hitters who would have to come to the plate before Duke would bat again.

It was that heritage within me that gave the conviction to fight for SAFECO Field (as it became known). I wanted the children of Seattle to have the same opportunity for baseball heroes that I had as a child in Brooklyn.

Could SAFECO provide a home field advantage to the Mariners? The fans would have the loudest say - *MS.*

	Chapter Five

May, 2001

"Boys, baseball is a game where you gotta' have fun. You do that by winning." - Dave Bristol, major league manager 1966-1980

After a record setting April, the Seattle Mariners were going to get their "comeuppance," so said the naysayers. Besides, Seattle had no stars, no icons and no obscenely overpriced prima donna athlete waiting for a chance to duck the fans.

Three game series at home vs. Boston (M's take 2)

The worst nightmare an American League hitter can have is that he will be facing Pedro Martinez in his next game. Unfortunately for Mariner hitters, they got to experience the nightmare as May got underway.

Even if he does wear another uniform, there's a certain awe inspired when Red Sox ace Pedro Martinez takes the mound. It is like watching Picasso paint. Pedro is an artist on the mound, and John Halama drew the opposing assignment.

May 1 A chilly, clear Pacific Northwest evening greeted the first Red Sox-Mariners battle of the 2001 season. Martinez, the Cy Young winner, strikeout king and ERA champ was matched by Halama as each pitcher held the opponent to few baserunners and no runs.

Martinez got the Mariners out with called strikes, swinging strikes, and surrendered only three weak singles. After eight innings, Martinez had struck out half the 24 outs recorded. In doing so, he fired 136 pitches to his catcher.

Halama got the visitors out on rising fastballs causing fly ball outs, and in eight innings had thrown only 98 pitches in his five strikeout, no walk gem. No Red Sox runner advanced past first base in the first five innings. But in the sixth, three Boston singles produced the only run Pedro would need.

Boston won 2-0. Martinez'career stats against the Mariners was an astounding 8-0 with a 0.89 ERA. Wow!

May 2 Boston's Hideo Nomo and Seattle's Aaron Sele were a marquis matchup. When the Japanese computer magnate, Hiroshi Yamauchi, became involved in team ownership, many wondered if there were going to be Japanese players in Mariner uniforms. While there had been several Japanese players in the major leagues, beginning with Masanori Murakami of the San Francisco Giants in 1964-1965, none had been particularly successful in the United States.

Kazu Sasaki, the Mariners' 32-year old AL Rookie-of-the-Year in 2000, took a step beyond anything that a Japanese player had ever accomplished in the major leagues. But there had never been a Japanese position player make it in America until Ichiro.

Boston's Hideo Nomo was the first pitcher from Japan in 30 years to make the major leagues, and he was going to face his countryman, Ichiro, in Seattle before one of the largest world-wide broadcast audiences to ever watch or hear a regular season baseball game.

Pancho Ito, a popular Japanese sportscaster was in Seattle to cover the game. He commented that Ichiro's exploits were "front page news" - not just sports news - nearly every day in Japan.

The Mariners had yet to lose two games in a row, but had also yet to face two such dominating pitchers as Boston's Pedro and Nomo. The M's, though, were up to the task.

Ichiro led off the bottom of the 1st intent upon getting a hit, but Nomo would have none of that. Ichiro didn't get a chance. Nomo plunked him in the back. Ichiro caught his breath, and took first base where he was stranded. Seattle fans were irate. How dare Nomo bean his own countryman!?! Especially since it was our guy!

Edgar Martinez later took the offense on his shoulders, driving in the M's first three runs. In the meantime, Sele was masterful, scattering seven hits in seven innings. Moreover, Sele extended his streak of not walking a batter to 22 innings, and picked up his fifth win against no losses. Nelson and Rhodes finished the game for the Mariners.

Nomo hit the showers after the sixth, having surrendered four hits, three walks and four runs to the home team. M's won 5-1.

Edgar Martinez – DH
Born: 01-02-63, New York, NY
Lives in Kirkland, WA with wife Holli and one child
5'11" 210
Signed through 2001

May 3 The rubber game of the series pitted Boston's Frank Castillo against Jamie Moyer, who was seeking to match teammate Aaron Sele with a 5-0 start. There is a kind of magic whenever Moyer is on the mound for Seattle: Mariner hitters get a quick start out of the gate.

The M's posted Moyer to a 2-0 lead in the bottom of the first behind Ichiro's double and steal of third, taking home on Edgar Martinez's sacrifice fly. Olerud then hit a solo shot. Later, Mark McLemore supplied the offensive power with a pinch-hit three run double. At that point, the "Mac of All Trades" was five for six as a pinch hitter. McLemore's positive attitude showed his character this early in the season. After requesting a trade in Spring Training to a team where he could start, McLemore accepted his role and made the best of it.

Ichiro collected three more hits and Cameron hit his third homer. Edgar collected his 1,000th career base-on-balls.

Moyer gave up three runs in seven innings and Charlton and Sasaki provided the finishing touches. The M's coasted 10-3.

Jamie Moyer – P
Born: 11-18-62, Sellersville, PA
Lives in Seattle, WA with wife Karen and four children
6'0" 175 lbs
Signed through 2002

Three game series at home vs. Toronto (M's take 1)
Seattle had won the first nine series of the season, and owned a daunting 22-6 record as they went into the three-game set with Toronto. The Mariners would win 127 games at this pace, but Toronto caused skid marks in Seattle's road to victory.

May 4 Mariner pitcher Paul Abbott chose to challenge Toronto strong man Raul Mondesi, but the Blue Jay got the worm here. Mondesi slammed two homers against Abbott, who pitched poorly in his second consecutive start.

Following Abbott's exit in the sixth, Norm Charlton and Jose Paniagua were unable to stop the visitors, who defeated the M's before 42,284 fans.

Mike Cameron hit a homer for the second consecutive night, and Ichiro went 2-4 extending his hitting streak to 11 games and raising his average to .348. Blue Jays 8, M's 3.

May 5 On a dreary, Seattle-gray day, the Mariners got back on track, but it took a pinch hit homer by Dan Wilson, who was mired in an 0-18 slump, to get things going.

The M's ace, Freddy Garcia, had his strike out pitch working, but not much else. He gave up seven hits and four runs in five innings; threw 106 pitches in the short outing; and was often behind in the count.

Nelson-Rhodes-Sasaki pitched four innings of relief, permitting one unearned run. Netting his 14th save, Sasaki's perfect appearance lowered his ERA to 3.45. Regardless of save numbers, to be a top closer in the league meant that Kazu couldn't maintain such a high ERA. But it was headed in the right direction. M's 7, Blue Jays 5.

Jeff Nelson – P
Born: 11-17-66, Baltimore, MD
Lives in Issaquah, WA with wife and four children
6'8" 235 lbs
Signed through 2003

May 6 Seattle went for its tenth straight series win sending John Halama to start against Toronto. The game was never in doubt as the Blue Jays had their way with Halama and reliever Ryan Franklin, scoring 11 runs on 14 hits.

Though Halama gave up five runs, only one was earned. Arare error, by third baseman Mark McLemore, opened a flood of two-out hits by Toronto spotting the visitors to a 4-0 lead. The Mariners would never catch Toronto, despite home runs by Bret Boone, his second, and Tom Lampkin, his third. It would later seem odd that Tom Lampkin led Bret Boone in homers after over a month of play.

Raul Mondesi continued his feasting on Mariner pitching and tremendous start with two more hits, including his 9th home run. He went 7-12 for the series and had nine RBIs. Blue Jays 11, M's 3.

Three game series at Boston (M's take 2)

May 8 Following the first series loss of the year, the Mariners flew across country to meet the Boston Red Sox. Game 1 of the set produced Seattle's first two game losing streak of the year. For the second straight game, the M's were pounded.

Three Mariner pitchers went to the mound and each of them was touched for runs, as the Red Sox had 14 hits, including four homers, and scored 12 times. Jamie Moyer suffered his first loss of the year, and Bret Tomko and Norm Charlton were ineffective, giving up five runs in 4 2/3 innings. Boston's Hideo Nomo avenged his loss in Seattle by taking the win.

Mike Cameron, the fence busting Mariner centerfielder, found out that Fenway's Green Monster doesn't give in. He left the game after slamming into the wall trying to catch Troy O'Leary's triple.

Mike Cameron – OF
Born: 01-08-73, LaGrange, GA
Lives in LaGrange, GA with wife
JaBreka and three children
6' 1" 195 lbs
Signed through 2003

With the loss, Seattle fell behind Minnesota for the majors' best record. One bright spot in the game: Ichiro went 2-5, extending his hitting streak to 14 games. Red Sox 12, M's 4.

May 9 Would the next game be the first time the Mariners lose three straight games? Not if the Mariners' 5-0 pitcher, Aaron Sele could help it. He pitched well enough through five innings to hold the hot-hitting hometown Red Sox to three runs on five hits. But reliever Arthur Rhodes, entering the game with an infinitesimal ERA of 0.69, surrendered two runs in less than two innings to let the Sox tie the game at 5.

Then the 8th inning arrived, and the M's exploded for five runs behind the timely hitting of Al Martin, David Bell and Dan Wilson. That trio started the game with a combined season's average of .177, but broke out of their slumps together with a collective seven hits. This Mariner team seemed to rise to the occasion with whatever was needed, and this game was a clear example of that.

Jeff Nelson got the win, and Kazu Sasaki threw one pitch to end the game on a double play and earn his 15th save. M's 10, Red Sox 5.

After the game, manager Lou Piniella revealed that the Mariners had videotaped Boston catcher Jason Varitek giving the sign to throw at Seattle's John Olerud. Perhaps it was in retaliation for the Red Sox Chris Stynes'breaking his cheekbone on an Aaron Sele pitch. Olerud wasn't beaned, but hit the dirt several times avoiding high and tight pitches. Such is the lot in the life of a baseball player. Bean balls happen. They're playing baseball, not chess!

May 10 The rubber game of the series at Boston was another fine performance by John Halama. Ascoreless tie was broken in the fifth when Al Martin, who was on first with a single, scored on a double by Carlos Guillen. The 6'2" 214 lb. linebacker look-alike was part of Piniella's aggressive baserunning scheme, and was forced to run through Boston catcher Jason Varitek to tag the plate. A huge argument ensued, with both Varitek and Boston manager Jimy Williams being ejected.

Halama pitched 5 1/3 innings of two hit ball. Nelson, Charlton and Sasaki only gave up two hits the rest of the way. Sasaki picked up another save – his 16th – and lowered his ERA to 3.12. Nelson's and Charlton's were at 1.72 and 3.00 respectively. M's 5, Red Sox 2.

Having recaptured the best record in baseball at 25-9, the M's packed their bags for Toronto, the only team to take a series from them so far.

> Speaking about Boston manager Jimy William's ejection, Mariner manager Lou Piniella said: "Jimy reminded me a little bit of me. I mean that in a complimentary way. The only thing he missed was kicking his hat. I sort of enjoyed watching him." Quoted in *Seattle PI*, May 11, 2001.

Three game series at Toronto (M's sweep!)

The resiliency of the Mariners to bounce back after defeat became obvious in the first 34 games of the season. While the series at Toronto wasn't crucial in the eyes of most baseball fans, it meant something to Mariner players. The Blue Jays had come to SAFECO just a week before and had embarrassed the M's. The 2001 edition of the Seattle Mariners wanted revenge.

May 11 The M's sent Paul Abbott, in search of his first win, to face off against the Canadian team's Joey Hamilton. Abbott and Hamilton were an even match through five innings, with Abbott giving up an unearned run.

In the top of the sixth the Mariners scored all the runs they would need on a three-run homer by Mike Cameron. Abbott gave up an additional run (this one earned) in 5 1/3 innings. Paniagua and Rhodes pitched 3 2/3 innings of scoreless baseball, striking out five along the way. The relief performance lowered the bullpen's ERA to 2.78 for the year. Ichiro was 2-5, stretching his hitting streak to 17 games. M's won 7-2.

Paul Abbott – P
Born: 08-15-67, Van Nuys, CA
Lives in Fullerton, CA with wife Yvette and four children
6'3" 204 lbs
Signed through 2001

May 12 Seeking to extend the team winning streak to four games, the Mariners trotted out ace Freddy Garcia against the Blue Jays' Cris Carpenter in game 2 of the series. This was not a day for pitchers, though, as Garcia gave up six runs in 4 2/3 innings. It was unfortunate for Garcia because the Mariners had given him a 7-0 lead.

The Mariners collected a season high 18 hits including 11 by the first three in the lineup: Ichiro (4 hits), McLemore (3) and Martinez (4). McLemore (who was a double short of hitting for the cycle) and Cameron homered.

Tomko got the win. Rhodes, Nelson and Sasaki sealed the victory. M's won 11-7.

May 13 Jamie Moyer was the next Mariner pitcher to try to get back on track as Seattle went for the sweep on Mother's Day at Toronto. Once again, timely Mariner hitting overcame poor pitching to secure the win.

Like it was supposed to be, Ichiro's presence was felt from the beginning of the game. He doubled to lead off the 1st inning and scored on Edgar's single. But, the Blue Jays came back to tie in the second. A Bret Boone homer in the third put the Mariners back on top, but Toronto rallied to tie the game at 5 in the fifth.

The win was vintage Mariners. Some called it "small ball," but Piniella said it's "just baseball the way it's supposed to be played."

In the top of the sixth, little used Charles Gipson singled for his first hit of the year. Ichiro followed with his own single, placing runners on first and third. A third Mariner single in a row by McLemore drove in a run, and kept runners on first and third. Then, the pesky Ichiro drew an errant pickoff attempt and came in to score.

With a lead coming into the late innings, it was bullpen time. Moyer couldn't go the distance, giving up eight hits, including three home runs, and five runs. The Mariner bullpen went to work. Franklin, Charlton, Paniagua and Sasaki pitched one-hit ball the rest of the way to slam shut any further Blue Jay comebacks. M's won 7-5.

Norm Charlton – P
Born: 01-06-63, Fort Polk, LA
Lives in Santonio, TX with wife Brenda
6'3" 205 lbs
Signed through 2001

Previously, the Mariners had set their club record for road victories in 1997 with 45. At 17-4 on the road, the M's could go 29-31 in the remaining 60 games on the road and still break that record.

Three game series at home vs. Chicago White Sox (M's sweep!)

Back in the friendly confines of SAFECO Field, the M's prepared for a six-game homestand against two of last year's playoff teams – the White Sox and the Yankees.

May 15 It was Aaron Sele's turn to pitch, and his opponent on the mound was Mark Buerhle. The White Sox jumped out with two in the top of the first, but as it seemed to happen all season, the Mariners immediately replied with a run of their own in the bottom half of the inning. It was a typical Seattle run – Ichiro single, a balk, and two ground balls for the run.

Mariner pitching then settled down giving up only one run the rest of the way, but it couldn't have happened without defensive gems. After the Mariners had gone ahead 4-3 behind the hitting of Bret Boone, Chicago made their move. Arthur Rhodes was on the mound when White Sox Josh Paul shot a liner into the right field corner. Ichiro recovered from a slip and caught up with the ball clanging around in the right field corner. He threw a bullet to cut-off man Boone, who wheeled, and seemingly without even looking, cast a laser beam to Mark McLemore at third base who put the tag on the sliding Paul.

But the Sox weren't finished. After a Ray Durham single, Mariner killer Jose Valentin hit a rocket down the left field line. Stan Javier raced over to cut the ball off holding Durham to third base. Javier's play didn't show up in the box score, but it saved the game.

Paniagua came in to get the final out. M's won 4-3.

Two streaks continued. The M's winning streak stood at six and Ichiro's hitting streak was at 20.

> "This is the best fundamental team I've ever seen. We move runners over. We put pressure on with our running game. We make the plays on defense. Our late inning relief pitching is great. These guys know how to play the game."
>
> -- Bret Boone,
> May 15, 2001

May 16 The M's Paul Abbott was looking for his first good pitching performance of the season, and faced Chicago's Rocky Biddle. The incredibly determined Abbott is an amazing story. In 16 years of professional baseball, he had been on the disabled list 11 times for arm, shoulder and knee injuries. He persevered. Teams dropped him enough so that he had to sign a total of six minor league contracts just to maintain a chance to play. Living out of a suitcase in towns such as Elizabethton, Kenosha, and Visalia made him strive for success even more.

In 2000, Abbott showed signs of finally making the grade. His 179 innings pitched were by far the most he had ever thrown in the majors. He finished at 9-7 with a 4.22 ERA; not great, but respectable. He started the 2001 season in a familiar place – the disabled list. Since then, he was an unimpressive 1-1 with a 4.70 ERA.

Abbott was vying for a spot in the Mariners' rotation, and his performance against the White Sox on May 16, 2001, would go a long way in manager Lou Piniella's eyes.

The 33 year-old righthander struggled with his control early in the game. He gave up two runs, but then found his stride and became nearly unhittable. In 6 1/3 innings, Abbott gave up just three hits, and struck out 10. When he reached the 100 pitch mark, Lou congratulated Abbott for a job well done. Charlton and Paniagua finished the game flawlessly.

For offense, it was the typical Mariner method. Ichiro was the catalyst, and any one of a number of Mariners finding a gap with two outs to drive in runs. All of Seattle's seven runs came with two outs. This time, the hitting heroes were Olerud and Guillen.

> **Without heavy lumber of their own, some say the Mariners are a boring team to watch. They score by advancing runners, bunts, sacrifices, hitting behind the runner. Nothing spectacular – but they win. Winning is never boring. -** *SE*

Ichiro extended his hitting streak to 21, and had hit in 37 of 39 games so far. M's won 7-2.

May 17 Mariner fans, coaches and players were all ready for would-be ace Freddy Garcia to pitch a good game. They weren't disappointed. Opposing Garcia was White Sox ace David Wells, the portly, $9 million/year lefthander.

The offense was, again, typical Seattle. In the first, Ichiro singled, stole second and third, and walked home on Edgar's single. Throughout the game, Bret Boone had a homer and a double, driving in three runs, increasing his batting average to .331.

But the game story was Freddy. He was dominating. In 7 2/3 innings, he yielded only six hits, one a solo homer to Paul Konerko, and walked one batter. Jeff Nelson closed out the game for Garcia, whose record stood at 4-0. M's won 5-1.

Off the field, Jose Paniagua, was suspended for three games for *nearly* hitting Boston's Manny Ramirez in a May 9th game at Fenway. The league was cracking down on high and tight pitches, but the Mariners were shocked that Paniagua was suspended and without hitting anyone.

In other off the field news, GM Pat Gillick was still in search of another bat. Al Martin still wasn't hitting well enough to be the regular left fielder. Stan Javier and Mark McLemore were too valuable as utility men, and Charles Gipson, perhaps the best athlete on the team, couldn't solve curve balls. It was uncertain when Jay Buhner would wield his mighty bat again. That left Gillick to continue the hunt.

> Don Drysdale and Bob Gibson were two great pitchers known for throwing inside against hitters.
>
> As said before it is a part of the game. But the best quote on the subject came from another great pitcher who wasn't known for beanballs. This Hall-of-Famer said: "Pitching is the art of instilling fear." Who made that chilling statement? Sandy Koufax Brooklyn and Los Angeles Dodgers. - *SE*

But at 31-9, with an eight game winning streak, was there any reason to fiddle with success? Rome wasn't burning, but the Yankees were coming to town. A three in a row world champion, the Mariners were not. Another hitter in the Mariners' stable wouldn't hurt.

Pat Gillick – General Manager
Born: 08-22-37, Chico, CA
Lives in Seattle, WA with wife Doris

Three game series at home vs. Yankees (M's take 1)
May 18 Last year's American League Championship Series contenders had two lefthanders, John Halama for the Mariners and Ted Lilly for the Yankees on the mound. Just about everyone who saw the game wished Halama and Lilly had remained in their respective dugouts.

By the end of the first inning, the score was 4-3 Yanks, and it only got worse. In three innings, Halama gave up eight hits and seven runs. His relief help, Bret Tomko, wasn't much better. He gave up seven hits and six runs in the next three innings. Overall, New York collected 19 hits and 14 runs.

On the Mariners side, they had 13 hits and 10 runs, including three more hits by rookie sensation Ichiro Suzuki. His hitting streak stood at 23 and his average had reached a lofty .375. Showing the aggressiveness that epitomized the 2001 season, the less than fleet-footed Dan Wilson stole his first base of the year. Yanks took the opener in a football score 14-10.

Dan Wilson – C
Born: 03-25-69, Barrington, IL
Lives in Seattle, WA with wife Annie
and their three children
6'3" 214 lbs
Signed through 2002

May 19 While the first game of the series had fans with strained necks watching the hits fly and runners dash around the bases so much it was like viewing a tennis match, game 2 of the series was a well-played pitching contest by two solid teams.

Jamie Moyer of the M's and Orlando "El Duque" Hernandez of the Yanks pitched remarkably. Hernandez gave up four hits and one run, striking out eight in eight innings. Moyer was even better – allowing no runs, one hit and walking none in seven innings.

The M's took a 1-0 lead going into the top of the 9th inning, a perfect situation for the Mariners to win. But the vaunted Mariner bullpen couldn't hold the reigning champions. Arthur Rhodes had pitched a perfect 8th, striking out two of the three batters he faced. Kazu Sasaki entered in the 9th to close it out, but the Yankees borrowed a page from the Mariners'book. Alfonso Soriano hit a one out single for the Yankees in the 9th, and then promptly stole second and third. After a Chuck Knoblauch pop-out, Derek Jeter came to the plate with two outs. Since Soriano had taken third, Sasaki was limited in throwing his nasty splitter, because a wild pitch would have brought in the tying run. Instead, Kazu sent a fastball to the plate, and Jeter laced it through the infield sending the game into extra innings.

In the 10th the Yankees played Mariner baseball again. Bernie Williams hit a leadoff double against Sasaki, and advanced to third when Tino Martinez guided the ball to the right side of the infield. Williams then scored on a ground out.

New York's Mariano Rivera, who set the benchmark for consistency out of the bullpen, threw only nine pitches to get the M's out in the bottom of the 10th securing the win, and chalking up the Mariners' second series loss of the season. For just the third time in the season, the Mariners had lost two games in a row.

Ichiro's hitting streak was stopped at 23. In presumably his last at-bat of the game in the 8th inning, El Duque escorted Ichiro to first base with a first pitch fastball in the back – not the kind of "hit" Ichiro wanted. Yankees 2, M's 1.

May 20 Seeking to get back in the win column, Seattle sent Aaron Sele to the mound against one of the best pitchers in baseball, the Yankees' Roger Clemens in game 3 of the series. The flame-throwing, multiple Cy Young award winner had more victories against the Mariners (21) than any other pitcher.

> **Mariners hitting coach Gerald Perry has been remarkable in developing patience at the plate. Hitters go deep into the count wearing down pitchers and causing more hittable pitches to be thrown. Mariner batters in 2001 have been superb in taking the plate away from opposing pitchers.**

But, this was a statement game for the Mariners. The patient Seattle batters made Clemens throw strikes, and after three straight walks in the 1st, Bret Boone sent a rocket into the right-center field gap, scoring three runs. By the end of the second inning, the M's had scored five times, handing Clemens his first loss of the season. In fact, Clemens wouldn't lose again until September.

Meanwhile, Aaron Sele made quick work of the Yankees, scattering eight hits and two runs over 7 2/3 innings. Rhodes and Nelson struck out three of the four batters they faced to lock up the win. M's 6, Yankees 2.

Acrowd of 45,953 - the largest regular season attendance in SAFE-

CO history – saw the M's improve to 32-11, a remarkable eleven games ahead in the AL West.

Two game series at Minnesota (split)

The mighty Minnesota Twins! Huh? Since when has Minnesota been referred to as "mighty?" Since the Twins, with the tiny-for-baseball-payroll, had the second best record at 29-13, that's when!

May 22 Paul Abbott took the mound for the Mariners and Brad Radke for the Twins. Between them, they would give up 18 hits and 15 runs, neither lasting more than 4 1/3 innings.

The third inning was a nightmare for the Mariners as eight Twins scored. Ryan Franklin relieved Abbott, shutting the door on Minnesota and giving Seattle a chance to come back.

And come back they did! The M's scored seven runs, getting nine hits from the 3,4,5 and 6 hitters (Martinez, Olerud, Boone and Cameron). With a one-run deficit going into the bottom of the 8th, it would seem the Mariners were poised to complete the comeback.

Bret Boone – 2B
Born: 04-06-69, El Cajon, CA
Lives in Orlando, FL with wife Suzi, and two children
5'10" 190 lbs
Signed through 2001

But Minnesota's young first baseman, Doug Mientkiewicz, hitting over .400 at the time, slammed M's reliever Norm Charlton's splitter for a single to drive in two more Twins runs.

With a seemingly insurmountable five run deficit in the 9th, the M's started the inning with three straight singles, loading the bases. A new pitcher came in for the Twins. After a force out at home, Carlos Guillen singled in two runs. Then Tom Lampkin doubled, driving in another run and sending Guillen to third. An Ichiro sacrifice fly made the score 12-11, Twins, with two outs and a Mariner in scoring position. But Mark McLemore struck out ending the one of the strangest games of the season. Twins 12, M's 11.

After the game, the Mariners made a roster move. Sometimes hard hitting Toronto Blue Jay Tony Fernandez was released. Pat Gillick, the former Blue Jay GM, was familiar with Fernandez's skills and considered making an offer. But the Brewers snatched him away, and Seattle promoted Ed Sprague from Tacoma. A veteran third baseman, Sprague was expected to spell Olerud at first, Edgar at DH and contribute in left field.

May 23 Two would-be All Star pitchers, Freddy Garcia and the Twins' Eric Milton faced each other at the Metrodome. Neither was particularly sharp. Garcia gave up seven hits, three walks and four runs before leaving in the 7th inning. Milton finished the 7th, giving up ten hits, two walks and four runs.

A clutch solo home run by David Bell in the 8th gave the Mariners the lead for good. Bell started the season slowly, and had steadily increased his average to .229. But his defensive play at third base made him a Seattle pitchers' favorite.

In the bottom of the 8th inning, Arthur Rhodes, who had relieved Garcia in the 7th, walked the first two batters. After a swinging bunt strikeout, Jeff Nelson came in to pitch to Minnesota's Torii Hunter who already had two hits in the game.

Nellie has a 95 mile-an-hour fastball; a wicked slider; and rarely gave up hits. But he was prone to handing out bases-on-balls, and on this occasion Nelson walked Hunter to load the bases with one out, the M's clinging precariously to a one-run lead.

Piniella stomped to the mound, snatched the ball from Nelson's hand and brought in Kazu Sasaki, in search of a strikeout. Jacques Jones was at the plate for the Twins and worked the count to 3-2. Sasaki fired a high and way-outside fastball, but the overanxious Jones swung and missed the errant pitch for strike three. Sasaki cruised through the next four hitters for his 18th save.

Kazuhiro Sasaki – P
Born: 02-22-68, Sendai City, Japan
Lives in Yokohama, Japan with wife
Kaori and two children
6'4" 220 lbs
Signed through 2002

Thank you, Jacques. Alittle luck doesn't hurt – no matter how good you are. M's 5, Twins 4.

Four game series at Kansas City (M's sweep!)
In any sport a team isn't great unless it beats the teams it's supposed to defeat. Against the lowly Kansas City Royals, the M's did just that, but it wasn't easy. No major league opponent is.

May 25 The M's staked John Halama to a lead in the 1st inning off an Edgar Martinez homer. In the 3rd, though, Halama came unglued. Halama yielded five runs in that inning without retiring a single Royal before rookie Ryan Franklin came in. Franklin proceeded to do a masterful job for the next five innings, but the Mariner had a huge 6-1 deficit to overcome.

Since the Mariners hit few home runs, big innings rarely happen. The M's were a "chip-away" team. With the strong bullpen work of Franklin, who threw first pitch strikes to 15 of the 17 batters he faced, Seattle had time to cut the lead; two runs in the 4th and 7th made it a one-run game going into the inning the Mariners have owned all season, the 8th.

Mike Cameron lead off the 8th with another patient walk, and took third on Tom Lampkin's single. Carlos Guillen hit a grounder to third, but Cameron got caught in no man's land, and was out at the plate. Then Bell reached base on a KC throwing error, scoring one run, with Mariners on first and second. The danger of Ichiro, even on a routine ground ball, then came into play. Ichiro slapped a one hopper to Royal pitcher Jason Grimsley. The pitcher could have gone to third for a force or to second to perhaps start a double play, but he couldn't decide what to do. So Grimsley opted to get the safe out, but when he turned toward first he was obviously surprised to find that Ichiro had almost reached the base. Grimsley hurried to throw the ball wildly over first baseman's Mike Sweeney's head allowing the winning run to score. The M's added two more runs in the 9th.

Paniagua and Rhodes pitched the bottom of the 8th, and Sasaki earned his 19th save with a perfect 9th. Franklin was credited with a well-deserved win. M's won 9-6.

May 26 Aaron Sele, 6-0, owning the league's second best ERA, took the mound for the Mariners against the Royals Brian Meadows, 1-5.

The Mariners jumped on top in the 3rd with characteristic Seattle "small ball." Olerud and Boone singled, and with men on first and second, Martin directed a grounder to the right side moving both runners into scoring position with one out. Guillen doubled them home, and Wilson singled Guillen home, for a 3-0 Mariner lead.

> *"This is a simple game.*
> *You throw the ball,*
> *You hit the ball,*
> *You catch the ball."*
> **Manager, Durham Bulls**
> **(*Bull Durham*, 1988)**
>
> **Or was it Lou Piniella,**
> **Seattle, 2001?**

That's all Sele needed as he sprinkled eight hits over seven innings. Jeff Nelson came in for the 8th and 9th. M's won 7-2.

May 27 Game 3 of the series was a nail-biter from start to finish. Jamie Moyer was effective, if not spectacular, in ceding seven hits and three runs in 6 2/3 innings.

Meanwhile the Mariners manufactured four runs of their own with singles and advancing runners.

Entering the bottom of the ninth, the M's had a 4-3 lead. That meant it was Sasaki time, and the Mariner faithful were ready to chalk up another win. Not so fast, though, as KC's David McCarty took a Sasaki forkball that didn't bite to the fountains at Kauffman Stadium, sending the game into extra innings.

Neither team scored in the 10th, but it was back to the manufacturing plant for the Mariners in the 11th. Edgar singled, and Gipson came in to run. Even when Edgar's legs are healthy, he's not exactly a sprinter. Olerud singled, but Gipson could only take second. Boone, the league's leading RBI man at the time, bunted the runners over one base. Ichiro was intentionally walked to get to Cameron. The popular centerfielder hadn't been hitting well over the past several weeks, and had already struck out twice in this game. But he knew he had to get the run in. His sacrifice fly accomplished his goal. "I went with the pitch instead of chasing what they threw me," said Cameron. Norm Charlton pitched two perfect innings for the win.

Was this a dramatic win in the overall scheme of the season? Probably not, but it was great baseball. The M's created runs through sheer smart, unselfish play. This was characteristic of what would happen all season long. M's won 5-4.

In the meantime, there was no indication that Gillick had stopped his desire for another hitter. The rumor was that he could be turning to Japan again. Kazuo Matsui, 26 year-old .340 hitting shortstop had major league potential according to scouts. The Mariners' popularity in Japan was rising daily, and because of that the M's may have the upper hand over other teams. Any deal involving Matsui, though, would probably have to wait until after the season.

May 28 In the Memorial Day final game of the series, Paul Abbott pitched for the Mariners; Chad Durbin for the homestanding Royals. It was an historic day for Abbott – his first complete game in the major leagues.

The Mariners scored 10 runs in the first five innings and had smooth sailing the rest of the game. Dan Wilson and Carlos Guillen continued their strong hitting. Wilson had raised his average to .248 from .193 on May 5. Over the same period, Guillen raised his average from .196 to .245.

Abbott yielded just six hits and three runs, striking out six. The understated Abbott said: "It will be nice to take that baseball in my living room and say I threw a complete game." M's 13-3.

Carlos Guillen – SS
Born: 09-30-75, Maracay, Venezuela
Lives in Aragua, Venezuela with wife
Amelia and one child
6'1" 200 lbs
Signed through 2001

Three game series at home vs. Baltimore (M's sweep!)

May 29 The Cal Ripken final tour came to Seattle for the last three games of May as the baseball season moved from *early-season* to *mid-season*. No longer could the M's be considered just "out to a fast start." The first game with Baltimore was going to be the Mariners' 50th game, and the moniker of *early* no longer applied.

Freddy Garcia and the bullpen pitched another gem, and Ichiro officially became **the** human highlight.

SAFECO Field, like many of the new ballparks, has little room in the extreme outfield corners. There is a scant 18 inches between the right field line and the stands at the 326' mark in right field. In the 3rd inning, Oriole star Brady Anderson hit a screaming line drive toward the right field corner. An all-out sprint to get to the ball would have run Ichiro into the wall, and likely left him injured and the ball roaming free. Instead, as Ichiro hit the dirt of the warning track and the baseline, he slid on his back reaching out his glove in foul territory to snag the ball inches from the ground and the side wall.

But Ichiro wasn't finished with his defensive heroics. In the sixth, Ichiro made another sliding catch in right field, but perhaps the best play of all was for the game's final out. Baltimore's Jerry Hairston lifted a shallow fly ball to right field. It would have been an easy decision for most rightfielders to have let the ball land, and hold the batter to a single. Instead, Ichiro put on his Superman's cape, flew in toward the ball, and left his feet. Turning his body in mid-air to get his glove out as far as possible, he caught the fly to end the game. Then Ichiro popped up, pumped his fist in a rare exhibition of emotion, and joined his teammates in the victory celebration.

In addition to his outstanding defense, Ichiro drove in a run on two hits raising his average to .358.

Garcia gave up four hits and one earned run in seven innings. Rhodes, Nelson and Sasaki, who got his 20th save, completed the win. M's won 3-2.

Seattle was 38-12; the 10th best record in baseball history for the first 50 games.

The first results from All-Star voting were in, and several Mariners were in good position to be selected to the 2001 game to be played at SAFECO Field. Edgar Martinez led in votes for DH, of course, and John Olerud and Bret Boone were second at their positions. Mike Cameron was sixth among outfielders, but the surprise was that Ichiro was second, only 41 votes behind the leader Manny Ramirez. The big part of the surprise was that Ichiro was listed by his last name (Suzuki), not the name the country's fans knew. Additionally, none of these ballots reflected returns from Japan yet.

May 30 Game 2 of the Mariners-Orioles set was a tight one until the M's took control in the -- you guessed it -- 8th inning. The bottom of the inning began with the home team ahead 5-3. Guillen doubled to lead off the inning, and David Bell got him to third with a deep sacrifice fly. Then the dam broke, and the flood was on. Wilson doubled, scoring Guillen; Ichiro doubled, scoring Wilson; McLemore singled, scoring Ichiro; Edgar doubled, moving McLemore to third; Olerud homered scoring everyone. Boone joined in the fun by following with his own solo homer. All told, the M's put a big seven marker on the board in the inning.

John Halama got the win, giving up nine hits and two runs in six innings. Mark McLemore stole four bases, extending his streak to 16 straight steals during the season. The M's had now won seven consecutive games going into the last of May. M's 12, O's 5.

John Halama – P
Born: 02-22-72, Brooklyn, NY
Lives in Brooklyn, NY with wife Christina
6′5″ 200 lbs
Signed through 2001

May 31 The odds were stacked for the Mariners with Aaron Sele at 7-0 and a 2.81 ERAgoing against the Orioles Jose Mercedes at 1-6, 6.11 ERA. The M's won, and Sele got his 100th victory, but it was far from a cakewalk.

Seattle's runs were scored in the usual Mariner method. A Bell single, Ichiro and McLemore patient at-bat walks, an Edgar sacrifice fly and a two out single by Olerud scored the M's two runs.

It was the pitching and defense, though, that provided the highlights of the game. Going into the top of the 8th inning with a 2-1 lead, Sele had only allowed three hits, one a Cal Ripken solo home run. The Orioles Melvin Mora led off the inning with a double and the next batter sacrificed him to third. With a one run lead, one out and a man on third, left-handed pitcher Arthur Rhodes relieved Sele to face left-handed hitter Brady Anderson. The M's infield pulled in, but what they really needed was a strike out. Rhodes couldn't find the plate, though, and on a two balls, no strike count, Anderson hit a shot in the hole between 1st and 2nd bases. Olerud dove to his right as Mora broke for home. The throw to the plate under those circumstances is an awkward one for lefthanders such as Olerud. Mariner catcher Dan Wilson blocked the plate and Olerud muscled the throw perfectly to tag the sliding Mora. It was a good thing the out was made at home, because the next Oriole batter singled, but no damage was done.

Sasaki pitched the 9th, gaining his 21st save, and lowering his ERA to 3.04. M's won 2-1.

It was the end of May, and the Mariners were an incredible 40-12; a full 14 games ahead of the second place Oakland Athletics. This was the largest lead going into June that any team had ever attained since the start of the three-division system. Seattle's record for the first 52 games was the sixth best in baseball history.

Amazing record. Amazing stats. Amazing Mariners.

May Magical Moments (20 wins - 7 losses . . . Season 40-12)
1. Edgar gets 1000th base on balls (3rd)
2. Mariners get 18 hits against the Yankees (12th)
3. Ichiro's 23 game hitting streak ends (19th)
4. Abbott pitches first career complete game (28th)
5. Ichiro catch to end the game. Rare emotional display (29th)

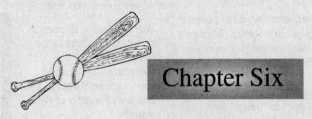

Chapter Six

June, 2001

"If I were playing third base and my mother were rounding third with the run that was going to beat us, I'd trip her. Oh, I'd pick her up and brush her off and say, 'Sorry, Mom,' but nobody beats me."
-- Leo Durocher, Hall of Fame Manager

The Mariners started June with an eight game winning streak, had won 77% of their games, and were on pace to win a record 125 games. Their victories were derived from starting pitching, relief pitching, defense, small ball, and an occasional home run. They had players having career years, such as Bret Boone and Mark McLemore, but every win seemed to have a different hero. Each player seemed to do what it took to win. It was as if the 25 players in Seattle uniforms all had the Leo Durocher attitude about winning. But the M's were genuinely nice guys and these 2001 Mariner nice guys certainly wouldn't finish last.

Three game series at home vs. Tampa Bay (M's sweep!)

June 1 Jamie Moyer, with a 6-1 record, squared off against Tampa Bay's Bryan Rekar at 0-6. The M's gave Moyer a 2-0 lead, as usual, on two walks and a Bret Boone double in the first inning. Moyer left the game in the 6th with a 5-4 lead, and had been victimized by a bad call in the outfield. Mark McLemore, playing left field, was judged to have trapped a line drive, which led to the first two Tampa Bay runs. The replay showed that McLemore had caught the ball, but the umpire, of course, wouldn't change his ruling.

The bad call didn't matter, however. Paniagua, Rhodes and Nelson pitched a scoreless final four innings for the win. M's won 8-4.

The season's one millionth fan was among the 41,094 at SAFECO.

June 2 Paul Abbott at 3-2 went against the Devil Rays'Ryan Rupe, 0-6. Greg Vaughn, the subject of numerous trade rumors, put the visitors ahead with a two run homer in the top of the first inning. That lead lasted exactly five Mariner batters. The first seven Mariners reached base on singles or walks, and the first five scored.

> The Mariners, in search of another hitter since the winter, led the American League in runs scored through the first two months of the season.

Abbott settled down, holding the Devil Rays to only two hits through the 5th inning. Ryan Franklin, Brian Fuentes (making his major league debut), Jose Paniagua and Kazu Sasaki went the rest of the way. M's won 3-2.

The M's win was their 10th in a row, tying the franchise's longest win streak, set in September 1996.

June 3 In another mismatch, Freddy Garcia won his sixth game without a loss. He pitched seven innings of one run ball, but tired in the 7th, yielding to Fuentes, and Nelson-Rhodes-Sasaki to finish. Ichiro, playing DH, was 3-4, with two runs, two stolen bases and an RBI. M's won 8-4.

Mark McLemore, who played third base, left field, center field, shortstop, and second base for the Mariners, missed his third straight game with a groin strain.

Three game series at home vs. Rangers (M's sweep!)
A-Rod came back to Seattle, but few cared to boo this time. The Mariners were 43-12, on an 11 game winning streak and were so far ahead of the rest of the AL West that it didn't matter who was in second. The Rangers, though, were 20-35, twenty-three games behind the Mariners, and led the planet in runs allowed.

June 4 Game 1 saw John Halama, and the Rangers Pat Mahomes take the mound. It was another game where the best pitchers weren't the starters.

Halama gave up six hits, two walks and six runs in 2 1/3 innings; Pat Mahomes was only slightly better and gave the Mariners eight hits, two walks and five runs through five innings.

The star of the night was Bret Boone, who drove in a career high seven runs on two three-run homers and a single to lead the Mariners to an 11-6 win. Boone took over the major league lead in RBIs, and was hitting a hefty .332. Ryan Franklin was nearly perfect out of the pen, striking out eight, walking one, and giving up only one hit in 5 1/3 innings. M's won 11-6.

June 5 The M's went for lucky win number 13 in a row by sending former Rangers ace, Aaron Sele to the hill against the Rangers current ace, Doug Davis.

Neither pitcher was particularly sharp, but kept their teams in the game. In the bottom of the 8th inning, with both starters having departed, Mike Cameron hit a two-run homer to give the Mariners their first lead of the game, 5-4. Cameron had entered the game mired in a 7-41 slump.

Kazu Sasaki pitched a 1-2-3 ninth for his 23rd save. M's won 5-4.

June 6 In the last game of the series, Jamie Moyer was seeking his 8th win versus the Rangers' Darren Oliver, who started the game at 4-1. The game was another Moyer masterpiece buoyed by the uncanny ability of the Mariners to give Moyer a lead. Edgar hit a solo homer in the first, and Moyer pitched seven innings of workmanlike, three-hit ball.

> While gone to Florida, Lou Piniella, watched his team on television. The M's won all four games the skipper missed. Lou said "It was fun to watch. I can understand why our ratings are so high."

But the Martinez home run was all the Mariners would get until the 8th, when Ichiro led off with a bunt single, and took second on the pitcher's throwing error. The Mariners then got six more hits in the inning off four rattled Rangers' relievers, and tallied six runs. M's won 7-3.

The M's won their 14th in a row and stood at 46-12. This is the second best 58-game start in history, trailing only the 1912 NYGiants.

Three game series at home vs. Padres (M's take 2)
The San Diego Padres came into town for the first set of interleague games in 2001. Manager Lou Piniella was back after having missed the previous four games while in Tampa with his wife, whose father passed away. And, Mark McLemore was back, having rested his strained groin.

June 8 Paul Abbott dueled the Padres'ace, Kevin Jarvis. The Padres got on top with a run in the first, but that was the last time San Diego was ahead. Edgar Martinez and Bob Boone homered in the M's first turn at bat. Then in the second, the Mariners were up to their old tricks, by not even bothering to start a rally until there were two outs. The M's got three more runs in the second, to lead 6-1.

Abbott pitched five hit ball for 7 2/3 innings, and Rhodes and Nelson closed out the game. The ERAs of Rhodes and Nelson hovered near the 1.00 mark for the season. Local sports-talk station KJR was taking friendly wagers on which of the two would have a sub 1.00 ERA first. Was it possible that Rhodes and Nelson would NEVER face pitching slumps? M's won 7-1.

Arthur Rhodes – P
Born: 10-24-69, Waco, TX
Lives in Baltimore, MD with wife and
two children
6'2" 206 lbs
Signed through 2003

June 9 Last year's Mariner baserunning catalyst, Rickey Henderson, provided the spark to halt the M's 15 game winning streak, handing Freddy Garcia his first loss of the season.

Garcia would struggle early in the game, something that would be an achilles' heel throughout the season. In the first two innings, Garcia's lack of control forced him to give the batters easy strikes to hit. The Padres went up 2-0 on a Rickey Henderson single who had been in a 2-43 slump prior to his run-scoring hit.

The M's tied the game in the 4th, and went ahead 3-2 in the 6th on a Guillen double, another Mariner sacrifice, and a Padre error. But the Padres took the lead for good in the 7th aided by a Phil Nevin single. Nevin, who was the apple of Seattle's eye over the winter and in spring training, was leading the team in batting average, home runs, slugging percentage, and RBIs. Padres 6, M's 3.

June 10 The Mariners'ability to bounce back after a loss was apparent all season. In game 3 of the Padres'series, John Halama pitched one of the best games in his career and the Mariners hit three home runs in an 8-1 victory.

Halama pitched seven innings of shutout baseball and the M's scored seven runs on dingers by Martin, Olerud and Ichiro before another capacity crowd at SAFECO Field. Rickey Henderson, who went 0-4, commented that Halama "had nothing" and he was looking forward to facing him again in San Diego. *(Kinda' makes you wonder what game Rickey attended.)*

The Mariners finished the homestand at 11-1, and stood overall at 48-13.

On June 6th, Seattle made a familiar name its top pick in the 2001 baseball draft, selecting shortstop Michael (Nomar's brother) Garciaparra.

The younger Garciaparra ultimately signed a contract with the Mariners, turning down a scholarship from the University of Tennessee.

Gillick Seeks No. 1

Surprising to some, GM Pat Gillick discussed his continued efforts to not only add another hitter, but also another pitcher to the Mariners' stable. He said: "If I can get a number one starter, I'd take a number one starter."

Immediately the pitcher who came to mind was the Chicago White Sox' David Wells. A veteran, playoff tested pitcher, Wells was just the type of ace Gillick described.

But Wells was known to be a clubhouse disaster, the kind of player who could cause problems for other players. Wells even went so far as to say that the White Sox slugger Frank Thomas was unwilling to play through minor injures. In fact, Thomas missed all but 20 games in 2001 due to a potentially career-ending injury. Wells' statements about Thomas were an indication of his unsuitability for Seattle.

Hall-of-Fame manager Sparky Anderson went on local sports radio station KJR and commented that Lou Piniella was a good enough manager to handle Wells. Anderson thought the $9 million/year overweight lefthander would be just what the Mariners needed.

To date, Piniella had been managing brilliantly. He was winning a record number of games without a known superstar; one of his best players (Mark McLemore) didn't even have his own position; his leadoff hitter was fourth in the team in on base percentage; but Lou won and got everyone enough playing time to be satisfied.

There was clearly a different feel in the clubhouse than in past years. Jay Buhner, second only to Edgar Martinez in Mariner longevity, on the disabled list but with the club nearly every game, commented: "There's a different feel about this team. There's no loud music in the clubhouse. There are no egos. We're just a bunch of guys who know how to play baseball, and we go about doing our jobs."

Lou Piniella, Manager
Born: 08-28-43, Tampa, FL
Lives in Tampa, FL with wife Anita
Signed through 2003

Regardless of Sparky Anderson's sentiments, bringing the cantankerous, high-maintenance David Wells to Seattle would have diverted Piniella's attention to one player. The M's were a team that depended on its closeness, camaraderie, and blue-collar work habits. To infest that balance with David Wells would have been a travesty.

Fortunately, Gillick ignored the advice of Anderson, some fans and sportswriters, and flatly rejected David Wells at any price.

To this point in his short tenure as the Mariner GM, Gillick had been nearly perfect. He handled the almost intolerable situation of Ken Griffey, Jr., admirably, bringing to Seattle a competent centerfielder, Mike Cameron, as part of the deal. In his first year, Gillick signed Aaron Sele, Arthur Rhodes and John Olerud; he brought in the rookie pitcher of the year, Kazu Sasaki; he recognized the need for veteran savvy, and brought in clutch performers Mark McLemore and Stan Javier; and he refused to break the bank on Alex Rodriguez. Only the Al Martin deal tasted sour, but Martin would improve his hitting and defense after the 2001 All-Star break.

In his second year, he signed Bret Boone and Jeff Nelson. Then, with the encouragement of part-owner Hiroshi Yamauchi, Gillick took a big risk in bringing across the Pacific Ocean the now hugely impactful Ichiro Suzuki. And perhaps his biggest signing was retaining manager Lou Piniella.

Another, less publicized, artist helping to paint the Mariner picture was Chairman Howard Lincoln. His leadership in retaining Piniella, and in signing Sasaki and Ichiro has not been well chronicled.

Lincoln had to give Gillick the tools to acquire the talent, but also had to persuade Mariner ownership that Gillick was making the right moves.

> **"If you want to get a ring, you have to have a number one starter."**
> **– Seattle GM Pat Gillick, June, 2001.**

Imagine two people on either ends of a teeter-totter, and Howard Lincoln is the fulcrum. Mariner upper management seemed as good as the team on the diamond.

In the meantime, the search for another bat and a number one starter continued. The Mariners' money pitcher was Freddy Garcia, Jamie Moyer or Aaron Sele. As good as they were, would they be the kind of pitchers to be mentioned with Roger Clemens of the Yankees, Pedro Martinez of the Red Sox, Randy Johnson of the Diamondbacks, or Greg Maddux of the Braves?

That answer was clearly no.

Howard Lincoln – Chairman/CEO
Born: 2-14-40
Lives on Mercer Island, WA with wife Grace

Three game series at Rockies (M's take 2)

Interleague play continued as the Mariners hit the road to Denver at the 2001 version of the launching pad, Coors Field. In interleague play, the home team rules apply regarding the designated hitter position. So, Edgar would get his view of the mountains from the bench.

First baseman John Olerud volunteered to play left field letting Edgar play first base to keep Martinez' bat in the game. Piniella rejected the idea as he had in 2000, reasoning that Edgar just wasn't the glove-man he used to be. And again, Edgar has a tendency to get hurt when he does anything other than hit. Edgar is a professional hitter with a capital "H." The M's were so far ahead of the AL West that a few days' rest for Mr. DH would harm the team.

June 12 Coors Field was like a pinball machine on this night. The hitters had flippers and the pitchers were serving the baseball and diving for cover. But the way the home runs were flying, the fans were ducking, too.

With the Rockies starting a lefthander, Brian Bohanon, Edgar did get to play at first base instead of John Olerud. He and Bret Boone hit 1st inning solo homers, but the Rockies matched the M's on a first-inning, two-run Todd Helton shot.

In the 2nd, it was Dan Wilson's turn with a solo homer, and the game stayed at 3-2 until the bottom of the 4th. Mariners'pitcher Aaron Sele didn't stop too many Rockies on this day, eventually giving up the lead and two runs, including a Ron Gant homer.

The Mariners'answered in the 6th, with Dan Wilson hitting a two run double, and Stan Javier gave his best imitation of Barry Bonds in hitting a two-run blast. The Mariners increased the lead to 9-4 in the 7th, scoring two runs, including another Boone moonshot.

But a lead is never safe at Coors, and the Rockies scored five times to tie the game at 9. Arthur Rhodes saw his ERAdouble by yielding three runs in 2/3 of an inning. Jose Paniagua's relief was no help, and it took rookie Brian Fuentes to calm the storm.

In the Seattle 9th, Mike Cameron, popular for his hustle, his smile and his contagious positive attitude, socked a Juan Acevedo fastball into the centerfield seats for the Mariners' win.

Kazu Sasaki picked up his 25th save, and preserved Fuentes' first career victory.

The game saw nine homers; six by the Mariners, a season high, tying a Coors Field record by a visiting team. There actually was a 10th homer hit. Todd Helton sent the go ahead home run over the left field wall, only to be snatched away by the leaping grab of the Mariners' Stan Javier in the 8th inning. Javier would make that catch again when it counted even more in October. M's 10, Rockies 9.

June 13 Rainout The next night, game 2 was rained out, but it was a good news/bad news kind of day. The good news was that Norm Charlton was coming off the disabled list. He had pulled a groin muscle two weeks before, enabling Brian Fuentes to get a shot in the show. Fuentes had pitched very well, 3 1/3 innings of hitless ball, but major league rosters are only as flexible as there are players with available options. Once the options are exhausted, the player must be made available to the other teams in the league or they must remain on the big league roster. That meant that Brian Fuentes would be going back to Tacoma, where he would get more innings, and develop his craft further.

The bad news, though, was that longtime Mariner outfielder and clutch-hitter, Jay Buhner, had to have surgery on his foot. His physician was guardedly optimistic that Buhner could see action by August 1.

In still other news, pitcher Jose Paniagua, who had several bad outings in a row needed something to change his fortunes.

> I don't like interleague play. It's like watching exhibition games. The uniforms of the opponents are funny. I don't recognize the players. I don't care what happens to the teams after they leave here. You hear people talking about "heated rivalries." You never hear them say "heated inter-league opponent."
>
> Let's forget interleague play, and give us more games against the Yankees or Red Sox - - - you know, those teams who are most fun to beat!   *- SE*

He accepted the suggestion from Mike Cameron that he needed to shave his head . . . donning that Buhner buzz-cut look. *Whatever it takes, huh?*

June 14 Game 1 The rainout necessitated a rare doubleheader. In the first game, the Mariners must have forgotten that whenever Jamie Moyer pitches, they are to give him a first inning lead. Instead, Rockies rookie pitcher Shawn Chacon looked like Tom Seaver, and held the Mariners to two hits and one unearned run. Moyer wasn't sharp. Rockies won 8-2.

June 14 Game 2 In the nightcap, the situation was reversed. The Mariners scored five runs before Mariners'pitcher Paul Abbott ever took the hill. The big hits were a bases loaded Al Martin triple and a David Bell two-run homer.

Abbott coasted through seven innings, and Arthur Rhodes pitched two innings of "Arthur Rhodes" type ball (no hits, two strikeouts), giving the M's the split. M's 5, Rockies 1.

To this point, of the 21 series Seattle had played, the M's won 18, lost two and split one. They were 50-14, two games behind the 1912 Giants.

Three game series at Padres (M's take 2)

June 15 The next part of the tour of pointless interleague play was at San Diego. Freddy Garcia, trying to rebound from his first loss, faced the very tough Padre pitcher, Bobby Jones. Despite a 3-8 record, Jones entered the contest with a 3.16 ERA, and since many Mariner hitters had never seen Jones before, it would be a difficult test.

Garcia, in addition to trying to get back in the win column, was pitching for the first time since the Gillick announcement of a search for a number one hurler. How Freddy would respond was on the minds of Mariner fans everywhere.

The M's 24-year old Venezuelan right-hander was awesome. He gave up four hits and one

> Throughout the season the Mariners' gaudy record was compared to the 1912 New York Giants.
>
> That pre-WWI team finished their season at 103-48, and lost to the Boston Red Sox in the World Series. Fred Merkle led the team in home runs with 11. Christy Mathewson was just one of the team's pitching aces. He was 23-12 and had 27 complete games. Oh, this same guy also led the team in innings (310) and saves (4).

unearned run in eight innings. He struck out six, and walked one – clearly the performance of a number one.

But this one game wouldn't make Garcia the money pitcher yet. There would be many more games to determine that.

Mariner hitters solved Bobby Jones early, scoring six runs in the first two innings. The M's finished with 15 hits. M's won 8-4.

June 16 Rickey Henderson got his wish from the earlier series with the Padres. John Halama took the mound for the Mariners, but Henderson didn't fare much better than the first time.

Rickey did get a two-out infield single against Halama in the 3rd. He collected another hit later in the game, to bring his batting average all the way *up* to a dismal .215.

The big story of the game, though, wasn't Halama's strong pitching, or the near perfect relief of Jose Paniagua and Norm Charlton. The story was John Olerud accomplishing one of the rarest feats in baseball: he hit for the cycle.

In Olerud's first at bat, he sliced a double to left field, and later scored on Al Martin's double. Then, in the 3rd, he tripled down the right field line. It was the Puget Sound native's 12th triple in 13 major league seasons. In the fifth, Olerud lifted a soft liner to center, landing just in front of the Padre centerfielder for a single.

Needing just a home run to complete the cycle, Olerud led off the 7th against former Mariner farm hand Tom Davey. Instead of a homer, Olerud hit a sharp grounder to first base which Padre Ryan Klesko couldn't handle. Olerud reached on an error.

By that time, the game was well under control by the Mariners. Under other circumstances, Seattle's first baseman would have gotten the rest of the night off, but manager Lou Piniella remained aware of Olerud's opportunity. Throughout the season, Piniella had gone a bit longer with a struggling starting pitcher in the 5th inning if the Mariners had a sufficient lead. Piniella wanted to help his pitchers get "W's," and also understood that personal accolades for hitters are important too.

So, Lou left Olerud in the game to get him one more bat. He had looked ahead to see that even if everyone in front of him made outs, Olerud would still get a chance with two outs in the 9th.

The Mariners'8th went quickly, but Mark McLemore led off the 9th with a double. After a Bret Boone line-out, John Olerud stepped to the plate against San Diego reliever David Lee. Olerud took a hard cut at a 1-1 pitch and hit a mammoth 464-foot home run to complete the cycle.

This was the second time in his career the 6'5" lefthander had hit for the cycle; the first time coming on September 17, 1997, with the New York Mets. It was only the third time that a Mariner had hit a single, double, triple, and homer in the same game.

Hitting for the cycle takes some luck involved. If a hit were to be just a few inches to the left or right, the double may have been a single, or even an out. The combination of pure hitting and luck, though, makes hitting for the cycle a treat to behold. M's 9, Padres 2.

John Olerud – 1B
Born: 08-05-68, Seattle, WA
Lives in Fall City, WA with wife Kelly
and two children
6'5" 220 lbs
Signed through 2002

June 17 The final game of the set had Aaron Sele pitching against San Diego's Woody Williams. Williams had been mentioned in trade rumors since before the season, but as the All Star break approached, was still a Padre.

The Mariners entered the game at 52-14, and needed to play .500 ball the rest of the way to reach 100 victories. Even if the M's slumped to that level, the second place Oakland A's, the overwhelming pre-season AL West favorite, would have to play .720 baseball the remainder of the season to catch Seattle.

But first the Padres. Sele was no mystery. He gave up ten hits, three walks and six runs in four innings, one of his worst outings of the year. The normally dependable Ryan Franklin did about the same, yielding three runs in two innings.

In the meantime, the Mariners rallied. In the 7th inning, facing a 9-5 deficit, Olerud hit a three run dinger and Boone followed with a solo shot to tie the game. But in the bottom of the 8th Jeff Nelson had his second straight poor performance, and gave up a two run homer to allow San Diego to salvage a win. Padres 11, M's 9.

The Mariners happily headed north to Oakland, and back to having Edgar Martinez in the lineup.

Four game series at Athletics (split)

The Mariner pitching staff was exalted because of the good starters and great relief staff. But the A's young phenoms may have been the best starting staff in baseball. Hudson, Mulder, Zito and Lidle will provide fits for hitters for years to come.

June 18 Jamie Moyer went head-to-head with A's lefthander Barry

Zito. Moyer had yet another strong performance, but it was wasted as Zito became the first pitcher to beat the Mariners twice in the season. Moyer gave up only two hits and two runs in six innings, and left the game with a 3-2 lead. But Norm Charlton couldn't close the door, as the A's played their own version of small ball to score the winning two runs in the bottom of the 7th. For only the third time all season the Mariners had lost two games in a row. A's won 4-3.

Off the field there were new All-Star results. Bret Boone had surpassed Roberto Alomar to lead in voting for second basemen. Ichiro was the overall top vote-getter, Edgar widened his DH lead, and Olerud was on top for first-base.

It was also announced that AAA pitcher Joel Pineiro would be one of the M's representatives at the All-Star Futures Game on July 8 at SAFECO.

Athletes in any sport need motivation to play at their highest level. Irrespective of the ridiculous salaries paid professional players (The Mariners payroll is about $3 million per player.), money isn't enough to provide the spark every day of a 162 game schedule. A pennant race would clearly make each pitch important to each player on the team in the race. But the tremendous lead the Mariners had over the Athletics meant the M's as individuals needed something else. No amount of money would suffice.

> **No More DH!**
> In my personal opinion, baseball was intended for a position player to hit and field. Fielding is a skill that was intended for all players. The American League initiated the DH because of its lackluster play compared to the National League. It was an artificial creation to inject excitement into the AL. The NL did not need this then and does not need it now.
> - MS

Preventing a third loss in a row was important to the Mariner players. Beating Oakland, clearly a talented team, at home was also on the M's minds. "The series against the A's is a big one," said reliever Jeff Nelson. "We've got to go in and play hard." Regardless of having nearly a 20 game lead, the M's were definitely not complacent.

June 19 In another one-run affair, the M's rebounded for the win 8-7. In order to gain the victory, the Mariners had to claw out of a four-run 1st inning hole, and then a two run deficit in the 9th.

With a 52-16 record, it would be fair to say that nearly everything had gone right for the Mariners so far. Yet, the M's were 0-13 to this point when behind after eight innings.

Trailing 7-6, and facing A's closer Jason Isringhausen, Ichiro led off the 9th with a single and advanced to third on a hit-and-run single by McLemore, who then stole his 22nd consecutive base.

> Oakland Coliseum is a challenge for all players. In the June 18th Mariners game there, the umpire crew chief had to stop the game to get a fan in centerfield to stop flashing a beacon attempting to distract Seattle batters. The human would-be lighthouse was escorted from the stadium.

Edgar pushed the ball to the right side for the first out, enabling Ichiro to score. But McLemore inexplicably stayed at second, shaking his head at his own mistake. Even the best teams of all time blundered occasionally. If this was really going to be the Mariners' year, they had to overcome mistakes.

Wanting to atone for not advancing, McLemore harassed Isringhausen into a bad pick-off throw, and took third. Olerud was then intentionally walked, setting up the double play. Bret Boone hit a deep sacrifice fly to drive in the winning run. Small ball wins.

Kazu Sasaki pitched a perfect ninth, getting Jason Giambi and John Jaha out on swinging third strikes, both of them flipping their helmets in frustration as they walked back to the losers' dugout. M's won 8-7.

June 20 It was a near picture-perfect setting for a baseball game. The sky was clear with a 70 degree game time temperature. There were 40,000 screaming fans and two good pitchers, Freddy Garcia for Seattle and Mark Mulder for Oakland, on the mound.

Garcia was in fine form. Except for a Jason Giambi two-run homer in the 1st, and an unearned run in the 6th, Freddy completely mastered the A's. In the 8th, when he turned the ball over to Jeff Nelson, the M's led 4-3. Seattle scored on home runs: Edgar's two-run shot and Boone's two solo homers.

Nelson held the lead, and then Sasaki, as usual, came in to close the door in the 9th. The A's got two singles, but also had two outs when Oakland's Eric Chavez came to the plate. Kazu expected to finish him off with another evil splitter.

Chavez, a left-handed pull hitter, took an outside Sasaki fastball and rifled it over the left field fence for a three-run, game winning homer. Only the day before, Seattle's closer Kazuhiro Sasaki was superb. This next day though, Sasaki blew the save. This inconsistency would become more than a mere matter of concern as the Mariners completed their season. A's won 6-4.

June 21 The fourth and final game of the Oakland series was a slugfest, reminiscent of games with the Rockies. The A's got six first inning runs against M's starter John Halama. In characteristic form, the Mariners started chipping away right after the Athletics scored, almost as if to say "it's just a matter of time before we catch you."

After seven innings, the score was 10-9 Athletics. Martin, Bell, Cameron and Boone had all homered to lead the charge back. An 8th inning two out rally, the Seattle Mariners'signature for the 2001 season, brought in the winning runs for the M's. After a Tom Lampkin ground-out, and David Bell popout, Ichiro lofted a single to center. On the first pitch, Ichiro took off for second and was safe. McLemore then walked, bringing Edgar up. Conventional wisdom had the baserunners staying put to give one of the league's most dangerous hitters the chance to do what he does best. But this is no conventional season, and Lou Piniella is no passive manager. On a 1-1 count, Ichiro and McLemore surprised Oakland by making a double steal. Edgar then drove in both runs with a hit to complete the Mariner comeback.

Jose Paniagua and Arthur Rhodes shared the last three innings for the win. The split with Oakland meant that the Mariners had yet to lose a road series. M's won 12-10.

> To date in the season, Edgar Martinez, who hasn't gotten a "leg hit" in over a decade, had an incredible .449 on base percentage. He led the team in walks and was second in RBIs. Edgar has done all of this without the benefit of Ken Griffey, Jr. hitting behind him.

Piniella hinted that the M's huge lead in the AL West would enable him to start to look to the postseason, especially with the pitching staff. Previously, the bullpen had normally been some combination of Nelson, Rhodes and Sasaki. Piniella indicated he was going to make a concerted effort to give Rhodes and Sasaki more rest. At age 31 in the 2000 season, Rhodes pitched in the most games of his career by far. And for every inning pitched in a game, a reliever throws at least two innings in the bullpen. Too much arm stress in June through September would mean ineffectiveness in October. Moreover, Kazu Sasaki was amassing big save numbers in April and May, but for him to be a strong closer in October, he must retain arm strength.

Piniella made his statements in view of the fact that starters rarely complete games due to the way today's game is played. That puts more reliance on the bullpen. Piniella's intimation was a clear signal that we would see more pitchers in Mariner uniforms as the season unfolded.

Three game series at home vs. Anaheim (M's win 1)
After ten games on the road, the Mariners were finally, back home!

June 22 Game 1 of the series with the division rival Angels was a dud. Aaron Sele was going along fine against Anaheim's Jarod Washburn until the fifth inning, but then he couldn't get anybody out. Nine of the first ten Angels reached base, as Sele looked like a pummeled boxer. Until after the game, it was incomprehensible as to why Sele wasn't taken out.

Mariner hitters couldn't solve Washburn at all, managing only five singles. Washburn entered the game at 4-4, with a 4.29 ERA. Angels won 8-1.

Following the game it was revealed that Norm Charlton would have to go back on the 15-day disabled list due to a reaggravated groin pull. That left Piniella with a very short bullpen, requiring Sele to "take one for the team." Brian Fuentes was recalled.

Chris Widger, Mariner backup catcher who had been on the disabled list all season was given a rehab assignment in Everett. But he was forced to have a second surgery, and wouldn't play in a big league game at all during the 2001 season.

Major League Baseball also announced that interleague play would change in 2002. AL West teams would be playing NLCentral teams, such as the Chicago Cubs and St. Louis Cardinals. *[Regardless of who is played, I still don't like it. – SE.   I don't either. - MS]*

June 23 Jamie Moyer deserved to develop a complex. Formerly the recipient of Mariner run support, Seattle just stopped hitting when Jamie pitched.

Moyer pitched eight innings of two-hit, no walk ball, but lost.

The Angels' Pat Rapp and three relievers held the M's to six hits, five of them singles. Reliever Troy Percival, boasting a 99-mile an hour fastball, and 0.96 ERA, closed out the win. A bright spot for the Mariners was another inning of hitless relief by young lefthander, Brian Fuentes. Angels won 2-1.

June 24 Ichiro was given the day off in game 3, and the M's picked up the slack. Mike Cameron replaced Ichiro in the leadoff slot and helped make quick work of the visitors. The M's tallied four runs in the 1st, countering the two scored by the Angels in their half.

The Mariners cruised the rest of the game behind Paul Abbott's four hit pitching, and relief help of Nelson, Rhodes and Sasaki (save 26). Thanks to the bullpen, the Mariners were 43-3 when leading after six innings.

> **"The two most impor-
> tant things in life are
> good friends and a
> strong bullpen."**
>   **- Bob Lemon,
> Hall of Fame pitcher
> and manager**

The Mariner bats were a welcome sight at SAFECO Field, with nine hits, including home runs by Boone and Wilson. M's won 7-3.

Three game series at home vs. Oakland
(M's take 1)
June 26 The Oakland A's came to town to renew the rivalry with Freddy Garcia matched against Oakland's Mark Mulder.

Mariner hitters garnered 15 hits. David Bell, who was hitting .343 over his previous 28 games, had three hits and two RBIs. Mike Cameron hit a three-run homer. Dan Wilson was 2-3 to increase his average to .273, and Carlos Guillen was 3-4.

Garcia was good, but not great. He scattered nine hits over 6 2/3 innings, and Arthur Rhodes and Jose Paniagua pitched hitless ball for the rest of the game. M's won 7-3.

David Bell – 3B
Born: 09-14-72, Cincinnati, OH
Lives in Seattle, WA with wife Kristi
5'10" 190 lbs
Signed through 2001

The Mariners announced another deal with Japanese baseball. Tacoma reliever Kevin Hodges, who pitched in 13 games in 2000, was sold to the Satoshi Iriki.

Tampa Bay released veteran outfielder Gerald Williams. A career .260 hitter, the M's would be interested in him if he would agree to platoon. Instead, Williams agreed to sit the bench for the Yankees. He must have believed that the Yankees were going to win the AL championship. Regardless, he wouldn't be on the postseason roster.

At the same time, the Mariners turned their attention to disgruntled Yankee outfielder Chuck Knoblauch. Seattle was dangling Al Martin and Bret Tomko as bait. Supposedly, the Yankees wanted Seattle minor league pitcher, Joel Pineiro as part of the deal.

Former Yankee Knoblauch teammate Jeff Nelson indicated he would welcome the Yankee leftfielder. "Chuck would become the player he used to be if he could get away from New York," said Nelson. This curious statement begs more questions. Was the Mariners' reliever saying that people play better AFTER New York? Or was this remark just about Knoblauch? Unfortunately, there was no further info.

Seattle also announced that all three games with Oakland were sellouts, bringing the total to ten consecutive sellouts at SAFECO.

The Mariners sellout crowd of 45,722 on June 24, 2001, was a record seventh in a row at SAFECO Field. Thanks to the fans' vocal participation, Seattle's beautiful home park has quickly become one of the most intimidating places for visiting teams to play.

June 27 Oakland's young righthanded ace Tim Hudson faced embattled Mariner lefthander John Halama. In the second, Halama gave up consecutive singles, and then hit the A's Eric Chavez, loading the bases. Ramon Hernandez then parked one over the bullpen in left field for a grand slam. Halama later gave up a two-run shot in the 5th and was done.

Manager Lou Piniella termed yet another weak Halama performance "dismal" but the lefthander who was acquired in the Randy Johnson deal with Houston disagreed. "I thought I threw the ball well," said Halama. With a 6-5 record, Halama had 25% of the total team losses to that point.

The M's knocked out starter Hudson with three runs in the 4th and 5th, but were stopped cold by four Athletic relievers. A's won 6-3.

June 28 Seattle and Aaron Sele hoped to bounce back in game 3 against Oakland. Mariner nemesis Barry Zito took the hill for the Athletics.

Sele pitched well enough to keep the Mariners in the game, but not well enough to win. He gave up six hits, an uncharacteristic four walks, and three runs in 6 2/3 innings.

Seattle's offense battled, forcing Mariner-killer Zito out of the game with one out in the 7th, but couldn't get past the Oakland bullpen.

Brian Fuentes gave up his first hit, first run, and had his first loss for the Mariners. Sele, who started the season 8-0, was winless in June. The loss to Oakland and the previous loss of two out of three to Anaheim, marked the first back-to-back series losses for the M's to this point in the season. A's won 6-3.

Just before the game the Mariners announced that John Halama was being sent to Tacoma to work on getting the ball down in the strike zone.

> Mariners in a slump? Seattle had lost 7 of its 11 games from June 17-28, giving up an average of six runs per game. But not all of those runs were earned. The M's defense had gone south with the pitching. None of these were attributes of a championship team. But all teams go through a slump, right?- *SE*

Three game series at Anaheim (M's sweep!)

June 29 It was back to business as usual for the Mariners, especially when Jamie Moyer was on the hill. Jamie hadn't thrown his first pitch yet and he was already staked to a six run lead. Ichiro led off with a single and Guillen homered. Edgar Martinez singled, and exhibiting the unselfish attitude of the Mariners, cleanup hitter John Olerud sacrificed Edgar to second. Then, a walk and three more singles, including Ichiro's second hit of the inning, produced the rest of Seattle's six first-inning runs.

When a starting pitcher gets an early lead like this, his game plan adjusts. Jamie Moyer, the savviest veteran of the Mariner staff, understands how to pitch with a lead. He's less concerned about nibbling around the corners, and more concerned with putting the ball into play. The opponent can score a few runs, but Moyer knows to not give a hitter a base.

Moyer bent but didn't break against Anaheim. He pitched five innings, and gave up some hits (8) but no walks. He did give up five runs, and this game didn't look good for Moyer's ERA, but there's a reason why Jamie Moyer is the major league's third winningest pitcher of the past five years – he knows how to win.

The Mariner offense continued to add the runs. Mike Cameron hit a home run that landed somewhere near Disneyland; Ichiro, Edgar, Olerud and Javier each had two hits; and Guillen, Cameron and Wilson each drove in two runs.

Just for kicks, the Mariners sent Nelson, Rhodes and Sasaki to pitch the last four innings. The results? 4 innings pitched; 1 hit; no runs; no walks; nine strikeouts. M's won, 9-5.

Off the field a new name popped up in trade talks: Yankee OF/DH David Justice. How would Justice adjust to yet another new team? Would he be ready to go back to the outfield and leave Edgar at DH? Would the Yankees be willing to let Justice go to a team they could meet in the ALCS?

Just like they say on *Days of Our Lives,* Stay Tuned!

The Mariners' race through history had them a full two games behind the 1902 Pirates through the first 78 games. Pirate centerfielder Ginger Beaumont led the team with a .357 batting average, but Honus Wagner, who hit .329 and drove in 91 runs, was generally considered the team leader. Jack Chesbro, with a 2.17 ERA, was 28-6, to lead the pitchers. The Pirates didn't hit many home runs, though. Tommy Leach led the team, which finished the season at 103-36, with only six round-trippers. Now that's small ball!

June 30 In game 2 of the odyssey at Anaheim, the Mariners experimented with newly called-up Denny Stark on the hill against the young Angels' righthander, Ramon Ortiz. The right-handed Stark was 9-1 with a 2.06 ERAat Tacoma.

Stark struggled, but any relative watching would sure have been proud of this 2001 debut. After 5 2/3 hard fought innings, Stark gave way to Paniagua and Sasaki who shut out the Angels from the 6th forward.

The Mariners finished with 10 hits, and a Tom Lampkin homer in the 6th was the game winner. M's won 5-3.

"This was a bullpen win," said Piniella, as the month of June ended. The Mariners stood at 58-21, so far ahead of everybody that it really didn't matter who was in second place.

The month of June was the Mariners' *worst* month so far. The M's were 18-9, which would translate to a 108-54 record for the season. Not too shabby. The mid-season classic was just around the corner, and it was somehow fitting that the Mariners'magical season would include the All Star game in Seattle.

June's Magical Moments (18 wins - 9 losses . . . Season 58-21)
1. M's complete 15 game winning streak (8th)
2. Halama shuts out Rickey who says "Halama had nothing." (10th)
3. Olerud hits for the cycle (16th)
4. Boone passes Alomar for all star second base voting (18th)
5. M's sell out for record 10th straight game at SAFECO (24th)

Chapter Seven

July, 2001 (Pre All Star)

"You can shake a dozen glove men out of a tree, but a bat sepa - rates the men from the boys."

- Dale Long major league first baseman, 1951-1963

The trading deadline was at the end of month and if the Mariners were going to find an impact hitter, it would have to come in July. In the shadow of the All Star game, with the Mariners firmly fastened to first place, the hunt would come down to the wire.

Continuation of three game series at Anaheim
(M's sweep!)
July 1 Eight games in eight days . . . all just before before the All Star break - Whew! The Mariners had already taken the first two games of the series in June from the Angels, and sent Freddy Garcia to the mound looking for his 9th win. Garcia had only one loss, and a victory would almost assure the young Seattle ace of a spot before the home fans on the All Star team.

Garcia tossed a knockout punch, but Carlos Guillen was the one who got kayoed. Freddy pitched a complete game shutout, scattering eight Angel singles. Boone's 21st homer led the offense. M's won 5-0.

In the 3rd inning, there was a scare that sent Guillen out of the game. Anaheim's Larry Barnes hit a low pop-up into shallow left field. Guillen went back, waving his arms, calling for the ball and looking up into the sky. Mariner leftfielder Al Martin came in, waving his arms, calling for the ball and looking up into the sky. They both arrived at the same time. Guillen made the catch, but also caught an Al Martin elbow to the side of his head. He seemed to black out for a brief moment, but then opened his eyes to see a worried friend, Freddy Garcia, hovered over him.

Guillen had to leave the game with a mild concussion, and would return several days later.

The collision involving Guillen was described by Martin as reminding him of his football playing days at USC. It was later learned that Martin never played football at USC, which marked yet another curious episode in Al Martin's life. Past accusations of domestic violence had been resolved in his favor, he said, but actually he was on probation for a domestic violence conviction in Scottsdale, Arizona. Yet another allegation – this one of bigamy – made headlines when he played at San Diego. The 33 year-old, $5 million/year outfielder remained an enigma to Seattle fans. People were cheering for him to achieve the results expected by GM Gillick, but Martin's off-the-field difficulties made it hard for him to be an endearing persona.

Another injury turned out to be a hoax – thank goodness! The Mariner postgame show on KIRO radio reported a rumor that Seattle elder statesman, Jay Buhner, had to be rushed to a Seattle hospital suffering from cardiac arrest. Trainer Rick Griffin heard of the incident and called Buhner's house to check on the condition of the idle slugger. It turned out that the only rushing going on was Buhner himself running between the barbecue grill and the telephone. Bone was home cooking a steak.

Jay Buhner – OF
Born: 08-13-64, Louisville, KY
Lives in Issaquah, WA with his wife
Leah and three children
6'3" 215 lbs
Signed through 2001

The Mariners were back on TV after a two-game hiatus. Prior scheduling commitments kept the M's off television for the entire weekend (June 29-30). Starved fans reported not being able to watch any other games because without the Mariners "it just wasn't baseball."

Remember the days when the only show Seattle baseball on television could beat was a hair removal infomercial? Bob Dylan sang it - *For the times, they are a-changing.*

All Stars picked

The biggest news of the day, though, was that four Mariners were elected to start in the All Star game. Ichiro Suzuki led all American leaguers in votes, becoming the first rookie to do so. John Olerud won the starting job at first base; Bret Boone won second base; and Edgar Martinez won Designated Hitter. Reserves and pitchers were to be named in several days.

Ichiro not only had the most votes in the American League, he also had the most votes of any player, receiving 3,373,035. Barry Bonds of the San Francisco Giants led the National League with 2,140,315.

Four game series at Texas (split)

Aaahhhh - Texas in July! There's nothing better than sitting at a night game in 98 degree heat. It would have been 110 earlier in the day. This could describe just about any day in July and August in Alex Rodriguez's new home.

July 2 With all encompassing heat as a backdrop, the Mariners sent Paul Abbott to face the hard-hitting Rangers. The game was one where neither team could hold a lead. The M's got up by three on an Edgar Martinez sacrifice fly and a Dan Wilson home run. But the homestanding Rangers came back to tie on two walks and three straight hits.

The game was tied at four going into the 7th when the Mariners went ahead on a Mike Cameron run-scoring triple. But in the bottom of the inning, Ryan Franklin relieved Abbott and promptly gave up three runs, to give Texas a 7-5 lead.

In the top of the 9th Tom Lampkin was hit by a pitch, but watched two outs being made without advancing past first. Ichiro then came up and promptly sent a two-out slider into the right field stands to tie the game. Ichiro hadn't started and came into the game after Stan Javier pinched a nerve in his leg. The Mariner singles-hitting right-fielder proved he could turn on a pitch and drive it, too!

The Mariners won the game in the 10th when All Star John Olerud doubled, went to third on a bunt single by All Star Bret Boone, and scored on an Al Martin single. Boone eventually moved to third and scored on a Mark McLemore sacrifice fly. Kazu Sasaki sent Texas down in order to earn the save. He struck out Ivan Rodriguez, and Alex Rodriguez to end the game. M's won 9-7.

After the game, Ichiro was overheard saying that he was ready to participate in the All Star home run hitting contest. Was he serious?

In off the field maneuvering, veteran utility man, Stan Javier, an important cog in the Mariner machine, went on the 15-day disabled list. He was being sent back to Seattle for an MRI. Joel Pineiro, right-handed pitcher, was called up. Pineiro was scheduled to start the All Star Futures game in Seattle on Sunday, but would miss that opportunity because he was in the major leagues instead.

 Stan Javier – OF
Born: 01-09-64, San Pedro de Marcoris, Dominican Republic
Lives in Santo Domingo, DR with wife Genoveva and three children
6'0" 200 lbs.
Signed through 2001

A minor league note: John Halama won his first start for Tacoma over Oklahoma City, 4-1.

July 3 Going for Seattle's fifth straight win, Aaron Sele was due after being 0-June in the win column. He received support in the top of the first on a Mike Cameron three-run homer. ADavid Bell homer gave the M's a 5-1 lead going into the 4th. But Texas had their own lumbermen wielding big axes. I-Rod and A-Rod hit back-to-back 430' shots to cut the lead. The Mariners had more power on this night, though, and smashed 10 extra-base hits.

Sele went 6 2/3 innings, and Jeff Nelson and Arthur Rhodes closed out the game. Nelson was shaky, though, not having pitched in several days. This was characteristic of the tall righthander throughout the season. On this night against Texas, Nellie gave up two walks, a hit and a run on 37 pitches in 1 1/3 innings. M's won 8-4.

The Mariners' win gave them a 61-21 record – 40 games over .500 with the All Star break just around the corner.

Meanwhile, there was another strong AAA Mariner pitching performance. Bret Tomko tossed a no-hitter. It was the first nine-inning no-hitter ever thrown by a Mariner AAA pitcher.

July 4 On Independence Day, the Mariners were never really in the game. Jamie Moyer gave up three doubles and three runs in the first, and a home run in the second. But the fireworks were saved for after the game.

In the top of the ninth, Ichiro was at bat with two outs, Bell on first base and Cameron on third. Texas led 6-3. Ichiro hit a routine ground ball to Michael Young at second. But no grounder hit by Ichiro is "routine" because of the pressure the Japanese rookie places on the defense with his speed and hustle.

Young bobbled the ball, and seeing that his only possibility for a play was at second, pushed the ball with his glove to Alex Rodriguez who was covering second base. Rodriguez grabbed the ball just as Bell was hitting the bag, and umpire Rob Drake screamed "Out!" for the game-ending play. Rangers won 6-3.

David Bell broke into a rage, claiming he was safe. He continued the argument long after all other Mariners had left the field. Local Seattle print and broadcast media discussed how Bell's hustle and argument showed the heart of the team. They didn't get it particularly right. The implication was that Bell's play was somehow unusual in that he cared so much about winning, regardless of the fact that Seattle had a huge lead over everyone.

David Bell did indeed represent what was so good about the 2001 Mariners, but it wasn't embodied in that one play in Texas on July 4th. Bell, like nearly every one of the Mariners, is a professional baseball player; an athlete whose sole goal is to win. The only challenge for such an athlete is the one of the moment. Anyone who has ever played a team sport at a level beyond grade school knows that the mindset of a true athlete does not include a season record. Making the right play at the right time is the goal. That's why baseball players don't have to be 6'6, 300 lbs. to be successful. Instead, though small in stature, but giant in mental toughness, a good baseball player is one who is strongest of mind.

The Mariners were blessed in 2001 to have one of the most mentally tough teams in baseball history. That's the biggest reason why the lack of a "superstar" such as Ken Griffey, Jr. or Alex Rodriguez on the Mariners was irrelevant. Oh Seattle had superstars – mental superstars, and they proved it by making the right plays at the right time, for a remarkable record of 116 regular season wins.

But even the best teams falter sometimes.

July 5 The Mariners played their worst game of the first half of the season in losing to the Rangers 14-2. And even with this crushing loss, there was a bright spot on the mound.

Rookie Denny Stark started for the Mariners, and in four innings, combined with reliever, Brian Fuentes, to give up 14 runs and 13 hits. The game was brutal. The heat was brutal. And the 4th inning was so brutal on the Mariners that they didn't even record an out until the Rangers had batted around. The game got so out of hand in the late innings that catcher Dan Wilson played first base; catcher Tom Lampkin played right field; and first baseman Ed Sprague, played catcher.

The positive part for the M's was the 3 1/3 innings of hitless relief by Joel Pineiro and Jose Paniagua. The rest of the season for both pitchers went in opposite directions . . . more on Pineiro and Paniagua later. Rangers won 14-2.

After the game, Stark was sent down to Tacoma and outfielder Scott Podsednik was called up.

Alex Rodriguez, the All Star starting shortstop, announced he wasn't going to participate in the All Star home run hitting contest. Bret Boone, on the other hand, was selected as the Mariner participant.

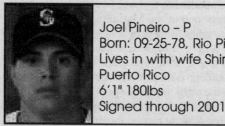

Joel Pineiro – P
Born: 09-25-78, Rio Piedres, Puerto Rico
Lives in with wife Shirley in Rio Piedras, Puerto Rico
6'1" 180lbs
Signed through 2001

Three game series at Dodgers (M's take 2)
It was off to Los Angeles to meet another National League opponent, the team with the major leagues' third highest payroll at just under $109 million.

July 6 Freddy Garcia pitched one of the best games of his career, and Mariner hitters made mincemeat of the Dodger staff. Garcia's fastball was blazing hotter than the summer LA pavement. He took a no-hitter into the sixth, and ended up permitting Los Angeles only four hits, one walk, and struck out five. It was Freddy's second consecutive complete game shutout, the first Mariner to accomplish this feat since Randy Johnson in 1998. Freddy stood at 10-1 as he prepared for his start for the American League in the All Star game.

On the hitting side, Ichiro stepped to the plate in the top of the first and promptly knocked a Kevin Brown pitch into the stands. This was Ichiro's first leadoff home run. The M's never looked back and collected 13 runs on 11 hits, including nine hits from the 6-7-8 hitters, Martin, Guillen and Bell. M's 13, Dodgers 1.

Al Martin - OF
Born: 11-24-67, W. Covina, CA
Lives in Scottsdale, AZ with wife Cathy
and one child
6'2" 214 lbs
Signed through 2001

July 7 Game two of the series at Los Angeles was unusual in that all the runs were scored on home runs – three of them, all solo shots. That meant the game was a pitcher's duel, all the way.

The M's Paul Abbott gave up only four hits. When Gary Sheffield hit a two-out home run in the 6th Jeff Nelson relieved. He sent the Dodgers to the dugout with a strike out, struck out the side in the 7th, and struck out the first batter in the 8th. Arthur Rhodes then relieved Nelson and struck out his first hitter for sixth consecutive K's from the relief staff.

In the meantime, young Dodger lefthander Terry Adams surrendered only a home run to John Olerud in the fourth. Matt Herges relieved Adams pitching the 8th and 9th, setting up the game for the Dodgers' bottom of the 9th with the score even at 1-1.

Jose Paniagua came in for the M's who sailed through the first two batters, but then gave up a home run to Adrian Beltre for the Dodgers' win. Dodgers 2, M's 1.

Boone's season-high 13 game hitting streak was stopped in the game.

Down at AAA Tacoma, John Halama pitched nine-inning perfect game . He was so perfect that there were no memorable defensive plays. He struck out 9.

July 8 The rubber game of the set and final game before the All Star break was another pitcher's duel until the Mariners broke open the game in the 7th. Aaron Sele took the mound for Seattle against the Dodgers' Jeff Williams.

Since AL pitchers bat in NL parks, Sele helped himself with a suicide squeeze bunt in the 2nd to score putting the M's in front 2-0. The game sped along with the Mariners holding a 3-1 lead going into the 7th inning, when Seattle's bats awoke from a two-game slumber. Starting with a lead-off home run by catcher Dan Wilson, the M's went on to score six runs on eight hits for an insurmountable lead. M's won 9-2.

The M's continued their mastery on the road, and took a few days off for the All Star game with a overwhelming 63-24 record.

In the meantime, the Yankees' pitcher Mariano Rivera had to drop out of the All Star game, and was replaced by the Mariners' Jeff Nelson. Mike Cameron was added to replace Tampa Bay's Greg Vaughn. With a huge smile on his face, Cameron beamed to fans, and said: "I'm going to enjoy it to the utmost. It's the ultimate dream for a lot a baseball players. It's great to get to be on the field with the best players in the game."

Alex Rodriguez, under pressure from Commissioner Bud Selig's office, changed his mind and decided to participate in the All Star home run hitting contest. Ichiro, however, would have to wait until another year.

In more off-the-field news, it seemed that Detroit outfielder Juan Encarnacion was the latest player in the Mariners' sights. As the All Star break neared, the 25-year old Tiger was hitting .253 with 10 home runs and 41 RBIs. Regardless of who was to be acquired, Tacoma speedy outfielder Scott Podsednik would be trying to stick on the major league team.

M's Midseason review
At 63-24, the Mariners had a phenomenal first half. Hitting had been a question all year, but it shouldn't have been. The Mariners were second in the AL in batting at .283; first in runs at 530 (over 6 runs per game!); first defensively with a team .985 fielding efficiency; and 4th in pitching with a 4.00 ERA.

Bret Boone was the foremost Mariner at bat, leading the league in

RBIs and the team in home runs. Mike Cameron was ahead of all AL centerfielders in slugging percentage. The bottom part of the order – Guillen, Bell, Lampkin and Wilson – weren't producing gawdy numbers like Alex Rodriguez, Troy Glaus or Ivan Rodriguez, but they were hitting in the clutch.

And then there was Ichiro. He was hitting .347, with 41 RBIs, 76 runs, 28 stolen bases, 134 hits, and was an amazing outfielder. By the half-time break, he had answered all the preseason questions and more about whether this Japanese star could cross the bridge to Major League Baseball.

"There is more respect for the game here than in Japan," Ichiro said in an Art Thiel column. (*Seattle Post Intelligencer*, July 6, 2001) "I can't even compare it. My feelings in coming to the ballpark are astronomically higher than when I was in Japan. I'm so happy to come here."

Ichiro also talked about how in Japan some managers and players would harass opposing hitters at bat. Even catchers got into the act, and Ichiro recalled the time a former major leaguer, playing in Japan, became so frustrated he grabbed the catcher after a pitch, threatening to hit him.

While the biggest adjustments, such as to culture, food, travel and pitching, have been manageable, day games present a problem to Ichiro. "Usually there's no pregame workout. I feel those days are difficult to prepare myself. I have to work out to prevent injuries."

Ichiro even adjusted to pervasive clubhouse hijinks. His locker was near Jay Buhner's, the team initiator of newcomers. Buhner didn't spare Ichiro, regardless of the star's on-the-field heroics. Several times the butt of Buhner's escapades, Ichiro's only comment was "I just pretend to laugh even though I don't understand the joke."

The only question left about Ichiro was whether he had the stamina to withstand a 162 game schedule.

One of the best statements about the impact of the Mariner first half came from Les Smith, one of the Mariners original owners. Smith, who enlisted his friend, Danny Kaye, to help bring baseball to Seattle many years ago, has been a season-ticket holder since 1977. Every year, Smith and his wife take off in mid-October for the paradise in Hawaii. But not this year. The 81 year-old former Mariners part-owner delayed the annual trip to the islands . . . just in case there were some World Series games in the Emerald City to attend at the time.

But the irony of all statements about the first half of the baseball season was actually made back on February 2, 2001. This was a time just before pitchers and catchers were to report to spring training, and there was no Alex Rodriguez. The Mariners hadn't landed another hitter. There were many, many questions about whether Seattle would field a team competitive with Oakland and Anaheim.

With just hint of bitterness over the off-season lack of moves, the excellent sports columnist, Art Thiel, said:
"In the first inning of the All-Star Game, when Rodriguez sends a Johnson heater over the center-field wall, only to see the ball snatched back by Griffey, the burning moment for the Mariner fans will need to be salved by a seven game lead in the AL West."
(Seattle Post-Intelligencer, February 2, 2001).

Little did Art know – little did any of us know – that the Mariners would have a 19 game lead over the A's at the All Star break!

Chapter Eight

All Star 2001

"The one constant through all the years, Ray, has been baseball. America has rolled by like an army of steamrollers. It's been erased like a blackboard, rebuilt, and erased again. But baseball has marked the time. This field, this game, is a part of our past, Ray. It reminds us of all that once was good, and that could be again. Oh people will come, Ray. People will most definitely come." Field of Dreams, 1989

The 2001 All Star Game was more than just nine innings of baseball on July 10th, and it was more than the Home Run Contest, the FanFest and Future All Stars. The game was the entire experience for the Mariners, especially because the extravaganza was in Seattle.

Getting there was another experience altogether. The Mariners had four starters elected: Ichiro, Edgar, Olerud and Boone. Freddy Garcia and Kazu Sasaki had been named to the team's pitching staff. It was certainly reasonable for the M's to have so many players on the team. They were on pace to break the all time record for wins as a team. To be in that position the Mariners had to have a significant number of players having remarkable years.

In fact the Mariners' season was going so well that Seattle sports radio station KJR marketed an initiative to just let the Mariners play the National League. Everyone on Seattle's team was playing like All Stars. Why not go for the victory with the history-making Mariners? While KJR's idea was just a promotion, there was a good argument that at least six Mariner pitchers – Garcia, Moyer, Sele, Sasaki, Nelson and Rhodes – and three position players – Bell, Cameron and Wilson – should be added to the four Mariners who were elected.

But All Star manager, Joe Torre of the Yankees, had other thoughts. He chose seven of his own pinstripers to don the All Star uniform, and ignored, among others, Aaron Sele, who was 9-1 with a 3.64 ERA, or Jeff Nelson with a 2.19 ERA, or Arthur Rhodes at 5-0 with a 1.95 ERA. After all, it was the Mariners'bullpen that turned "r-e-l-i-e-f" into "v-i-c-t-o-r-i-e-s." Or Torre could have gone for center-fielder Mike Cameron, who had 15 first half-homers, 57 RBIs, 18 steals, and was playing gold-glove outfield.

By the time the All Star game arrived, both Nelson and Cameron were All Stars.

Fan Fest
This was a magical exhibition from July 6-10. Set up like a trade show, Fan Fest was a dream for baseball fans. The exhibits covered thousands of square feet and attracted 180,000 people. In fact, it was so full, that people had to get tickets to go in. That's nothing unusual, but the tickets were for specific times. To do it in any other way would have the mighty hordes overflowing.

> "With all those votes from Japan, Ichiro doesn't deserve to start in the All Star Game. And, who wants to see Mike Cameron or Al Martin or David Bell play in the All Star Game?"
> - Dan Patrick, ESPN radio, July 8, 2001

Former Mariners Alvin Davis and Harold Reynolds were named by Major League Baseball as official spokespersons of Fan Fest. Essentially, they were good will ambassadors, and all they had to do in Seattle to draw a crowd was show up. Just about any player connected with the Mariners, present or past, made the locals come alive.

"Heavenlike" may be a better term than magical if a baseball fan were describing Fan Fest. Fans could learn the secrets of sliding home, hitting a curveball or flashing the right sign, as major league players, managers and other experts of the game offered their insights at "the Diamond." This was an authentic downsized baseball diamond complete with chalklines erased in the dirt. Warren Spahn, Lou Brock, Tommy John and Bob Feller were just a few of baseball's luminaries occupying this area.

Think you could strike out Edgar Martinez? At "The Bullpen" fans got to toe the rubber and hurl a splitter to virtual major leaguers.

Just 60' 6" away from the Bullpen was the "Video Batting Cage." Fans could step into the batter's box and hit real baseballs thrown by major league pitchers. OK, the real pitchers weren't there, but technology made you think they were.

There was even a "Steal Home Challenge" where the fan on third would race against family and friends to try to beat the ball to the plate.

Everything didn't cause you to lace up your old spikes, though. For the engineers, there was an exhibit ("Making of the Game") which showed how baseballs, bats, uniforms etc. are made. For would-be Dave Niehauses, there was "The Week in Baseball Fantasy Broadcast Booth" where fans could add their own level of excitement to baseball's greatest plays. For the Griswolds of the world, there was the "World's Largest Baseball," a 12 feet in diameter hardball ready for Paul Bunyan to hit back to Minnesota.

Probably the biggest hits for baby boomers, though, were the exhibits relating to baseball collectibles. Baseball cards, bats, baseballs, jerseys, hats - - all kinds of memorabilia that bring quiet smiles of remembrance or scenes of youth that seemed like they were yesterday. Many of the game's stars of just a few years ago were there to sign something for you. . . . stars, such as Frank Robinson, Harmon Killebrew and Ernie Banks.

If all a fan wanted to do was transform into a sponge, soaking in the images, the "National Baseball Hall of Fame & Museum" and "Negro Leagues" exhibits provided an ocean of memories.

Tickets to the Slugging Contest and All Star Game were so scarce that Fan Fest was all most people could see. People spent hours - sometimes even days - standing in line to get tickets. But the lines were almost rites of passage into this abundance of baseball. Then the thousands of people spent more hours combing the exhibit hall floor. Smiles of near reverent appreciation were abound as each person found his or her own field of dreams.

Workout Day and Home Run Derby
You would think that going to watch players take batting practice would be only for those most avid of baseball fans. Well there were around 40,000 of them sitting in the SAFECO Field stands on a chamber of commerce day.

I was seated about 15 feet past 3rd base just 11 rows up. There was a feeling of awe – not of idolatry for the players on the field – but of being part of the experience. As I glanced from home plate to right field and across the outfield, I noticed many children on the field. These were the children of players out having a good time with their dads.

I spotted a player and a few children wrestling in left field, only a few feet from me. The player seemed almost like he was in his back yard playing roughhouse with other neighborhood kids. As I looked at the scene of normalcy in a family setting (but very dif - ferent for a baseball field) I couldn't help but think of wrestling with my own dad many, many years ago. When the kids finally gave the poor player some relief and let him up, I noticed the unmistakable steely blue eyes of Cal Ripken, Jr. On that moment, Ripken wasn't baseball's iron man. He wasn't the guy who broke the record that couldn't be broken. He wasn't even an aging play - er whose best days were in the past. On this day, Cal Ripken was just another dad playing with his son. And it all seemed so right.
                                                                  - SE

There were children giggling all over the field, and one of the rarest highlights was provided by the Mariners' own Jeff Nelson. He and his four young daughters on SAFECO Field were a sight to behold.

The Home Run Derby was to be held later that day, but all the play-ers were getting a chance in the batting cage. And most of the pitch-ers were in the outfield milling around trying not to work too hard. Mostly, they were just talking with friends.

Baseball's glamour position for baby boomers was centerfield. That's where Willie Mays and Mickey Mantle played. Today's glam-our position is shortstop, and there stood two of the great shortstops of the game – Alex Rodriguez and Derek Jeter just biding time like it was a summer's day with nothing to do but chat.

A star of Seattle's past – 6'11" Randy Johnson – and a star of Seattle's present – 5'7" Ichiro Suzuki – shook hands and exchanged pleasantries. Shortly after that, Johnson was interviewed in a live broadcast on the huge centerfield screen. The Big Unit commented how he wasn't sure if he was looking forward to facing Ichiro or not. He would get that chance the following night.

With the players taking batting practice, much of the focus was on the sluggers. Alex Rodriguez, who received mostly cheers this time, hit a few balls into the deep left field seats, but it was Sammy Sosa who cranked one so far into left centerfield, that only the upper deck held the ball in the park. Mammoth home runs were flying out of the diamond into SAFECO seats. Fans in the outfield needed their baseball gloves for protection regardless of whether they caught anything.

Even with the players hitting moon shots during batting practice, there seemed to be calmness, like in the eye of a storm. Then a swarm of cameras and microphones all reaching to a central point appeared. It was a throng of reporters coming from the steps of the American League dugout moving toward the batting cage were in a circular pattern – like a school of piranhas ready to absorb the prey. But the seas parted and out came Ichiro to the batting cage. With his hat on backwards and sunglasses glaring in the brightness, Ichiro found serenity at the plate.

His first few swings were typical Ichiro hits: a bouncer through the middle, a soft liner to left field. But then Ichiro stepped out of the batter's box and steadied his eye on right field, almost as if to impersonate Babe Ruth. The next pitch came to the plate and with a quick flick Ichiro put it in the right field seats. On the next three pitches, Ichiro provided more souvenirs for the right field fans. Then, after four straight home runs, the rookie stepped aside and looked around, as if to say "See? I can do it too."

Maybe A-Rod was right when he said that Ichiro was so good that he could have won the Home Run Derby if he wanted to.

It was Derby time, and the fans were ready to see more moonshots. Jason Giambi satisfied! He hit an All Star record 14 home runs in the first round. Several of the shots went over the *Hit It Here Café* into the upper deck in right field. Best of all, these were Ruthian-like home runs -- high rainbows where you could watch the eyes of the fans following the hit traveling almost into space and finding an upper deck seat for a landing spot.

Giambi's home runs continued to mount. Players from both leagues stopped, stood on the dirt around the dugouts and watched in awe as the Oakland Athletic first baseman gave a lesson in slugging. Pitch after pitch came into Giambi, and pitch after pitch went soaring toward the concessions behind the right field stands. Finally, an exhausted Jason Giambi was finished, and the Seattle fans gave a standing ovation to the power hitter from their fierce rival.

After that initial display, Giambi was clearly spent. The Arizona Diamondback Luis Gonzalez, unknown to many fans, showed why he was hitting .355 with 35 homers at the break. He won the 2001 All Star Home Run Derby, but it was Jason Giambi who provided the memories.

All Star Game
It was billed as "An International Celebration of Baseball" and the Mariners were certainly a great example of that theme. A Puerto Rican, Venezuelan, two Japanese, and four native-born Americans, including a player of African descent, represented Seattle in the 2001 All Star game.

A low roar was present from the moment of entering the stadium. Then as each player was introduced, the crowd noise grew louder. With the coaches and reserves having been introduced, it was hard to tell who got the loudest cheer, but when the announcements of the starters were done, the clear winner in the fans' hearts, mirroring the All Star voting, was Ichiro.

The Yankees' Roger Clemens started for the American League and quickly got the National Leaguers out in the 1st inning.

When the bottom of the first came, the crowd got strangely quiet. They were awaiting the duel between Ichiro, the left-handed slap hitter, and Randy Johnson, the most feared left handed pitcher in baseball. Would Ichiro fare better than former Phillies' star Jon Kruk against Johnson? Could he even get a touch of the ball with the bat?

It didn't take long, because Ichiro welcomed a Randy Johnson fast ball and actually pulled it down the 1st base line. Colorado Rockies' first-sacker Todd Helton dove for the screamer, and made a tremendous stop. As Helton scrambled for the ball, Johnson broke for the bag, and Ichiro raced toward first. Helton threw; Randy caught; but it was too late. Ichiro beat out the play, earning a single on his first All Star at bat.

But the day belonged to Cal Ripken. In the top of the first before the first pitch, the AL's top vote-getter at third base was approached by shortstop Alex Rodriguez. A-Rod wanted Ripken to move to shortstop, the position where Ripken played for most of the 2,632 consecutive game streak that broke Lou Gehrig's record. The move had already been approved by manager Joe Torre, showing it wasn't only the fans who honored Cal Ripken. It was also his fellow players who showed their respect by having him start his final All Star game in the spot on the field where he became famous.

As in most All Star games, the top pitchers were the bane of the best hitters. Mariners' starter, Freddy Garcia, showed he deserved to be among the top pitchers by hurling a perfect 3rd inning. Garcia's performance was but a serving of what he wanted to do to National League hitters if the Mariners made it to the World Series.

In the American League half of the third inning, Ripken sent a blast into the left field bullpen for a home run. He would later say that even he got goosebumps as he rounded the bases, to the cheers of fans and players alike.

Former Mariner player and now broadcaster Dave Valle retrieved Ripken's historic homer. That ball soon found its place on the Ripken family mantel.

For the rest of the game, the noise that started almost as background moved to the front row. Fans were screaming from the crack of Ripken's bat until the final out in the 9th. The fans were shouting for Mike Cameron when he hit a double into the gap. They continued to yell when Jeff Nelson set down the senior circuit in the 7th. And they were ecstatic when Kazu Sasaki pitched a 1-2-3 9th to end the game. In all, a Mariner got the first hit (Ichiro), got the win (Garcia) and earned a save (Sasaki). And the Mariner closer's mother, Nobuko Sasaki made her first flight out of Japan to see her son play.

....

The decision was simple. Do I attend my first All Star Game and pay way too much for a seat where I couldn't see as well at home on television? This was Cal Ripken's and Tony Gwynn's last All Star Game. I've followed their careers since they were rookies, pushing veterans to retirement. My boyhood hero was Duke Snider of the Brooklyn Dodgers. That dates me, and to have the chance to see the Duke Sniders of today would make me feel like a kid again.

The more I considered what to do, the more it became clear, and I give this advice. If you ever have the opportunity to go to an All Star Game, do it. I scraped together the money and bought a 12th row seat. It would be a great extravaganza at SAFECO Field and I wanted to remember this day as vividly as possible.

It was worth every penny. I was looking down the line when Cal

Ripken connected. I was sure it was a home run as soon as it left his bat. But this All Star Game was much more than between the lines. The Opening Ceremony to honor the international nature of the game showed that baseball could be a unifying institution not just of communities but of people from around the world. Major league baseball is continuing to grow in its global scope and pop - ularity. What a better place to showcase the best than at the All Star Game!

It was a day all 50,000 fans at SAFECO Field will always remem - ber, and it reflected what is best about baseball. - MS

After the game, Ichiro indicated he was humbled to be on the same field with the other All Stars, and particularly hitting against Randy Johnson. "I'm honored to face Randy in an All-Star game rather than the fact that I got a hit. He's a great pitcher and wore No. 51 before me for the Mariners. I always keep in mind that I must wear this No. 51 with dignity."

While the media swarmed around Ichiro, the Mariner who had the most fun had to be Mike Cameron. Remarking that it "felt like Christmas" as he entered the All-Star clubhouse, the immensely likable Mariner centerfielder was giddy. "When I walked in there and found my jersey, it was like a little kid getting his first bicycle."

Cameron clearly enjoyed his All Star experience, and ordered his Seattle teammates leather jackets. "The way this team was going, I wanted everyone to be a part of it," said Cameron.

For the Seattle Mariners, the 2001 All Star Game was perfect. The weather was sent from Heaven. The AL won the game. Each Mariner got to play, and several were involved in key events leading to the victory. It was better than a Hollywood script . . . and it was time for the Mariners to prove that the first half of the season wasn't a fluke. As the All Stars departed for the start of the second half of the 2001 season, the Mariners awaited Barry Bonds and the San Francisco Giants.

Chapter Nine

July, 2001 (post All Star)

"I told [GM] Roland Hemond to go out and get me a big name pitcher. He said 'Dave Wehrmeister's got 11 letters. Is that a big enough name for you?'"
— Eddie Eichorn, Owner, Chicago White Sox, 1985

Major league baseball shifts into a different gear after the All Star game. The first several weeks after the break are consumed with trade possibilities. Contenders want players who can help win the pennant. The teams out of contention are looking to unload expensive talent. They want young players who can help in the future, and who don't cost as much.

At 19 games ahead, the Mariners were more than a contender. They were a shoo-in for the playoffs, but were still looking for another hitter. GM Pat Gillick had been seeking that hitter since before Spring Training, and continued to hold an empty bag. It was a plus, though, that halfway through the season, the M's had plenty of trade bait.

First on the list was Bret Tomko, the 28 year old right-hander with major league experience. Also available was Al Martin, a career .280 hitter in the National League, who had yet to find his way in the AL. Martin's $5 million salary made him a difficult trade. John Halama, a left handed Jamie Moyer-type, was about to be recalled from AAA. He was said to be available.

Other teams were interested but believed that the Mariners were not in a good trading position. These teams wanted Jose Paniagua, who Seattle management believed was the closer of the future. The other teams wanted Joel Pineiro, Denny Stark and Robert Ramsay. They even wanted two of the injured youngsters, Gil Meche and Ryan Anderson. Pineiro and Anderson were clearly not on the table.

The Mariners, meanwhile, were still interested in Jermaine Dye of

Kansas City, Chuck Knoblauch of New York and Phil Nevin of San Diego. But two players who seemed to be most attainable were from the same team. Shannon Stewart and Jose Cruz, Jr. of the Blue Jays appeared to be highest on Seattle's wanted list.

Gillick no longer seemed interested in finding a new number one pitcher. Freddy Garcia had earned that spot. CEO Howard Lincoln indicated that he would be willing to expand the payroll for the right player, but Gillick was not one to take a blind leap. "At this point [July 12], we're three weeks from the deadline and everyone still has a pretty high price for their players," said the Mariners GM.

So, with the All Star break over, the team roster was filled with the same hitters as before, and with John Halama back in Seattle, the Mariners' five man rotation was Garcia, Moyer, Sele, Abbott and Halama.

The M's first half had been tremendous. They were 20-5 in April, 20-7 in May, 18-9 in June and were 5-3 in July so far. Whether it was a weekday or a weekend, the Mariners had a winning record on every day. By the All Star game, the Mariners could play sub-.500 (37-38) and still reach 100 wins.

The fans were coming by the thousands! Seattle was on pace to draw 3.5 million fans. That meant revenue was up. With the contracts of several veterans, including Aaron Sele and Bret Boone, coming due at the end of the season, more money in the coffers wouldn't hurt.

But all of that would have to wait. There were victories to be had and records to be broken. Bring on the Giants!

Three game series vs. Giants (M's take 2)
July 12 A packed house, just like at the All Star game, awaited the Mariners and San Francisco Giants at SAFECO Field as the second half of the 2001 season got underway. In fact, it was the Mariners 16th straight sellout, and the team announced that the entire six game homestand was already sold out. In game one against the visitors from the Bay Area, Paul Abbott started for the M's against Kirk Reuter for the Giants.

It didn't take long for Barry Bonds to acquaint himself with the right field fans. In the first inning, Bonds sent a towering drive to the right-center field seats for his 40th home run of the season, and his first in 13 games.

The Mariners scored runs in the 2nd and 3rd in typical Seattle fashion: singles and sacrifices, but the Giants took a 3-2 lead on a Rich Aurilia home run in the 6th. Exit Mr. Abbott. The game stayed that way behind the relief pitching of Paniagua and Franklin, and the Mariners had their last chance in the 9th with the bottom of the order coming up. With one out, David Bell took an 0-2 pitch from Giants reliever Felix Rodriguez and literally crushed a high line drive just left of the center field sod area to send the game into extra innings.

In typical Seattle fashion, Sasaki came in and held the Giants to nothing. By the 11th inning, Arthur Rhodes had relieved and struck out the only two batters he faced. In the bottom of the frame, with two outs and Mike Cameron on second, the Mariners'Tom Lampkin, batting a meager .091 against lefthanders, hit a dribbler into centerfield against Giants' lefty reliever Chad Zerbe. Cameron scored and the Mariners won the game - - just as they had done 63 times in the first half.

So, the M's started where they left off. Ichiro got his hitting streak going. Boone had 2 hits. Edgar drove in a run. The bullpen stopped San Francisco cold. M's won 4-3.

As it had been, it was to be again.

Tom Lampkin – C
Born: 03-04-64, Cincinnati, OH
Lives in Vancouver, WA with wife and five children
5'11" 195 lbs
Signed through 2001 (club option for 2002)

One thing would be changing, though. The deluge of Japanese reporters had turned into paparazzi. One overly inquisitive correspondent was standing in Ichiro's driveway interfering with the rookie outfielder's car. Kazu joined Ichiro that afternoon in releasing a statement that they would no longer talk to Japanese media until their "privacy is respected." Though the Mariners were generating substantial support from Japan, the team released its own statement in full support for its players.

July 13 It was Friday, the 13th and the black cats were running all over SAFECO Field bringing bad fortune to the home team. Jamie Moyer had his third straight bad outing, surrendering ten hits in six innings. His ERA over those three games was 6.88, and he had lost four of his past five decisions.

But the shadows weren't over only Moyer. Bell, Guillen and McLemore all had defensive miscues in the fourth inning, driving a stake through Mariner hearts. When the dust cleared, the Giants had a 5-1 lead with Ramon Ortiz on the mound, and that was all they needed. Giants won 5-3.

Off the field, Norm Charlton was in Tacoma for a rehab assignment. His groin pull was not healing as well as hoped. Jay Buhner wished he was ready for a rehab assignment, but team trainer Rick Griffin wasn't willing to give the green light yet.

July 14 The M's were looking to rebound with newly-declared ace Freddy Garcia on the mound. An overflow crowd of 49,809 was on hand to see if Freddy was the Mariners'money pitcher. The Giants' Shawn Estes, one of the team's top pitchers, took the hill for San Francisco.

Freddy didn't disappoint. He gave up only three hits, two of them solo homers, in seven innings. Meanwhile, the hustle of Bret Boone and timely hitting of Edgar and Cammy brought Mariners to home plate.

Ichiro provided the biggest highlight, though, with his defense. In the fourth inning, Jeff Kent hit a shot to deep right field. Ichiro went back, turned and kept retreating. Then he turned back again, leaped up, stretching his glove as far out as it could go. Kent's drive went over the wall, but Ichiro's climb was just high enough as he made the catch with part of the "white" showing. Ichiro hadn't found his offensive groove, though. He was hitless in nine straight at bats.

The bullpen was flawless. Jeff Nelson, Arthur Rhodes and Kazu Sasaki pitched the final two innings, yielding only a Nelson walk. It was Sasaki's 30th save. The Mariners' win gave them their 22nd series win of the 29 played, and had a game record of 11-5 over National League opponents. M's won 3-2.

Three game series vs. Arizona (M's take 2)

The mighty Arizona Diamondbacks, one of the National League's best teams, came to town. Home Run Derby champ Luis Gonzalez was looking to make those dingers count for more than just *"oohs and aahs."* Randy Johnson's team – probably the last organization for the Big Unit - was going to help Seattle celebrate the second anniversary of SAFECO Field.

The new outdoor baseball stadium had been very successful for the Mariners. In its first two years, the average attendance was 40,373 fans. Of the 78 sellouts to date, 24 had been in this baseball season. In addition to Mariner games, SAFECO had hosted high school graduations, proms, weddings, career fairs, company meetings, and a fund raiser for then presidential-hopeful George W. Bush. In SAFECO's young life there had been great moments, and there were many more to come in 2001.

July 15 It is rare to start a series on a Sunday, but such is the lot in the life of interleague play. Aaron Sele pitched one of the best games of his career in game 1 of the series.

Sele threw a two-hit complete game shutout, earning his 11th win against only one loss. He struck out five, walked one, and retired 23 of the final 24 batters he faced.

The Mariners' offense provided plenty of support with 13 hits, but the game was only 3-0 until the 7th when rookie Scott Podsednik broke the game open. Pinch-hitting for Ed Sprague, Podsednik lined a rocket into the gap in left-center for a bases loaded triple to put the game out of reach.

But all wasn't good for the home team. Ichiro was 0-5, extending his hitless streak to 13. Edgar Martinez left the game in the 3rd inning with a strained quadricep and would be evaluated on a day-by-day basis. This strain, though, would hinder Edgar the remainder of the season. At Tacoma, Norm Charlton wasn't ready to take his pulled groin muscle to the mound yet. He could throw the distance, but the contours of the hill made him not capable of pitching. M's won 8-0.

Meanwhile, Bret Tomko was obvious trade bait. Even Manager Lou Piniella, who rarely commented on personnel matters, stated "There's going to be a lot of scouts watching Bret pitch."

Piniella appeared on *ESPN's Sunday Conversation* and commented that Ichiro was "quicker than what I thought and a much better hitter." He added that Ichiro was learning English and fit in well in the Mariner clubhouse. Piniella sounded surprised to relate, though that he and Ichiro communicate in yet another language. "I speak Spanish with him," said the manager. "He picked it up quicker than English."

As for his own metamorphosis, Piniella admitted to being older and wiser. "I'm more patient. I don't argue with umpires as much. There comes a time in anybody's life when you turn corner."

July 16 John Halama got his first start for the major league club since June 28 and looked to pitch in the bigs as he had in his stint in Tacoma. His charge at AAA was to rediscover how to keep the ball down in the strike zone. He got the ball down against the Diamondbacks all right, except it was down 400 feet from home plate.

Reggie Sanders, Damian Miller and Steve Finley hit rockets off Halama, who gave up five runs on six hits and two walks in just three innings. Halama's record stood at 6-6.

Joel Pineiro pitched four scoreless innings of relief for the Mariners. After the game, Manager Lou Piniella indicated that Halama was going back to the bullpen for more work. Speculation was that Pineiro might get a chance to take the fifth starter's spot in the rotation.

Ichiro was 0-5 for the game, and now on an 0-18 slide. His batting average had dropped to .333. Diamondbacks won 5-3.

July 17 The M's looked to rebound with Paul Abbott on the mound, seeking his sixth straight decision. Abbott did not disappoint, and was a hit with his teammates. Abbott would end the year with the highest run support of any starter in the American League. He scattered six hits over 6 1/3 innings, giving up just one run, as Seattle completed interleague play with a 12-6 record.

Ichiro was in the DH spot with Edgar's sore quadriceps keeping him on the shelf. The Japanese rookie broke out of his slump in the first inning with a single. He took third on a Guillen double, and scored on a Boone sacrifice fly. Guillen later scored on a Cameron sacrifice fly, giving the M's a 2-0 first inning lead. That was Mariner baseball. When Ichiro gets on base, good things happen!

Boone and Bell both homered, and Ichiro added a double and his 31st stolen base. Arthur Rhodes and Ryan Franklin pitched 2 2/3 innings of near-perfect relief, extending the Seattle bullpen's scoreless streak to 19 innings. M's won 6-1.

Off the field, Kazuhiro Sasaki and Ichiro Suzuki announced they would begin speaking to Japanese media again. The policy was changed despite the fact that two Japanese, who weren't identified as reporters, had tried to enter Sasaki's apartment a few days previously. Sasaki indicated that he learned the security guard at his apartment complex had even been offered a $500 bribe for entry into Kazu's home. The two Japanese Mariners stated that part of the reason for wanting to play in the United States was to get away from the Japanese paparazzi. The stars regretted their time of silence because it punished legitimate reporters.

The team headed for Kansas City without All Star centerfielder Mike Cameron, who stayed behind to be with his pregnant wife, who was experiencing labor pains.

Two game series at Royals (split)

July 18 Jamie Moyer broke out of his pitching slump, but his work of art on this evening was matched by Kansas City's Chad Durbin. Moyer, who had won only one of his previous seven starts, threw just 73 pitches in eight innings, giving up four singles, one walk and no runs.

But Mariner hitters couldn't get on track until the 10th, when four singles and an intentional pass yielded two runs. Jeff Nelson, who pitched a scoreless 9th, got the win, and Kazu Sasaki, who pitched a scoreless 10th, got the save. The Mariner relief staff had a 21 inning scoreless streak. M's 2, Royals 0.

As noted before, Ichiro had drawn a huge media presence. The media crush didn't impact just Ichiro and Sasaki. It affected Manager Lou Piniella as well. He commented that it wasn't just the Japanese reporters. The problem came from all the radio and TV sports networks as well. "There's so many of them now that I have to protect my own privacy as well as that of my players," said the manager. "It's a hard line to draw between the responsibility to the public of being accessible and avoiding distractions to be able to perform on the field."

It turned out that JaBreka Cameron was having false labor pains. Husband Mike boarded a plane for KC to join the team the next day.

July 19 Even though the Royals were 5th in the AL's Central Division, they were among the league's leading hitters. Mariner ace Freddy Garcia found out the hard way just how good the Kansas City hitters were by surrendering six runs on nine hits – six of them for extra bases – in only four innings. This was Garcia's shortest outing since opening day, as his record fell to 11-2.

Brian Fuentes, John Halama and Jose Paniagua were bright spots, however. They continued the relief staff's scoreless inning stretch by four in the Mariner loss. Ichiro was 0-5, dropping his average to .331. Royals 6, M's 3.

After the game, Seattle headed north to face the surprising Minnesota Twins.

Four game series at Twins (M's sweep!)

At 68-27, the Mariners were still wowing their fans and the entire baseball world. The 5-3 record after the All Star break was a bit of a slow down from the first half and Ichiro's average had dropped by 20 points. But Seattle still had not lost a series on the road and had not lost three games in a row. Despite not having the Randy Johnson or Roger Clemens type of dominating pitcher, the Mariners' versatility sheltered them from losing streaks.

July 20 The key number for this game wasn't Aaron Sele's seven shut-out innings, or the bullpen's two shutout innings, or even Mike Cameron's 17th homer. The key number in this game was 700. The Mariners' 4-0 victory at Minnesota was Lou Piniella's 700th victory as the Seattle manager. Only Atlanta's Bobby Cox, Minnesota's Tom Kelly, and San Francisco's Dusty Baker had more wins with their current teams.

The game itself was never in doubt as the Mariners jumped on top 2-0 in the second. Sele was masterful, with only one troublesome inning. Seattle's defense snuffed out a would-be Twins' rally in the 2nd with an unusual double play. With men on first and second, Minnesota's Chad Allen hit a sharp grounder to deep short. Carlos Guillen fired to second for the putout, but the relay to first was too low. The ball went rolling away from Mariner first baseman John Olerud. Seeing this action, the Twins' Brian Buchanan had rounded third and started home. Olerud quickly recovered and threw home, where catcher Dan Wilson built a fortress around the plate and applied the tag for the out.

Once again, Ichiro was 0-5, dropping his average to .327. M's 4, Twins 0.

July 21 Joel Pineiro got his first start of the season but it was John

Halama who was the pitching star for the Mariners. Posted to a 4-0 first inning lead on a John Olerud run-driving single and an Al Martin three run homer, Pineiro should have been able to coast to the win. But it wasn't to be. He gave up two hits and four walks in two innings, and seemed to struggle with each hitter. Rather than postpone the inevitable, Piniella came with the quick hook which, in retrospect, was a good decision.

Beleaguered lefty John Halama pitched well with good control in Minnesota's homer-dome, giving up only one run in 4 1/3 innings. Rhodes, Paniagua and Sasaki pitched the last 2 2/3 innings surrendering only one hit. Though the bullpen's scoreless streak was stopped at 32 1/3 innings, Halama was effective during the middle innings. Arthur Rhodes continued his outstanding pitching, and had retired 25 of the last 26 batters he had faced over about a two week period. M's 6, Twins 3.

Mark McLemore and Mike Cameron stole bases in the game, giving the Mariners the league lead in stolen base efficiency at 83%.

The trading deadline was less than two weeks away and speculation was that Jose Cruz Jr. seemed to the Mariners' prime target. Cruz' teammate, Shannon Stewart, and Kansas City's Jermaine Dye were also coveted, but neither seemed attainable. Detroit's Juan Encarnacion, 25, was also of interest, but general managers of all the teams were saying they weren't in a "fire-sale" mode. Stewart was considered the most unreachable of all due to the high price the Jays wanted.

Another player in the M's radar was the Tigers' Roger Cedeno. A leadoff hitter, Cedeno had been sought by Seattle in a Randy Johnson deal, and since he had turned down a three-year $13.5 million offer from Detroit, was considered available.

Interestingly, the question was posed of Lou Piniella as to Mark McLemore becoming the regular left fielder. His hitting, defense and baserunning were all very significant in Seattle's success. Piniella gave a typically direct response. "McLemore's too valuable to play just one position."

What about those other position players, such as Boone, Cameron and Olerud? Oh well, we knew what you meant, Lou. You're right. McLemore IS too valuable to play just one position. – SE

July 22 For the second straight day, the Mariners beat the Twins 6-3. Paul Abbott took a two-hit shutout into the 9th innings to earn his seventh straight decision, raising his record to 9-2. Jeff Nelson finished the game, lowering his ERAto 1.93.

Mark McLemore played shortstop and right field, collected two hits, drove in four runs, and was rumored to have sold popcorn in his spare time. The versatile veteran was asked once again to name his favorite position. "Wherever I can get four at-bats," he replied.

Ichiro found yet another way to help the Mariners in the game. In addition to his two hits, which signaled he was coming out of a post-All Star slump, Ichiro was on first when McLemore's fly ball to shallow right field was caught. The less than fleet-footed Dan Wilson, who was on third, broke for home. Seeing that Wilson was tagging, Ichiro went back to first base, and broke for second on the catch. A surprised Doug Mientkiewicz, the Twin first-baseman, cut off the throw to go after Ichiro. Meanwhile, Wilson was breaking for the plate; Ichiro stopped to get into a rundown.

While the Twins played catch, Wilson snuck home. Seeing that Wilson would cross the plate, Ichiro gave up. He had accomplished his goal. The official scorer had the play 9-3-6-3-4-6 for the tag out of Ichiro, and Wilson with a run scored. "It was a smart play by Ichiro," said Piniella.

This was a time where getting in a rundown was good for the team. M's 6, Twins 3.

July 23 The Mariners completed the four-game sweep of the Twins at Minnesota behind another strong pitching performance from Jamie Moyer, with relief help from Arthur Rhodes and Kazu Sasaki. Ichiro, Olerud and Guillen provided the offense with two hits each, but the key of the game was Charles Gipson's version of "The Throw."

The Mariners clung to a one-run lead in the bottom of the 8th. Arthur Rhodes was on the mound, and Lou Piniella had just inserted Gipson into centerfield for defense. Mike Cameron was the DH for the night. Mark McLemore had started in centerfield. With one out, the Twins' Chad Allen hit a double to right field. Then, Corey Koskie lined a clean single to center. Allen took off from second on the crack of the bat, but Gipson charged the hit. He picked it up cleanly off the Metrodome turf and shot a zinger all the way to Dan Wilson at home plate for the tag on Allen keeping the Twins from scoring.

"I charged it, got a good bounce and made the throw," said Gipson matter-of-factly. The play made manager Lou Piniella look like a genius for the defensive replacement. The winning skipper stated: "He's got a strong accurate arm. That's one of the reasons I put him in there." M's 3, Twins 2.

Charles Gipson - OF
Born: 12-16-72, Orange, CA
Lives in Orange, CA with wife Mikhael and three children
6'1" 195 lbs
Signed through 2001 season

The game was a benchmark for Ichiro. His 450th plate appearance in the 5th inning activated a $2 million incentive clause in his contract. At game's end, Ichiro was batting .327 with 32 stolen bases.

Anyone selling Ichiro merchandise was cashing in, too. Limited edition Ichiro rookie cards were selling for as much as $1,000. With Ichiro Bobblehead Day approaching, merchants and fans alike were ready to have the bouncing face of Ichiro adorn their mantels or fatten their bank accounts.

Three game series vs. Royals (M's take 1)
The Mariners had just swept the Central Division leading Twins at Minneapolis. But the Central Division's 5th place team, the Kansas City Royals, would prove to be a more worthy opponent in Seattle.

July 24 Another packed house at SAFECO Field (17th straight sellout) was on hand to see the Mariners with ace starter Freddy Garcia thrash the visiting Royals. Only it didn't happen that way.

Second-year right hander Kris Wilson held the Mariners at bay and earned the term "Mariner killer." This was Wilson's second victory over Seattle in a week, and Garcia's second straight loss. Royals won 6-1.

But the big story of the day was outside the gates. As Mariner tickets became more scarce, scalpers became more popular - - including with the police. Scalping is illegal in Seattle city limits, and in a recent three-day homestand, an undercover sting netted 30 arrests with 151 Mariner tickets being confiscated.

The team also warned of a scam whereby tickets that had already been used for entry were being re-sold. Since tickets were no longer torn at the SAFECO turnstile, but instead scanned, an unwary purchaser on the street wouldn't know that the ticket had already been used. The bar code on the previously used ticket would reveal through scanning that the ticket was no longer valid for entry.

Interestingly, it was discovered that the Mariners' organization operated a service on its web site for season ticket holders who lived outside the Seattle city limits. The team essentially brokered tickets for whatever price they could get (a/k/a scalping). Mariner management justified the service on the ground that only non-Seattle residents sold the tickets for more than the face value, thereby avoiding a violation of law. *Hmmmm. . .*

July 25 Kansas City wished it played the Mariners at SAFECO every game. When the Royals come to Seattle, their pitchers are like Cy Young, their hitters like any of the Bronx Bombers, and their fielders like Willie Mays. It was Royals' pitcher Paul Byrd's turn to baffle Seattle's hitters on this night. With a newfound screwball as part of his arsenal, Byrd distributed six hits and held the M's scoreless until the bottom of the 9th.

On the other side of the diamond, Royal batsmen peppered Aaron Sele for nine hits and five runs. Kansas City won 5-1.

With less than a week before the trading deadline, the Athletics acquired a player the Mariners wish they could have had – the Royals' Jermaine Dye. The A's outfield of Johnny Damon, Terence Long and Dye made the Mariners feel fortunate to be 19 games ahead of the green and gold from Oakland.

But the M's still coveted Jose Cruz, Jr. who was starting to appear unattainable. The Blue Jays' demands were still too high. So, Seattle turned its attention to Juan Encarnacion. A new name surfaced as well – Mark Quinn, the 27 year-old Royals' left fielder.

July 26 In one of Seattle's best played games of the season, the Mariners offense came alive, and their pitching and defense were near perfect baseball in a 4-0 victory. Seattle's Joel Pineiro surrendered only one hit, no runs and walked none over six innings.

Rhodes, Nelson and Sasaki each pitched one inning to preserve the shutout. Seattle batters collected 11 hits on the way to the win. Ichiro, Olerud and Bell each had two hits.

Al Martin's eight-game hitting streak was stopped when he popped out as a pinch-hitter. Martin was batting .328 over the previous 28 games but continued to hear the clamor for a new left fielder. "I know I was horrid," said Martin, referring to his near .100 April and May. "You want to earn your keep which I haven't done. Nobody wants to stink."

Deadline Deals

In 1998, the M's made a trade deadline deal sending pitcher Randy Johnson to Houston for prospects Freddy Garcia, Carlos Guillen and John Halama. The year before, a Mariner deadline transaction found pitcher Derek Lowe and catcher Jason Varitek going to Boston for reliever Heathcliff Slocumb. Back in 1988, Seattle sent slugging first baseman Ken Phelps to the Yankees for pitching hopefuls Rick Balabon and Troy Evers, and young outfielder Jay Buhner.

Three game series vs. Twins (M's sweep!)

The Twins came to town in a tie with the Indians at the top of the Central Division. The Twins post All Star drop was Titanic, and playing the Mariners wouldn't float them.

July 27 The M's made the Twins think they were playing in the Kingdome as Seattle scored eleven runs and had four home runs. John Olerud, Stan Javier, Bret Boone and Ichiro Suzuki all hit round trippers as the M's made Paul Abbott the fourth Mariner starter to reach double-digit wins. At 10-2, Abbott joined Sele, Garcia and Moyer as Seattle improved its record to 74-29 and a franchise record 45 games over .500.

Norm Charlton was activated and pitched two innings, allowing just one hit. Mariners won 11-4.

Off the field, Seattle trade prospects were looking grim. GMs had high demands for Seattle's young pitchers, but Pat Gillick wasn't parting with Joel Pineiro, or Ryan Anderson and Gil Meche. The question for Gillick was "Do we go for the ring now or preserve talent for the future?" Mark Quinn of the Royals and John Vander Wal of the Pirates were still available. Carlos Lee of the White Sox was added to the catalog of Mariner potentials. Just three days were left to trade. It appeared that the M's may find the well empty in the search for another bat.

July 28 THE day was finally here. What day was that? Ichiro Bobblehead Day!

The Mariners were cautious, fearing the anticipated multitudes as if they were raiding 13th century Mongols. The team issued these rules:

Ichiro Bobblehead Day Info

• Guests may being lining up at midnight, Saturday, July 28
• Queuing prior to 10:00 a.m. will be allowed only on the plaza next to the parking garage.
• No overnight parking is available at the SAFECO parking garage
• In fairness to all guests, no one will be allowed to hold places for additional individuals
• Anyone "cutting" in line will be sent to the back of the line
• The Right Field Gate and Home Plate Gate will open at 10 a.m. All other gates will open at 11:00 a.m.
• Bobble heads will be given to the first 20,000 fans, first come, first served.
• Guests with multiple tickets must go to the back of the line to receive additional bobble head dolls.
• Guests who wish to exit the ballpark must do so via the "exit gate" at the Home Plate entrance.
• Uniformed Seattle Police officers and Mariners security staff will be present overnight to patrol the area and handle any problems that may arise.
• Tully's coffee and Oh Boy! Oberto will be on hand to provide refreshments for guests.
• Bathroom facilities will be provided on the parking garage plaza.
• Any collectors soliciting bobble head dolls inside SAFECO Field or on ballpark property will be ejected.

Even before midnight, people lined the sidewalks outside SAFECO Field. Donavan and Leslie Tappe of Bothell, Washington, were first in line. The bobblehead craze had swept baseball to the point where fans were vying for retired players' bobbleheads. Rod Carew bobbleheads in Minneapolis and Willie Mays' bobbleheads in San Francisco were fan favorites.

At SAFECO for Bobblehead Day

The enthusiasm over a plastic doll with an oversized head sup - ported by a spring had swept the country. I remember seeing those dolls as a kid in New York, but they were ceramic then. And today, people were going to wait in line all night just to get a chance to possess a 2001 bobblehead doll. This was too good an opportuni - ty to pass up. I had to talk with these early birds. I haven't gotten out of bed before 10 AM in a decade, but Saturday, July 28th, found me at SAFECO Field at 6 AM, microphone in hand.

Proudly wearing a Mariners' cap, **Barry** *from Federal Way, WA said: "I didn't ever expect to be in line waiting for a doll. Frank, over there, who is with me gave me the tickets. So I'm going to give my doll to him. I dragged my friend to get here at 4 AM. It's amazing to see how much enthusiasm this Ichiro doll craze is bringing to Seattle."*

Jerry *from Kalama, WA, said his son Garrett, wanted a doll. "It's a two hour drive here from home, and we'll go to seven games this year. We came up last night, and since we were here, we decided to come early to get a chance to take the doll home and keep it."*

Christopher *from Omaha was visiting his aunt in Seattle. "My Auntie Linda is a season ticket holder and she gave six of us the tickets. We're going to give all six of them to her because she's a baseball fanatic. I was just a Nebraska Cornhusker fan until now, but with this count me in as a Mariner fan."*

Debra *from Seattle got her ticket about a month ago, and didn't spend the night at the park because of the rain. "I got the ticket just because this was Ichiro Bobblehead Day. Ichiro is the 'Brad Pitt' of baseball."*

"Only in America could a bunch of people from Seattle line up at 6 in the morning to get a bobblehead doll from a company owned by an enterprising Australian and made in China of a Japanese player," commented **Mike** *from Queen Anne in Seattle. "My wife and houseguest were very excited about the Ichiro bobblehead because he's so cute. I never imagined myself doing this, but I saw this coming. That'why I got the ticket."*

Mike *from Des Moines, WA was specifically at SAFECO as part of Ichiromania. "This is my kids'first baseball game ever. So what better way than to get them something they'll have the rest of their* *lives, and then pass them on through generations."*

Rick, *who had driven up from Portland, Oregon, donned a Philadelphia Athletics blazer. "I've collected baseball cards for 40 years. I bought these tickets about four months ago because I read in Sports Collectors Digest about the Ichiro bobblehead. We're sitting in centerfield, but who cares. Just to get in is excit - ing I knew a little about Ichiro's history in Japan. I thought he would be at least a hit in the US, if not a sensation. So I picked up some early cards of him from eBay, and had a hunch. The people in Portland are crazy about him too. When I was growing up it was so dominated by Yankees, and I was 12 during the Maris-Mantle thing of 1961 – that was big. But this is bigger than that. I thought Camden Yards was great, but SAFECO is a great, super ballpark. Everything is perfect."*

Kevin *from Lake Stevens, WA had lost all track of time. "I don't know when I got in line. My brother slept here in a tent. I don't know how he's going to get the tent inside Safeco. I got these tick - ets two months ago for this day, and for Kazuhiro bobblehead night too. Ichiro and Sasaki are great ballplayers and I'm glad they came here to be Mariners."*

"We came to the game last night and got home about 11 PM. We stayed there about an hour and came right back," said a Mariner's fan wearing a # 51 Ichiro jersey. "We have a 15 game package, and sit right behind Ichiro in right field. He waves at us. We miss Jay [Buhner], especially his power, but Ichiro fills in quite well. We've had about two hours sleep, and if we get our bobblehead, it will be worth it. It's great to see the Mariners doing this well, but you don't think any team could be this good."

Don *from Bothell, WA, was first in line. He got to SAFECO at 7 PM the night before. "I wanted an Ichiro doll to add to my Ichiro memorabilia collection. I'm just a big Mariner fan!"*

But **Todd**, *also from Bothell, was a bit more cynical. "I'm here for the stupid plastic doll. I got here 11:30 PM last night and I'm tired. I'm going to get my doll and go back home to bed. Then I'm going to sell the doll on eBay for $1500." Todd added "How will the Mariners do this year? They're overrated. Cleveland will win. Even the A's will beat the Mariners."*

The line moved rapidly after the gates opened. **Dave** *from Seattle* *was just excited to be there, and got an Ichiro bobblehead doll. "I haven't even looked at the doll yet. I'm more interested in seeing the Mariners beat Twins. I'm big fan of Mariners, but this is my first bobblehead. I remember when it didn't matter what seat you had at the Kingdome. You could always get a better one – sit wher - ever you wanted. Now at SAFECO, this is great!"*

I stood here for several hours myself talking with people. The line to get in the game said so much about what a baseball team can do for a community. Every kind of person was here: old, young, male, female, every ethnic group, in wheelchairs. But you better not break line because four people who tried were removed. It was a great feeling being here. The Mariners have been a unifying force for Seattle, and it has been building ever since SAFECO Field opened. - MS

The Ichiro bobbleheads were predicted to be all-time favorites. Gary Engel, a Japanese baseball memorabilia dealer, bought $25,000 worth of Ichiro merchandise from Japan when he heard that Ichiro had signed with the Seattle Mariners. He knew that the seven-time Japanese batting champ would be a good investment, but he never dreamed there would be a phenomenon called "Ichiromania."

"I got more callers asking for Ichiro items the day after The Throw than any other time," Engel was quoted by *ESPN.com* as saying.

Rob Fitts, a New York-based Japanese card dealer said that his business has tripled due to Ichiro. In the fall of 2000, a complete set of 1993 Takara Orix Blue Wave cards sold for $50. That was Ichiro's rookie year, and by the summer of 2001, just Ichiro's rookie card from that set was selling for $1,800.

But that wasn't the record – by far. A2001 Ichiro Fleer E-X card was sold to Bruce Gaston of SportsCardInvestor.com for $22,000! Like the stock market, value is based on the present and future projections.

Even Manager Lou Piniella got caught up in the Ichiro Bobblehead rage. "My wife said she had to have one. So I got one for her," said the giddy new bobblehead doll owner.

Oh yes, there was a baseball game on July 28th, too. Ichiro "Mr. Bobblehead" Suzuki went 3-4 with two RBIs and a stolen base. Jamie Moyer kept the ball in the park, giving up only one run on five hits in 6 1/3 innings. Jeff Nelson and Arthur Rhodes closed out the game with 2 2/3 innings of scoreless relief. It was the M's seventh straight victory over the Twins who fell out of first place in the Central Division. M's 5, Twins 1.

July 29 The only heads bobbling on this day were of the Twins' batters watching Freddy Garcia spin sliders and change-ups by them. Garcia pitched a complete game five hitter, giving up only one earned run and walking two. The win stopped Freddy's two-game losing streak.

Bret Boone, Stan Javier and Ed Sprague had ten hits among them, with Boone driving in three, Javier scoring three, and Sprague driving in four, matching his season total. M's 10, Twins 2.

The series sweep was the Mariners' 12th of the year, a team record.

Wild Card Dealers

Changes in baseball postseason have impacted deadlines trades. In the past, a team 19 games back, such as Oakland wouldn't even consider trading prospects. With a wildcard playoff spot available, and with Oakland having the second best record in the AL, not winning a division would give the A's as good a chance as any team to get to the World Series.

Detroit GM Randy Smith explained that teams were so payroll heavy, they were waiting to the last possible moment to make deals. "When Seattle traded Randy Johnson, people said that it was a good deal for Houston. But Seattle filled a lot of holes, which we're seeing this season."

Three game series at Detroit (M's take 2)
July 31 The Mariners went back on the road to end the month of July, and former 21 game winner Jose Lima regained his form by holding Seattle to six hits. Only one of those hits was for extra bases, an Al Martin double, and the Mariners were all but out of the game from the first inning.

Aaron Sele was on the mound for Seattle, and gave up three hits, a walk and two runs in the first frame to put the Tigers ahead to stay. The Mariners ended their four game winning streak, but Ichiro continue his climb back up with two hits, raising his average to .330. Tigers 3, M's 2.

The trading deadline came and went for the Mariners. In one last effort, Seattle reportedly offered Denny Stark and John Halama to Detroit for Juan Encarnacion. The Tigers said OK, as long as Joel Pineiro and Ramon Vazquez, the Mariners' shortstop at Tacoma were included. *Fat chance!*

Standing pat didn't disappoint skipper Lou Piniella. "We didn't want to mess with the club's chemistry. Our players have done pretty darned good, and unless you improve yourself a whole lot, you shouldn't tinker with them," said the first place manager.

Lou had a point. The M's went 11-4 without all-world DH Edgar Martinez. One of the Mariners' best players was a man without a position, Mark McLemore. A "this is my last year" player had overcome early season injuries to hit nearly .500 as July ended - Stan Javier. Essentially, this was a team that did what McLemore said. "We just take care of business on a day-to-day basis."

July's Mariner Moments (18 wins - 11 losses . . . Season 76-30)
1. Mariners hit 40 games over .500 (3rd)
2. Freddy beats Kevin Brown, the $15 million man (6th)
3. Everything All Star (6th - 10th)
4. Lou's 700th Mariner victory (20th)
5. Gipson nails runner at home (23rd)
6. Ichiro Bobblehead Day (28th)

Chapter Ten

August, 2001

"You can't sit on a lead and run a few plays into the line and just kill the clock. You've got to throw the ball over the plate and give the other man his chance. That's why baseball is the greatest game of them all."

- Earl Weaver, Hall-of-Fame manager, 1968-1982, 1985-1986

The roster was set. It was time for the stretch run. No new hitter was found. The Mariners had been consistent all season long, but if another bat was going to join Seattle, he would come off the waiver wire or from within. Every other team that needed a hitter made a trade for one. Many other teams needed pitchers, a source of abundance in the Mariner system. As the leader in scoring, the M's chose to not make their own deadline deal.

Continuation of three game series at Detroit
(games 2 and 3)
August 1 Paul Abbott won his ninth straight decision, tying a club record, with a 7-1 win over the homestanding Tigers.

The lopsided score belied the fact that Abbott suffered control problems during the game. He threw 103 pitches in only 6 2/3 innings, and was rescued from a bases-loaded, no-out situation in the 3rd. Ichiro and Carlos Guillen provided defensive gems. Ichiro's reputation kept the runner at third base on a medium fly ball to right field. It was a good thing because the Mariners' phenom threw a frozen rope all the way to Tom Lampkin at home plate that would have clipped the Tiger runners' paws. Guillen's play was skill of the mind and body, as he deftly avoided catching a soft line drive. He chose to let it bounce, picked it up, touched second and fired to first for the inning ending double play.

On the offensive side, Seattle collected 14 hits. Every Mariner with an at-bat got a hit. Boone had three hits and captured his 100th RBI.

The only negative of the night was that the Mariners were on the receiving end of their first triple play since 1997. In the 4th, with Lampkin on first and Ichiro on second, a hit-and-run play ended the inning. McLemore's liner to second made the triple play the only winning trifecta for Detroit. M's won 7-1.

August 2 The Mariners starting pitching staff in the future will probably include Joel Pineiro. The 2-1 win, a four-hit, no walk, seven innings gem, showed that the 22 year-old right hander may have just moved the future to the present.

Pineiro was a heavily sought-after commodity as the trading deadline neared just the week before, but Manager Lou Piniella sat squarely in the Puerto Rican native's corner. "I told Pat [Gillick] how much I liked him. I'm glad he wasn't traded," said Piniella.

Pineiro got valuable tips from starter Aaron Sele, who went over the Tiger lineup hitter by hitter to help Pineiro get ready for the game. The young righthander was 2-0 with a 0.74 ERA.

Tigers' lefthander Adam Pettyjohn was almost as good, though. The dependable Stan Javier, hitting leadoff for a resting Ichiro Suzuki, and Bret Boone had three hits a piece to lead the offense. Detroit's Jose Macias homered in the 3rd for the Tigers only run.

Mariner relief was strong once again. Jeff Nelson struck out the side on 11 pitches in the 8th, and Kazu Sasaki earned his 300th career save with a scoreless 9th. The triumvirate of Nelson, Sasaki and Rhodes hadn't allowed a run in the past 39 innings. M's won 2-1.

The win over Detroit meant that the Mariners were the first team in the 33 year history of division play to go 100 games without losing three in a row. The Mariner stood at 63-3 when leading after six innings, and 72-3 when leading after eight. *My oh my!*

Four game series at Cleveland (M's take 3)

A short flight took Seattle to the home of its likely first postseason hurdle, Cleveland. The Indians' lineup was loaded. The league's leading hitter (Roberto Alomar), home run leader (Jim Thome), and RBI leader (Juan Gonzalez) were surrounded by speed and power at nearly every position. Most preseason picks had the Indians at the top of the Central Division, and by the time Seattle arrived, Cleveland had displaced Minnesota in first place. The best hitting team in the American League eagerly awaited the arrival of the Seattle Mariners.

August 3 The Mariners had a few good hitters of their own, and the lead-off game of the series that pitted Jamie Moyer against the Indians' Bartolo Colon could have been a slugfest, based on the numbers. Moyer had struggled of late, and Colon sported an ERA of 4.30. The battle, though, was Moyer vs. Colon.

For the second straight night, the Mariners won 2-1, and Jamie Moyer was brilliant. Over seven innings, he gave up only two hits, no walks, and struck out five. No Indian got past second base. But Colon was nearly as brilliant. Through seven, Colon had given up only one hit, and walked three. Outfielder Kenny Lofton aided Colon in Cameronesque fashion by robbing Carlos Guillen of a homer in centerfield.

In the 8th, though, Mariner magic was on stage as David Bell led off with a single. Lampkin sacrificed him to second. Ichiro, hitless to that point, noticed Indian third sacker Travis Fryman playing back. Ichiro cleverly laid down a bunt, surprising Cleveland. Since Fryman had to play the ball, there was no one to cover third. When the dust cleared, Ichiro stood on first with a bunt single and Bell was perched at third.

Yet again, Manager Lou Piniella was giving Ichiro credit for heads-up play. "He caught Fryman a few steps back and got the bunt down. Give Ichiro credit. It was a smart play," said Piniella.

A visibly shaken Colon barely kept the ball in the park as McLemore drove in Bell with a sacrifice fly, while Ichiro took second. Martinez, in his first game in 18 days, then walked, and Olerud drove in Ichiro with a single.

Sports columnist Mike Bauman commented on the contest, between the two most potent offenses in the league, stating:
"But in keeping with the theme of the evening, Ichiro won this game for the Mariners not with muscle but with a combination of brains and speed. . . . It felt like an old game, but a new and inter - national game, all at the same time." [Flawless execution Seattle's edge, MLB.com, August 4, 2001.]

The Indians eked out a run on the Nelson, Rhodes and Sasaki trio, but Seattle held on for a 2-1 win.

August 4 The offenses of both teams returned in the second game of the four-game set with the M's coming out on top 8-5. Freddy Garcia got his 13th win, against three losses, but surrendered ten hits and three runs in 6 2/3 innings.

Four straight singles and aggressive baserunning yielded three Mariner runs in the 4th. The M's added three more in the seventh on Dan Wilson's seventh home run.

Jose Paniagua came on to pitch the 8th and was totally ineffective. He gave up three hits and a walk in 1 2/3 innings, but Arthur Rhodes slammed the door shut by striking out Jim Thome with the tying run at the plate. M's won 8-5.

The win was Seattle's 80th, against 30 losses. It was the Mariners 22nd straight win when scoring four runs or more. To this point in the season, Seattle led the major leagues in runs and fewest errors while ranking third in fewest runs allowed, behind only the Cubs and Braves.

August 5 Mt. St. Helens erupts in Cleveland! OK, losing a base-ball game isn't that bad, but the loss on national television was one for the ages. The specific age was 76 years, because it had been that long since a team had lost a game after leading by 12 runs.

Aaron Sele started for the Mariners and Dave Burba, who wasn't having a stellar year, started for the home team. Burba lasted only two innings, but it didn't matter who was pitching for the Indians. The Mariners collected 17 hits and were running the bases at will.

The scoring started in the second. Al Martin hit a one-out double and was driven home by Mike Cameron's double. David Bell walked and Tom Lampkin hit the third double of the inning scoring Cameron. Ichiro then singled, driving in Bell and Lampkin. After two complete innings, the Mariners led 4-0.

In the M's 3rd, Edgar, Olerud and Martin loaded the bases with consecutive singles. Mike Bacsik relieved Burba for the Indians. Cameron greeted the new pitcher with a double scoring two runs. Guillen followed with a single scoring two more runs. Bell singled, and Lampkin was hit by a pitch, loading the bases again. Ichiro hit a long fly to center, scoring Guillen. McLemore walked, and Edgar was safe at first on Omar Vizquel's throwing error, while Bell and Lampkin scored.

The Indians failed to score in their half of the third, and after three innings the score was Seattle 12, Cleveland 0.

Sele, meanwhile, had surrendered a hit in each of the first three innings, but no runner had reached second base. Juan Gonzalez led off the 4th with a single, and Jim Thome followed with a gargantuan home run to right center. Marty Cordova reached first on the Indians' third hit of the inning, but was erased by the Mariners' second double play. At the end of four innings, the score was 12-2, Seattle.

The Mariners were at it again in the 5th. McLemore and Martinez singled. With Olerud due up and Seattle maintaining a comfortable ten run lead, Manager Lou Piniella started substituting. He sent Ed Sprague to hit for Olerud who promptly singled in McLemore. Martin drove in Edgar with a ground out. At the end of five the score was Seattle 14, Cleveland 2, for the M's second 12-run lead.

It's a normal occurrence when a game gets out of hand for managers to get other players into the game. In the top of the 6th, Indians' manager Charlie Manuel replaced Roberto Alomar at second and Travis Fryman at third. In the bottom of the 6th, Piniella sent in Charles Gipson to right field, replacing Ichiro. In the meantime, Eddie Taubensee pinch hit for Juan Gonzalez, taking over the Cleveland DH spot. Neither team scored in the 6th.

In the 7th, Stan Javier replaced Edgar Martinez at DH, but Seattle failed to score. In the bottom half of the inning, Cleveland's Russell Branyan, who started the game at left field, but had moved to third base, led off with a home run. Sele got the next two out, but Einar Diaz then singled, and Kenny Lofton and Omar Vizquel drew consecutive walks. After 6 2/3 innings, giving up eight hits and three walks on 116 pitches, Sele was done. John Halama came in with the bases load, two outs and the second year right handed hitter, Jolbert Cabrera at the plate. Cabrera singled, scoring Diaz and Lofton. At the end of seven, Seattle was content with a 14-5 lead.

The Mariners were held scoreless in the top of the 8th, but Jim Thome led off the Indians' half with his second homer of the game. Halama then beaned Branyan and yielded a two-run homer to Marty Cordova. After a ground out, Diaz and Lofton singled. Piniella signaled to the bullpen to bring in Norm Charlton to face Vizquel. "Little O" hit a double over first base, scoring Diaz. At the end of eight, Seattle still had a comfortable five-run lead at 14-9.

Seattle, scoreless in the 9th, brought Charlton back to the mound in the bottom of the inning to put an end to the too-long game. Taubensee led off the inning with a single, but Charlton retired the next two hitters and kept Taubensee at first. With one on, two outs in the 9th, and Seattle enjoying a five run lead, Jeff Nelson was throwing in the Mariners' bullpen presumably just to get some work. The Indians' Marty Cordova then doubled, leaving runners at second and third. Nelson hurried in to the game, and handed Will Cordero a free pass to first. Einar Diaz, then took a 3-2 pitch for a single to left driving in both runners. The score was then 14-11, Seattle.

The M's bullpen became frantic. Ace closer Kazu Sasaki was quickly readying to perform his specialty. He came in to face Lofton, who promptly singled loading the bases and bringing Vizquel up to the plate again. The Indians' manager had already reminded Vizquel of patience against Sasaki, and told him that the first base line was open. Indeed it was. Ed Sprague had the first baseman's mitt for the Mariners, and inexplicably was playing off the line. Sprague and Mariner field coaches forgot or ignored the situation, or simply believed that Vizquel couldn't pull the ball against Sasaki.

Omar worked the count to 3-2, and drove a Sasaki dropping split-fingered fastball down the vacant first base line for a triple, scoring all three baserunners, and tying the game at 14.

Neither team scored in the 10th, and in the 11th, with Jose Paniagua on the mound for the Mariners, the Indians hit three straight singles to make the final score Cleveland 15, Seattle 14.

The game lasted four hours and eleven minutes; 29 runs were scored; 40 hits were collected, 12 pitchers entered the game; and 27 position players saw action. The only error was by Cleveland's gold-glove shortstop Omar Vizquel. John Rocker, who struck out the side in the 11th got the win. Paniagua took the loss.

Prior to losing a 12-run lead for the second time with only seven outs to go, the Mariners hadn't blown more than a three-run lead all season. In the month before the game, Seattle's bullpen had given up only eight runs, but allowed 10 runs in this game alone. Sasaki, the master of the Mariner bullpen hadn't blown a save since May 27, hadn't given up a run since June 20, and had allowed only one of the previous 30 batters he faced to reach base.

Piniella said it all postgame: "What can I say?" *Again, Lou was right.*

Seattle 14   August 5, 2001   Cleveland 15

Hitters	Pos	ab	r	h	rbi	bb	so
Suzuki	RF	3	0	1	3	0	1
Gipson	RF/LF	2	0	0	0	0	1
McLemore	2B/LF	5	2	2	0	1	1
Martinez	DH	4	2	2	0	0	0
b-Javier	PH/DH	2	0	0	1	0	0
Olerud	1B	3	1	2	0	0	0
a-Sprague	PH/1B	3	0	1	1	0	0
Martin	LF/RF	6	2	3	1	0	0
Wilson	C	0	0	0	0	0	1
Cameron	CF	6	2	3	3	0	1
Guillen	SS	6	1	1	0	1	1
Bell	3B	5	2	1	2	0	1
Lampkin	C	4	2	1	1	1	0
c-Boone	PH/2B	1	0	0	0	0	1
Totals		**50**	**14**	**17**	**13**	**2**	**7**

a-singled for Olerud in 5th; b-flied to right for Martinez in 7th; c-struck out for Lampkin in 11th

Batting: 2B-Martin, Cameron (2), Lampkin. SF-Suzuki

Fielding: DP-2 (Guillen-McLemore-Olerud 2)

LOB-7

Pitcher	ip	h	r	er	bb	so
Sele	6 2/3	8	5	5	3	3
Halama	2/3	5	4	4	0	0
Charlton	1 1/3	3	2	2	0	2
Nelson	0	1	2	2	1	0
Sasaki (BS)	1/3	2	1	1	0	0
Rhodes	1	1	0	0	1	2
Paniagua (L)	1/3	3	1	1	0	0

Hitters	Pos	ab	r	h	rbi	bb	so
Lofton	CF	6	3	4	0	1	0
Vizquel	SS	6	0	4	4	1	0
Alomar	2B	2	0	0	0	0	0
Cabrera	2B	5	0	2	3	0	1
Gonzalez	DH	2	1	1	0	0	0
a-Taubensee	PH/DH	4	1	1	0	0	1
Thome	1B	5	2	2	3	1	0
Burks	LF	2	0	0	0	1	1
Branyan	LF-3B	3	2	2	1	0	1
Cordova	RF	5	2	2	2	1	1
Fryman	3B	2	0	0	2	0	1
Cordero	LF	3	1	1	0	0	1
Diaz	C	6	3	3	2	0	0
Totals		**51**	**15**	**23**	**15**	**5**	**7**

a-popped to second for Gonzalez in 6th

Batting: 2B-Vizquel, Cordova. 3B-Vizquel. HR-Thome (2), Branyan, Cordova.

Fielding: E-Vizquel

LOB-11

Pitcher	ip	h	r	er	bb	so
Burba	2	7	7	7	1	2
Bacsik	6	9	7	6	1	2
Rodriguez	1	0	0	0	0	0
Wickman	1	1	0	0	0	0
Rocker (W)	1	0	0	0	0	3

Game length 4:11; Attendance 42,494; Weather 78 degrees, clear; Wind 7 mph in from center

August 6 The Mariners needed starter Paul Abbott to give the bullpen a break in light of the previous night's debacle. It wasn't pretty, but Abbott accomplished the task. Earning his 10th straight win, the gutsy Seattle right-hander gave up six runs on seven hits and four walks, but pitched seven innings giving the bullpen the rest it needed. Abbott's 124 pitches were the most of any Mariner pitcher during the season.

Mariner batsmen were in full attack mode for the second straight night. Seattle won 8-6 on 13 hits. Ichiro led the Mariners with three hits and two RBIs, while Boone, Cameron and Wilson each added two hits.

Norm Charlton and Jose Paniagua pitched two scoreless innings, much different than the night before. Charlton admitted he felt "a little extra pressure to make sure Sunday night's game didn't happen again." M's 8, Indians 6.

Even though early August will probably be remembered for the Mariners' twelve-run collapse, the road trip was a solid 5-2. This included beating one of baseball's best teams (Cleveland) three of four games at its home field. As the Mariners came home to face Toronto, the M's were half-a-century above .500 at 81-31.

Three game series at home vs. Blue Jays (M's take 2)
The Mariners were back home and it was announced that Jay Buhner was cleared to start his rehabilitation. He was to run the bases for the first time under the observation of trainer Rick Griffin before going to Tacoma to get some game action. Though on the disabled list all season long, Buhner's leadership had been present. The team was anxiously awaiting the Buhner bat of the past 13 years. But even when Bone did return, it would be like Spring Training for him. He had been off for nearly a year, and it would be tough to return to form quickly.

August 7 The Toronto Blue Jays came to SAFECO at third place in the AL East, but six games under .500. Joel Pineiro pitched seven strong innings of three-hit, one-run baseball. He struck out 11 and lowered his ERA to the barely visible 0.86. He left the game in the hands of Seattle's heralded relievers with a 3-1 lead. But Jeff Nelson and Arthur Rhodes uncharacteristically gave up three runs in the 8th inning to give Toronto the lead. The Toronto runs included a Carlos Delgado homer off Rhodes that was hit so far it must have landed on a ferry boat going to Bainbridge Island!

The Mariners had not been a team of 9th inning comebacks in the 2001 season. They didn't have to because they were normally ahead. But on this night Seattle was facing one of the toughest relief pitchers in the major leagues, flamethrower Billy Koch.

Mike Cameron led off the inning with an infield chopper over the mound just in front of first base. The hustling Mariner centerfielder beat out the throw. He took second base when a 100 mile-an-hour Koch fastball wasn't handled well by Blue Jay catcher, Darrin Fletcher. Seattle had hit well all year with runners in scoring position, and this night was no exception. Carlos Guillen muscled a single to drive in Cameron sending the game into extra innings.

The inconsistent John Halama who had relieved in the 9th held the Blue Jays scoreless through the 14th inning. He was stingy with his pitches, making the visiting batters hit the ball into the ground. Though Halama allowed seven base runners over his six innings pitched, the Blue Jays weren't close to scoring against him.

But Seattle wasn't close to scoring on Blue Jay relievers either. As the clock neared midnight, the Mariners were coming to bat in the 14th inning. With one out, Stan Javier reached first on yet another hustling infield single. Sprague then struck out, but Olerud and Boone were intentionally passed, to bring up Cameron. Mike Dewitt, the seventh Toronto pitcher of the night, threw a strike, but then three straight balls. With nowhere to put Cameron, Dewitt bore down, and started throwing fastball after fastball, daring Cameron to hit it. The Mariner All Star centerfielder got a piece of the next two offerings from Dewitt to bring the count to full. The fans (Many of the 45,636 were still in the park.) were screaming *"A walk is a win! A walk is a win!"* They kept getting louder and louder as Cameron stepped out of the box to let SAFECO Field have its say. Then, after four hours and thirty-seven minutes, the game ended when Cameron drew ball four to force in the winning run.

In his excitement, Cammy just started jumping as if it were a playoff victory. Mariner first base coach John Moses nearly had to drag Cameron to the base because if he had left the field without tagging first, it would have been another out. M's 5, Blue Jays 4.

August 8 The 24th consecutive sellout crowd at SAFECO Field was treated to a fireworks display from Mariner bats in a 12-4 win over Toronto. Edgar Martinez drove in the 1,000th run of his career with his 16th homer in the 4th. Ichiro got four hits to raise his average to

.337, and Dan Wilson also got four hits, as the Mariners collected 19 hits overall. Perhaps skipping pregame batting practice had something to do with it, but it was clear from the first two innings, when the M's built a 5-0 lead, that Seattle wasn't going to let too many pitches pass by without a Mariner bat on them.

On the mound for Seattle was the guy who had leads all season, Jamie Moyer. He went the distance for his thirteenth win against only five losses. Normally, Piniella would have relieved Moyer after seven innings, but with the bullpen having worked so much over the past week, the Mariner manager asked the veteran lefthander to pitch as long as he could. It was Moyer's first complete game since September 19, 1999, who commented: "It's not important at all for me to have a CG beside my name, but it was important because our bullpen's been used a lot lately." *Like we said before, with Moyer, it's all about winning.*

The M's won 12-4, improving their record to 83-31.

August 9 Another sellout at SAFECO and Freddy Garcia was on the mound. Even though he got the loss, Garcia showed that he deserves his "ace" moniker as he battled for seven innings. Garcia gave up 11 hits and walked two in his stint on the mound, while permitting only two earned runs. But the Seattle defense was a bit porous, as two unearned runs came in on errors by Boone and Bell. When Garcia left in the 8th, the Mariners were behind 4-3.

Jose Paniagua, who had relieved Norm Charlton in the 8th, quickly dispatched of the first two Blue Jays in the 9th. Then, three straight Toronto hits extended the visitors' lead to 6-3 before the Mariners came to bat in the bottom of the 9th.

Seattle had earned the "Two outs ... So what?" slogan this year, and almost came through again. With two outs in the 9th, down by three runs, Ichiro hit a routine ground ball to second base. Stan Javier, who was on first from a single, was running on the play. Toronto second baseman Homer Bush fielded Ichiro's grounder, glanced at second and realized he couldn't get Javier out. So he tossed to first to get the sure out. Ichiro was a lightning bolt down the line, and beat the throw with sheer hustle. McLemore then hit a bullet through the hole to left to load the bases for Martinez. The Mariners' All Star DH singled home two runs, but Olerud ended the rally with a ground out. Mariners lost 6-5.

This game exhibited a problem that would haunt the team in the second half of the season. The failure of the bullpen to keep a game close effectively took the bat out of the hands of the potent Mariner offense. Instead of having to get one run to send the game into extra innings, Seattle would have to score three. Mariner reliever Jose Paniagua had clearly been a disappointment throughout the year, but was getting progressively worse. His ERAhad risen to 4.28, and his control was nonexistent. In 1 1/3 innings, Paniagua threw 31 pitches, and allowed three runs on two hits. Paniagua had been dubbed the Mariners' "closer of the future," but his continued inability to get hitters out brought that title into serious question.

In the meantime it was announced that Jay Buhner had been designated for a rotating rehabilitation assignment where he would play for Tacoma and Everett. Not only would the longtime Seattle fan-favorite be getting back into the batter's box, but he would be in a new spot in the outfield - left field. Buhner, in typical Bone manner, minced no words: "I'm nervous as hell about playing left field." He adamantly added, "I'm going to come back to the big league club and contribute in any way I can."

Three game series vs. White Sox (M's take 2)

As Chicago's southsiders came to Seattle, Bret Boone was loudly being discussed as a leading MVP candidate. With a .328 batting average, 26 homers, 104 RBIs and a gold glove at second base, Boone had a chance to be the first AL second sacker since Nellie Fox in 1959 to win the MVPaward.

Lou Piniella, who first managed the All Star infielder in 1992 before Boone was traded to Cincinnati, said that Boone was a more disciplined person in 2001. Also, "He has a much better approach to hitting with two strikes than he had. And he's gotten much stronger."

Both Boone's improved strength and two-strike hitting were obvious to any onlooker. In the Mariners Magical Season of 2001, whenever Boone got two strikes, he would open his stance, and crouch lower. Plus, he added 15 pounds of muscle in the off-season, giving him Popeye-like arms. Boone signed with Seattle for only one year, and his future will be a big topic of upcoming winter conversation.

August 10 Aaron Sele must have started thinking that Kazu Sasaki didn't like him. For the second straight outing, Sele lost a win and Sasaki blew a save – in a big way.

The Mariners were behind 3-1 going into the bottom of the 6th inning. It was a typical Sele game where he gave up a few hits, but didn't add to the problem by walking anyone. In the meantime, the White Sox starter, Jon Garland, was wild, but the M's couldn't gain a toehold to score more runs.

Alan Embree entered the game for Chicago in the 6th and found immediate trouble. Al Martin led off with a triple; Guillen walked; Wilson hit a sacrifice fly that scored Martin; Ichiro hit a bunt single and McLemore walked to load the bases. Embree was done after five batters and getting only one out - that on a long sacrifice fly.

Rocky Biddle came in to face Edgar Martinez, who had been on a tear since coming off the disabled list. He continued that mode. Edgar took a 2-0 pitch and hit a high fly ball. This was a Ruthian hit. It traveled to straight away left field and there was so much time to watch the ball that it was clear it was either going to be caught or it would be a home run. Would this ball ever come down? The bullpen crowded around the fence. The leftfielder went to the base of the wall, looked straight up, but didn't raise his glove. The ball touched down five feet beyond the fence on the TV cameraman's landing. Even if you didn't have a radio, you could hear Mariners' announcer Dave Niehaus shouting *"Get out the rye bread and mustard Grandma. It's grand salami time!"*

The shot gave Seattle a 6-3 lead going into the 7th inning. Sele surrendered a meaningless single to the White Sox in the 7th, and took the mound for the top of the 8th. Often, managers will change pitchers in the middle of the inning, sending the starter to the showers early. Mariner manager Lou Piniella didn't seem to share that philosophy, and would allow the starter to get the first out of the inning to hear the applause of the fans. Or maybe Lou was giving the fans an opportunity to cheer the pitcher who did so well. Regardless, Piniella showed, once again, that he understood the human psyche well, both the individual mind and group awareness. *Kudos Lou.*

Sele got the first man out in the 8th and handed the ball to Piniella, who brought in Jeff Nelson. The capacity crowd gave Sele a standing ovation. Sele's numbers for the game weren't great: 7 1/3 innings, seven hits, three runs, no walks, eight strikeouts. But they were winning numbers, which was Sele's forte.

Nelson got the next two hitters, and turned the game over to Sasaki. It was to be Sasaki's worst inning pitched of his entire pro career.

After a Carlos Lee popout, the next three batters reached base on two singles and a walk. With the bases loaded, the light hitting Herbert Perry walked in the first run of the inning. Ray Durham struck out, but with two outs and the bases still loaded, Jose Valentin and Magglio Ordonez hit consecutive doubles to score four more runs, giving Chicago the lead, 8-6.

Sasaki took the loss, and ironically, Rocky Biddle, who gave up the mammoth Edgar Martinez bases full home run, got the win. At this point, Sasaki seemed to be in a slump, very similar to early in the season. He was a pitcher who needed to work often, but with the huge lead, and the Mariners' starting pitching performing well, Sasaki would need to get most of his work on the sidelines. White Sox 8, M's 6.

Edgar's grand slam, meanwhile, and attaining his 1,000 RBI a few games earlier, caused discussion as to whether Edgar would be/should be voted into the Hall of Fame. Edgar's hitting statistics are comparable to Hall of Famer Kirby Puckett's. And Martinez didn't become a regular until he was 27 years old. But, Edgar is a designated hitter – the best DH the game has ever known.

Edgar, a career .320 hitter and run producing machine, hits more doubles than homers, but does more than just swing the stick. He wears pitchers down with his batting eye. Perhaps that is why he has a career .426 on base percentage. Five years after Edgar has retired, he could just be the first person to enter the Hall of Fame as a DH.

August 11 The Mariners made a roster move by placing Ed Sprague on the disabled list and bringing up Ryan Franklin. The young righthander had been a successful long reliever earlier in the season but had been sent to Tacoma only because he had options left. Franklin gave Seattle twelve pitchers, and Piniella the option as to who to keep at playoff time.

Solid pitching by White Sox rookie Dan Wright caught the Mariners' attention for the first eight innings. In 7 2/3 innings, Wright scattered five hits, and left the game with a 3-1 lead. On the other side of the diamond, Paul Abbott had surrendered only five hits, but suffered control problems again. Abbott added five southsiders to the base paths on walks, and was relieved by Franklin after seven innings.

Franklin got the win. The M's new arrival held Chicago scoreless for two innings, giving Mariner bats a chance to reach White Sox closer

Keith Foulke. The third largest crowd in SAFECO history saw the bottom of the 9th start with a Bret Boone single, followed by an Al Martin walk. Mike Cameron struck out extending his streak to 22 games in which he had owned a "K." Guillen made the second out on a fly ball to left, and with two down, two runs behind and two on base, local boy Tom Lampkin worked Foulke for a walk. Ichiro came to bat wearing an 0-4 collar at the time. It was vintage Ichiro Suzuki, watching a pitch for a strike, refusing to bite on two waste pitches, and then fouling off a pitch to the screen. On the 2-2 count, Ichiro took a low outside Foulke sinker over the shortstop's head to drive in the tying runs. Mark McLemore continued his "do anything and everything" season by driving home the winning run with a single to center. M's 4, White Sox 3.

With the win, the M's were 84-33, and maintained a 17 game lead over the streaking Oakland Athletics.

August 12 It was Joel Pineiro's turn to start, but Mike Cameron stole the show even before the game. The All Star centerfielder and fan favorite with an infectious smile, showed his appreciation to his teammates by delivering to each of them an All Star T-shirt and leather jacket. Spending nearly $5,000 on the gifts, Cameron said that the All Star experience was a team event for him.

Pineiro continued his amazing run, by giving up only three hits and one run in 7 1/3 innings. Rhodes got the final two batters out in the 8th, lowering his ERA to a microscopic 1.65. Mariner bats were held in check as well, scoring only on Ichiro's grounder in the 3rd.

But the M's took the lead in the 8th in typical Mariner fashion. A Carlos Guillen double was followed by an Ichiro bunt single. The bunt was supposed to be a sacrifice to get Guillen to third base, but Ichiro out-hustled the throw, giving the Mariners' runners on first and third with nobody out. After Martinez received an intentional walk, Olerud drove in the go ahead run with a long fly to left.

The crowd couldn't help but gasp, though, as Kazu Sasaki took the mound with the lead in the 9th in a save situation. The slender 6'4" righthander from Sendai City, Japan, revealed a new pitch to the White Sox – a curveball. He had primarily been a fastball/splitter pitcher, but the curve would provide a change of speeds with a different break. How Sasaki could develop a new pitch during a season was a mystery, but it would be hard to argue with Sasaki's past success . . . omitting the previous two appearances.

This time, Kazu was the Sasaki of old. He retired the side in order. No White Sox hitter was even close to reaching base. The save was his 36th, and the win went to Arthur Rhodes, who improved his record to 7-0. M's 2, White Sox 1.

The next day was for travel to the east coast, but in Tacoma there was a big event. Jay Buhner was coming to the plate.

Jay Buhner in action at Tacoma

A long line of cars waited to enter the parking lot at Tacoma's Cheney Stadium, the home of the AAA Tacoma Rainiers. It was the first time I had been in that stadium and it reminded me of so many of the minor league parks I had seen around the country. It has an intimacy about it which is a drawing appeal of minor league base - ball. I was there to cover the rehab assignment of Jay Buhner. Jay had said how much he missed being on the field and contributing to this incredible season even though his Mariner teammates felt his mere presence was a contribution.

A much bigger crowd than normal was abuzz with excitement. It reached a crescendo when this announcement came over the PA system: "Now batting for the Tacoma Rainiers, number 50, Jay Buhner." With each word, more people stood and cheered, and by the time Buhner took one mere step toward the lines of the batter's box, the entire stadium was standing in appreciation for this long time major leaguer who personified the work ethic of this year's big league club.

Jay stepped to the plate with his bat held high, swaying slightly as if to invite the pitcher to throw something close. He peered out at the mound seemingly over the goatee he has worn for over a decade. You could tell Buhner was anxious because he swung and missed an inside fastball. He swung again at the next pitch, send - ing the ball careening into the third base stands. Then he settled down a bit, taking 2 balls, but he couldn't hold up on another pitch out of the strike zone, and struck out.

Throughout the game, Buhner continued getting great ovations from the fans. In his second at bat, he grounded out to third. It was obvious that he was running at half speed down to first. In the 7th he popped out to first, but in the 8th he had one of the most unusu - al at bats I have seen in watching baseball since the Duke Snider days in Brooklyn. With an 0-1 count Buhner seemed to go around on the next pitch, an inside breaking ball. The umpire, though,

*said Buhner had been hit by the pitch, and should take first base.
Buhner started arguing, showing the umpire that the pitch had
actually hit the bat, not him. The argument continued as Jay
unhappily walked to first base. The visiting team got in the com -
motion and asked for an appeal to the second base umpire who
had a view from behind the pitcher. The Stingers won the appeal,
and Buhner was sent back to the plate with a count of 0-2, since
the ball hitting the bat would have been a foul strike. The manag -
er of Tacoma couldn't then argue because his own player had been
saying that he hadn't been hit.*

*Anyway, Buhner got his wish – a chance to hit the ball. He wasn't
successful, but Jay made his point: "Let me hit!"*

*Yet another occurrence in this AAA game showed the importance
of Jay Buhner to a clubhouse. A Salt Lake batter had been hit in
the knee by a pitch, and ambled to first base. Obviously in pain,
the team trainer called time out to attend to the injured player.
During the time where the trainer was tending the player, the PA
announcer shouted "B – o – o – r – r- r – i – n – g!" Jay immedi -
ately popped out of the home team dugout firing an icy glare at
toward the press box. He was justifiably angry as were many oth -
ers at the discourtesy of the announcer. It was, in a sense, a fitting
tribute to Jay Buhner who showed concern about a fellow ball
player, even though he was a minor leaguer whom Jay did not
know. That was revealing about the passion of this man for the
game, and gave insight into why he is a Mariner team leader.*

– MS

Three game sets at Boston and New York would test the mettle of
baseball's best team in 2001. Comparisons between the Mariners and
the 1998 Yankees who won an AL record 114 games were so often
made that players from both teams sounded the same. The Bronx
Bombers' All Star shortstop Derek Jeter stated:

*"You can't compare until the season is over. They spread their
offense around; they're getting good pitching; and have a strong
bullpen. So in that respect the teams were similar, but they haven't
done what we've done."*

Mariners All Star reliever Jeff Nelson, who was a member of the
1998 Yankees team, agreed:

*"We're having a great season and a lot of fun. But we realize we
haven't won anything yet. Any team that goes to the World Series
knows it has to beat the Yankees."*

Three game series at Red Sox (M's take 2)

Many players, coaches and management personnel were getting credit for the Mariners' stellar season, but few talked about hitting coach Gerald Perry. Leading the league in hitting, runs scored and sacrifice flies should be a clue that somebody somewhere has a good handle on what it takes to be a good major league hitter.

Veteran major leaguer Tom Lampkin complimented Perry for his ability to deal with individuals. "Ichiro, Edgar, Olerud and Wilson all have different hitting styles and Perry is able to reach each of them."

Al Martin, was one of the most successful of Perry's in-season projects, commented that "He's always there for you. He helps you to want to be more successful than you ever thought you could."

August 14 The game went 11 innings at historic Fenway Park. But the memorable thing about the game was the bizarre behavior of Boston's Carl Everett.

Jamie Moyer was on the mound for Seattle against the Red Sox, who still had postseason hopes. Hideo Nomo, the Sox # 2 starter, took the hill for the home team.

It was a typical Moyer game. The M's jumped on top 2-0 in the 2nd on Mike Cameron's 18th homer. But in the bottom half of the inning Boston's Carl Everett brought buffoonery to the national pastime.

Everett stands nearly on top of the plate when he bats and was doing so in the first inning against Moyer. If the batter's box isn't erased by the time he gets to the plate, Everett finishes the jobs by mixing the chalk into the dirt with his foot. He wears heavy padding on his right elbow, which he cocks out over the plate at the time of the pitch. As a result, Everett gets to take first base often by getting hit, or he forces pitchers to throw the ball out over the plate, giving him good pitches to hit. It's a good plan when he can get away with it.

In Everett's first at-bat, Moyer wasn't willing to give him the plate, and pitched inside. His last pitch nicked the padding on Everett's arm. The Boston outfielder immediately grew a smirk on his face and tried to taunt Moyer as he took first base. "Tried to" is appropriate because Moyer paid no attention to Everett, and instead was complaining to home plate umpire Mark Hirschbeck about Everett standing outside the batter's box on the plate.

Everett didn't stop jawing while he was at first base. First baseman John Olerud, though, was his normal stoic, unflappable self, and ignored the juvenile Everett.

In the 3rd, Everett grounded out to third on Moyer's fifth pitch, but between pitches continued trying to draw Moyer into a barroom brawl on the baseball field. Again, Moyer ignored Everett's childishness. In the 5th, Everett hit a home run over the Green Monster. This time, on his way to first, Everett stopped to admire his home run and grabbed his crotch. He pointed at Moyer and yelled, in behavior reminiscent of an insolent child. Again, Moyer didn't bite.

Moyer pitched seven innings, gave up two runs on six hits, but left with the game tied at 2. Both teams scored another run to send the game into extra innings. In the 11th, after an Ichiro Suzuki infield single and Mark McLemore walk, Edgar Martinez lined an 0-2 pitch off a light pole behind the Green Monster for an M's 6-3 win.

After the game, Moyer was asked about Everett's ridiculous behavior. "I didn't pay any attention to him. I just did my job," said Moyer, a consummate professional. He added that he should have refused to pitch until Everett was required to follow the rule and stand in the batter's box. An American League representative indicated that umpires were instructed not to enforce the "too close to the plate rule" unless the opposing team requested enforcement.

Everett refused to talk with the media, and Boston manager Jimy Williams said that Everett was an adult and could speak for himself. Williams had been burned by trying to discipline Everett previously, seemingly overruled by Red Sox GM Dan Duquette.

Had Everett been a Mariner, the behavior would have been handled differently. Early in Ken Griffey, Jr.'s career, he made a gesture toward then Detroit Tigers manager Sparky Anderson after Griffey hit a homer off a Tiger pitcher. Detroit had been avoiding the lethal Griffey bat with walks. That evening Mariner manager Lou Piniella had a stern talk with the Seattle superstar and the next day, Griffey apologized to Anderson, his own teammates and the fans for his actions.

The players must respect baseball and the fans. The game is their livelihood and the fans provide the funds. Carl Everett's impish behavior should have been disciplined by Red Sox management in the same way a parent would discipline a poorly behaving child. It does the child and the household in which he lives harm to be allowed to act rudely and to not have it pointed out to him. The Red Sox allowed Everett to embarrass himself, the organization and the Red Sox fans. If club owners really want to draw younger fans, they will have to make all the teams keep Everettesque behavior from the diamond.

August 15 Freddy Garcia took the mound for Seattle, and did what every ace pitcher must do. He pitched well enough deep into the game making sure the bullpen didn't have to pitch too many innings. He battled every hitter, and ended the game with very impressive stats: eight innings pitched, two runs, three hits, two walks, and seven strikeouts. He won his 14th game against four losses. Edgar Martinez hit a three-run homer for the second night in a row. Meanwhile Carl Everett wasn't talking. M's won 6-2.

August 16 Ateam in turmoil, the Boston Red Sox replaced manager Jimy Williams with pitching coach Joe Kerrigan. Boston was 65-53 when Kerrigan took the reigns. The Sox finished at 82-79. The end of Kerrigan's first night, though, was perfect. That meant the night didn't end well for the Mariners' Aaron Sele, a former Boston starter. And when a night ends poorly for a starting pitcher, it normally means the night goes poorly for the entire team.

Mariner hitters stroked 13 hits, three each by Ichiro, Bell and Javier. Ichiro's batting average had improved to .344. Going into the bottom of 8th inning, Seattle had a 4-3 lead.

Sele was still in the game, with a low pitch count. Boston's Nomar Garciaparra, older brother of the Mariners' 2001 first round draft pick, Michael, doubled. After an intentional walk, Dante Bichette took Sele deep for a three run homer. Whether it was Lou giving in, or Sele being persuasive, Seattle's starter pitched to one man too many. It wouldn't happen again. Red Sox won 6-4.

The M's took their season long streak of not losing a road series to Yankee Stadium.

Three game series at Yankees (M's take 2)
With the Mariners in the media hub of the world, and the season over 60% completed, attentions turned to the MVP award. *ESPN.com* ran a poll and Ichiro finished slightly in front of Bret Boone – not for the Mariners' MVP, but for the entire American League.

ESPN baseball editor David Schoenfield questioned the choice, admitting that Ichiro is one of the best players in the league, but not deserving of even being an MVP candidate.

"MVP winners are usually among the best offensive players in the league, and OPS (on base percentage plus slugging percentage) is an effective quick and dirty method to assess a player's overall offensive value. Ichiro was fourth on his team in that rating, behind Martinez, Boone and Olerud." [ESPN.com, August 17, 2001 Is Ichiro an MVP candidate?]

Raw statistics, though, don't show the offensive value of Ichiro Suzuki. Ichiro completely took over baseball games during the 2001 season. The opponents threw quicker when Ichiro is running to first base, thereby increasing the chance of mistakes. Ichiro's bat control was so good that when he was at bat, and Mariners were in scoring position, there was nearly a 50-50 chance that Seattle would score. That put tremendous pressure on the opponent's defense and pitcher. It did no good to keep a book on how to pitch Ichiro because he hit everything pitched to different parts of the park and often with different types of swings. After he got on base, even though he hit mostly singles, he put more pressure on opposing pitchers and the defense with the threat of stolen bases. This gave hitters after Ichiro better pitches to hit and turned Ichiro's singles into extra bases.

Basically, Ichiro was an enigma to every aspect of the opposition except in the field. After "The Throw," runners didn't challenge Ichiro's arm. The rest of his defensive play was legendary.

August 17 New York manager Joe Torre commented on the upcoming series with the Mariners: "It's important. Seattle is the best team in the game right now, and we can measure ourselves against them. Hopefully, we'll come out on top," commented the veteran Yankee manager.

First game pitcher Mike Mussina granted Torre's wish, beating the Mariners 4-0. He permitted only five singles and one runner to reach second base in seven innings. Mike Stanton and Mario Mendoza mirrored Mussina in effectiveness on the mound in relief.

Paul Abbott started for the Mariners. Yankees' leadoff hitter Derek Jeter greeted him in the first inning with a home run. The home team hit two other homers, accounting for all four Yankee runs.

But the big story was the accusation by the Mariners that New York was creating a near swamp out of the infield in a clear attempt to slow Seattle's running game. "It started in Boston and I guess we haven't been getting enough rain because the groundskeepers have been soaking everything pretty good," said Manager Lou Piniella.

New York media quickly spread the charges, calling the Mariners' "mudslingers." Yankee manager Joe Torre: "We've had some problems in front of home plate in the last year or two, but it's not anything we tried to do," Torre said with a smile. "But if I did it, I'm not going to tell you anyway." [*New York Daily News, August 18, 2001 Lou: Water Keeps M's from Running.*]

Even though the front of the home plate was dubbed the Yankee Marsh, Mariners reliever Jeff Nelson waded to receive his 2000 World Series ring. In a ceremony before the game, Nelson was handed the ring by Joe Torre, his former manager. As he looked at the year "2000" on his new possession, Nelson's mind was set on 2001.

August 18 The Mariners took game 2 of the series 7-6, but the Yankees won the moral victory. In a nationally televised Saturday afternoon game, Seattle ground Yankees' starter Ted Lilly into flour by scoring seven runs in 1 1/3 innings. Knocking six hits and reaping the benefit of third baseman Clay Bellinger's error, the M's built what should have been an insurmountable lead. Seattle's Joel Pineiro, nearly unhittable to this point, was on the mound, and looked to make a lasting impression on the Yankees, the massive TV audience and the near 56,000 fans in the stands. Instead, Pineiro gave up eight hits, walked three, and permitted five runs in 4 2/3 innings. He didn't last long enough to get the win, and breathed life into the reigning world champions.

What should have been a cakewalk turned into a struggle. The score stood at 7-5 until the bottom of the 9th. The bullpen team of Norm Charlton, Jose Paniagua, Arthur Rhodes and Jeff Nelson held the Yankees scoreless. The Yankees' bullpen squad of Randy Choate, Mark Wohlers and Mike Stanton did the same to the M's.

Kazu Sasaki took the hill for Seattle. Paul O'Neill led off with a ground out, but then things got nasty for Sasaki. The next three Yankees reached base, including a Jorge Posada line shot off Kazu's thigh. The dangerous Gerald Williams came to the plate with one out and the bases loaded, and was promptly plunked by Sasaki, forcing in a run and keeping the bases full. Shane Spencer hit two wicked fouls giving the screaming home crowd hope. But Spencer struck out leaving Alfonso Soriano to keep the Yankees at bat. The freeswinging New York rookie infielder took an 0-2 low outside "thang" from Sasaki to left field for the final out. The Mariner reliever breathed a long sigh, as Seattle evened the series.

Arthur Rhodes got the win, for an 8-0 record. Mike Cameron was 3-4 with a walk and Edgar Martinez was 2-2 with three walks.

August 19 The final game of the regular season between the champions of 2000 and the best team in baseball in 2001 wasn't close. It featured an incredible offensive performance by Seattle's Mike Cameron and another steady pitching performance by Jamie Moyer.

Cameron was 4-4 with two home runs – one a grand slam – and eight RBIs. The Mariners collected 15 hits and ten runs, most of them off Yankees ace lefthander, Andy Pettitte. Cameron also ended his streak of 26 straight games with a strikeout.

Moyer was stingy in allowing only five hits and one run, with no walks, over seven innings. Ryan Franklin pitched the final two innings. M's 10, Yankees 2.

Seattle had won five of six at Yankee Stadium and six of nine overall against New York in 2001. The victory capped the Mariners 21st straight non-losing road series and had the New York media abuzz. Under a headline "*Count Bombers As M-barrassed*" Anthony McCarron, Daily News Sports writer, found the Yankees very talkative.

Joe Torre: "Whether it's a statement or not, if we get to meet them again, I don't think that anything up till now is going to matter." All Star outfielder Bernie Williams: "There's no doubt about it. They can be beat." Slugger David Justice: It was a great series to see where we're at . . . I feel all right about it and we know they're a great team, but October is October." [New York Daily News, August 20, 2001.]

After the 4-2 road trip at Boston and New York, the Mariners flew home to face Detroit.

Four game series vs. Tigers at home (M's take 3)
As Seattle prepared for a seven game homestand against Detroit and Cleveland, Mark McLemore was finally receiving his due. Peter Gammons of *ESPN* called McLemore the "unsung hero who sparks the Mariners on and off the field." In addition to being the best

dressed Mariner (according to his teammates) McLemore had a .392 on-base percentage with 33 steals. Manager Lou Piniella indicated that McLemore was close to the M's "most valuable person. . . . Wherever we want to rest someone, Mac plays there." Piniella added that in addition to his defensive versatility, McLemore "takes pitches for Ichiro in the two-hole, he bunts when we need a bunt, he hits behind runners, but maybe the most important thing is that he brings something to the clubhouse every day." McLemore himself explained that "If I see guys are a little down, I get on them." The Mac of all trades – Mark McLemore.

Concerned that Kazu Sasaki may be tipping his pitches after his 33 pitch inning in the 9th inning of the 7-6 victory over the Yankees, Mariner pitching guru Bryan Price studied games films. His conclusion was that Sasaki wasn't giving the signs away, but may be letting the hitters see his grip on the ball in the glove before he throws to the plate. Since the grip is different for the fastball and the split-finger, knowing which of the two pitches is coming helps the hitters. Price promised to work with Sasaki on a fix.

August 20 The largest regular season crowd in SAFECO history - 45,972 – was on hand to welcome the M's back home. Steve Sparks, the knuckle-balling Tiger righthander was his own one-man welcoming committee. He performed *déjà vu* magic on the Seattle, reminiscent of his August 15, 2000, shutout of the playoff-bound Mariners. In 2001, Seattle was able to score one run on five hits – the run coming on a double play.

> **27 Straight**
> Going into the Detroit series, Ichiro had a hit in 27 straight starts. His hitting streak would have been at 28 were it not for his recent appearance as a pinch hitter. He smashed a vicious line drive to third base for a double play. Ichiro is the first major-leaguer in over 20 years to have three hitting streaks of 15 or more games in a season.

In the meantime, Freddy Garcia had early control problems leading to three Tiger runs. It wasn't that Garcia was walking batters. It was that his control inside the strike zone was poor, enabling Detroit to rough him up for eight hits and three runs in the first three innings. Garcia righted himself, though, pitching seven innings, but the M's couldn't come back. Tigers won 4-1.

August 21 It was a pitcher's duel between Seattle's Aaron Sele and Detroit's Jeff Weaver for seven innings. Sele was the best he had been all season. He gave up only three hits, including Juan Encarnacion's solo homer. He walked none and threw a remarkably low 76 pitches (55 for strikes) in eight innings.

Weaver gave up one run through six innings, but was constantly in trouble. In the 1st, 2nd, 5th and 6th innings, Weaver had several Mariners on base. But Seattle wasn't hitting in the clutch until the 7th when Mark McLemore and Edgar Martinez had two-out hits scoring three runs. Sele's win was his 13th against four losses. M's won 4-1.

> **International M's**
> The Mariners added more international appeal by signing a player from China. Right handed pitcher Chao Wang, sixteen years-old, 6'4", 160 pounds was to head to the Mariners extended spring training program at Peoria, Arizona. *August 21st*

The win was the Mariners' 90th of the season and the 1,200th of Lou Piniella's managerial career. Ichiro hit in his 18th straight game and 28th straight start. The game was sold out for at SAFECO yet again.

August 22 This game was cruel to the Tigers. Seattle scored six runs in the bottom of the first inning on the way to a 16-1 thrashing of lowly Detroit. Bret Boone and David Bell were only one hit shy of hitting for the cycle. Bell had his first five-hit game. Altogether, the Mariners had twenty hits. John Olerud had two homers. Ichiro was 3-4, upping his average to .345. Edgar was 2-4 with five RBIs.

Abbott pitched five shutout innings, but left with a slightly pulled groin muscle. He would miss his next start. Franklin gave up the lone Tiger run. Charlton, Nelson and Rhodes combined for three hitless and scoreless innings, while striking out five. M's won 16-1.

August 23 Joel Pineiro was nearly back on top of his game, and David Bell went deep twice to lead the Mariners to their 92nd victory. Pineiro gave up only one run in five innings, before yielding to a bullpen quartet of Halama, Nelson, Rhodes and Sasaki. The relievers held the Tigers hitless and scoreless for the last four innings.

Bell was 3-4 with two RBI and was hitting .343 for the month of August. Ichiro was also 3-4 and was batting .348. M's won 5-1.

The win broke the single-season franchise record. By winning 92 of their first 128 games, the M's had the fifth best start in history.

Three game series vs. Indians (M's take 2)
August 24 Jamie Moyer took the mound against Cleveland, the team many felt owned the most potent offense in baseball. At age 38, Moyer was having one of his best years. After an 0-5 record at St. Louis in 1991, the Chicago Cubs released him at the end of spring training 1992. The soft-throwing lefthander went home to Indiana to ponder his future.

Moyer began working out with the Notre Dame baseball team and sent tapes to Japan. No interest. Then he heard about a team in Italy but Moyer didn't think the European league took baseball seriously enough at that time. So he kept working on his own, waiting and hoping. He landed with AAA Toledo and had a respectable season.

By 1993, he won a tryout with the Baltimore Orioles. After starting 6-0 with AAA Rochester, Moyer went to Baltimore where he was 12-9 with a 3.43 ERA. Moyer persevered in his comeback and since coming to Seattle in 1996, the crafty lefthander has been one of the winningest pitchers in baseball.

It would take all of Moyer's best slow, slower, and slowest speeds to defeat the Indians. The contrast between Moyer's pitching style and that of the opposing hurler, Cleveland's Bartolo Colon, couldn't have been greater. Colon was a fireballing righthander and very emotional on the mound, another stark difference with the stoic Jamie Moyer.

> **Moyer's real job**
> Upon getting cut in 1992, Moyer's father-in-law, former Notre Dame hoops coach and *ESPN* commentator Digger Phelps, told him to "stay home, finish school and get a real job."

Seattle won the game and Moyer won the duel. Moyer efficiently ran through the powerful Indian lineup inning after inning. After seven, Moyer had given up only three singles. The lone Cleveland run came via small ball with a walk, a hit-and-run, and a sacrifice fly. On the other side, Bartolo Colon was laboring but successful. Edgar Martinez doubled in two runs and Bret Boone hit a solo shot. Ichiro was 3-4 again, raising his average to .350. Norm Charlton pitched two perfect innings to preserve the 4-1 win.

August 25 "Ty Cobb must be rolling over in his grave." That was the headline on Jim Caple's article on *ESPN.com* (August 29, 2001) about this game between Seattle and Cleveland. The game was tight, and the stands were packed for yet another sellout at SAFECO. Two of baseball's best scoring teams – two of the best teams in baseball period – played an 11 inning, 3-2 nailbiter. Seattle starter, Freddy Garcia, was excellent, allowing only two runs and six hits in eight innings. Chuck Finley, who pitched a scoreless first two innings for the Indians, was pulled as a result of back spasms. The Indians bullpen kept the game even with the Mariners at two runs.

So why, then, would Ty Cobb be rolling over in his grave? In the top of the 9th inning, Mariner closer Kazuhiro Sasaki's thigh became stiff as a result of being hit several days before. Arthur Rhodes was summoned to replace Sasaki to pitch to switch hitter Omar Vizquel. Ahigh afternoon sun shone down as Rhodes walked in from the pen. Meanwhile, Vizquel was having a chummy conversation with the home plate umpire. Vizquel was pointing in Rhodes' direction, and suddenly, just as Rhodes was about to step onto the infield, umpire crew chief Tim McClelland stopped Rhodes in his tracks. He then asked Rhodes to take his earrings out. It was obvious to the Mariner flamethrowing lefthander that Vizquel had initiated the altercation and took it one step further.

Rhodes was clearly irritated. "A little scrawny hitter like him? He's a midget! Why is he telling me to take my earrings out? When I face him again, I'll go right at him!" shouted Rhodes. McClelland asked Rhodes to take his earrings out because they were shining brightly in the sun distracting the hitters. Rhodes became irate and refused to take them out. The umpire gave Rhodes a choice – take out his earrings or leave the game. Rhodes was steadfast and so was the ump. Arthur Rhodes was tossed from the game without even getting the ball in his hand.

John Halama came into the game, *sans* any kind of earlobe accoutrement, and pitched 2 1/3 hitless and scoreless innings.

The game wasn't settled, though, until the bottom of the 11th inning. John Rocker, of New York's Number 7 train fame, became the Indians' seventh pitcher and promptly got into trouble. John Olerud led off with a walk, and gave way to Al Martin to pinch run. Mike

Cameron singled to put runners on first and second. David Bell came up and bunted to the third base side of the mound hoping to sacrifice. Rocker hurried to field the bunt and slightly slipped as he picked up the ball. Martin and Cameron were running on contact and Bell was hustling down the first base line. Rocker took a quick glance at third and noticed he had no time to get Martin. So he wheeled and fired to first, but the throw went into right field, allowing the winning run to score on Rocker's error. M's won 3-2.

Piniella couldn't help but chuckle after the game about the earring incident: "Rhodes has had those on all year. I guess Arthur didn't take it too kindly."

In a minor league note, Juan "Large Human" Thomas, led Seattle's AAA affiliate Tacoma Rainiers to a 4-3 victory over Tucson, clinching the PCL Division title.

August 26 The series and regular season finale against Cleveland was one of Aaron Sele's best games of the year. After surrendering a leadoff home run to Kenny Lofton, Sele gave up only five more hits and one unearned run. He left after seven innings with the game tied at two. In the bottom of the 8th, Mark McLemore hit a solo shot to straight away centerfield to put the Mariners ahead 3-2.

Ichi-dolls

Ichiro doll mania had raised its bobblehead again. Safeway sold a new version of the phenom's bouncing miniature for $11.99. The store had a limit of one doll per purchaser and sold all 30,000 in less than 24 hours.

It was the top of the 9th and the Mariners were looking to put away their sixth straight victory. Jeff Nelson came in to pitch and hit Marty Cordova, but got the next two out. Cleveland's Eddie Taubensee singled, putting men on first and third. Freeswinging catcher Einar Diaz couldn't reach Nelson's wildness, and walked to load the bases. Kenny Lofton stepped to the plate, already with three hits in the game. Arthur Rhodes came in to relieve Nelson. It had been a rare occasion that Rhodes, with his 1.50 ERA, couldn't hold a lead, but Lofton had the hot bat. A single up the middle scored two runs and put the Indians ahead.

In their turn, the Mariners ended the game with the bases loaded. Ichiro and McLemore couldn't drive in the tying run as both ground out. Seattle's winning streak and Ichiro's 21-game hitting streak were finished. Cleveland won the game, but Seattle won the season series 5-2. Indians 4, Mariners 3.

Three game series at Devil Rays (M's take 2)

As the Mariners made the cross country trip to Tampa Bay, Devil Ray General Manager Chuck LeMar was remarking at how Seattle was winning: "The team plays the game all of us wish our teams played – unselfish, outstanding defense, great pitching, and timely hitting. . . They're going to be good for a long time." The Devil Rays had the worst record in baseball at 46-84 as the teams took the field for the first game of the series.

August 28 The Mariners must have left their bats on the plane, because Tampa pitcher Paul Wilson looked like an All Star, holding the visitors to a measly six singles in a 6-0 shutout. Joel Pineiro was ineffective for Seattle, surrendering nine hits and four runs in 5 1/3 innings. Ichiro reached a milestone, though, collecting his 200th hit.

August 29 Without three losses in a row all season, Seattle came back the next night with another strong pitching performance by Jamie Moyer. It was Moyer's seventh straight win, and was typical Moyer magic. Oh yes, the M's did give him a first inning lead. Ichiro singled, stole second and then scored on the catcher's throwing error while stealing third. Then, a Martinez single, Olerud double and Boone ground out to the right side of the infield produced a second run. Moyer gave up only three hits, no walks, one run, and threw just 89 pitches in seven innings. Rhodes and Sasaki closed out the victory, but Kazu did give up a 9th inning run. M's won 5-2.

> **Wilsons Rough on Mariners**
> The Mariners were 0-3 against pitchers named Wilson, losing to Tampa Bay's Paul Wilson and twice to Kansas City's Kris Wilson.

August 30 Freddy Garcia made sure Seattle retained its streak of not losing a road series. The Devil Rays touched him for hits (eight in 6 2/3 innings), but the 25 year-old from Caracas, Venezuela, pitched well from the stretch and didn't walk a batter. Norm Charlton, Jeff Nelson and Arthur Rhodes continued the scoreless pitching. All the Mariner runs were scored, uncharacteristically, on home runs. Bret Boone hit a three run blast and David Bell a solo shot for a 4-0 win. With the win over Tampa Bay, the M's broke the 1906-1907 Chicago Cubs record of 26 straight road series without a loss. Off the field, it was announced that two Mariner right-handed hitters would come off the disabled list on September 1: Ed Sprague and Jay Buhner.

Three game series at Baltimore (M's take 2)

The quick trip from Tampa Bay to Baltimore gave three Mariners time for visiting friends. Tom Lampkin, John Olerud and Ed Sprague got a chance to visit the president, arranged by a Lampkin Pentagon buddy. President Bush, former owner of the Texas Rangers, talked baseball with the players, but also asked about the labor situation. Sprague had been to the White House before, as a member of a World Series champion team (Toronto in 1992), and Olerud commented that he was looking forward to visiting again for the same reason.

August 31 Noah's Ark couldn't have saved the Mariners against the Orioles this night. The Mariners left their bats on the plane again. Managing only six singles, Seattle's clutch hitting had suddenly evaporated. On the road trip so far, the Mariners were 3-22 with runners in scoring position.

> **Another Nasty**
> The Mariners signed 38 year-old former World Series MVP Pat Borders as a backup catcher, and brought in 37 year-old Randy Myers for a workout. The former "nasty boy" with Norm Charlton at Cincinnati, will look for a 2002 spring training tryout.

Seattle's Aaron Sele pitched reasonably well, permitting seven hits, two earned runs, and struck out seven in six innings. But without runs no pitcher can win.

In the top of the 9th with two outs, the clouds burst over Camden Yards and had everyone literally running for cover. In a keystone cops-like scene, the Oriole groundskeepers were trying to get the heavy tarp over the infield but the gusting winds and sheer volume of water made the cover too heavy to move. As the clouds emptied from the sky, the grounds crew kept getting more drenched. They tugged and pulled all they could on the massively cumbersome tarp only to slide in the soaked outfield grass. Meanwhile, the dirt of the infield was turning into a soup, and the water was draining so quickly in the stands that a river of cups, hot dog wrappers and popcorn boxes flushed toward the dugouts.

After 45 minutes, the umpires gurgled that the game was called, giving the Orioles a hard-swum 3-0 victory.

August's Magical Moments (20 wins - 9 losses . . . Season 96-39)
1. Losing 12 run lead to Cleveland (5th) *
2. Cameron's midnight walk for a win (7th)
3. Edgar's 1000th Mariner RBI (8th)
4. Cameron's two homer, 8 RBI day at Yankee Stadium (19th)
5. Lou's 1,200th managerial win (20th)
6. M's break franchise win record (23rd)

* Not all magical moments are good ones!

Chapter Eleven

September 1-10, 2001

*"I just don't have that first-step explosion anymore." . . . in a
game a few years ago after tripping on the dugout steps and
falling face-first onto the field on his way to argue a call.*

- - Lou Piniella, Seattle Mariners, Manager

The Seattle Mariners were in an unusual position as the final
month of the regular season got under way. At 96-39, the M's
were 17 games ahead of the second place Oakland Athletics
(79-56). Of the 27 remaining games, the Mariners would play 19
against teams with losing records. Thus, manager Lou Piniella's job
for September was to get the team ready for the playoffs.

Several Mariners were on fire in August. Al Martin hit .322 and Stan
Javier hit .367 off the bench. Edgar Martinez hit .353 with 30 RBIs
and Ichiro had his best month at .429 with a .461 on base percentage.
*[Ironically, preseason critics doubted that Ichiro could withstand the
162 game major league season. It seems Ichiro surprised everyone
but himself. - SE]*

Jay Buhner and Ed Sprague were coming off the disabled list and
ready to prepare for the postseason. Edgar would get a chance to rest
his aching quadricep. The insurmountable lead would permit Piniella
the luxury of setting the pitching rotation for the Cleveland Indians,
who was the likely first round playoff opponent.

But all was not well in Marinerland. Jeff Nelson, nearly untouchable
April through July, did a total turnaround in August. His 7.71 ERA
out of the bullpen was a cause of concern to Piniella. Jose Paniagua
was still striking out opposing hitters, but continued to walk as many
as he struck out. When he couldn't find his control, he would groove
pitches. Then Seattle's outfield would get plenty of work. Aaron Sele
had only a slightly better August than his horrific June and Carlos

Guillen wasn't hitting.

With all of this in the background, the games in September did matter . . . but just not as much as they would if there were a tight pennant race. Thus, Piniella's challenge over the last month was to get the Mariner engine running on all 25 cylinders.

Continuation of three game series at Baltimore
(games 2 and 3)

September 1 The Mariners came back from a three-run deficit to win 6-4 and preserve the road series streak. Ichiro and Mike Cameron led the offense in a four-run sixth. Jay Buhner made his 2001 debut by driving in a run on a bases loaded walk.

Paul Abbott gave up all four Oriole runs in just five innings, but Ryan Franklin, Norm Charlton, Jeff Nelson and Kazu Sasaki combined for four innings of hitless relief. Sasaki earned his 40th save.

September 2 If this game had been in a pennant race, it would have been one for the ages. Seattle rookie Joel Pineiro and Baltimore rookie Rick Bauer, in his major league debut, matched each other pitch-for-pitch. Pineiro allowed four singles and no runs in seven innings. In the 4th inning, Baltimore's Jeff Conine foolishly challenged Ichiro's arm, but was cut down at the plate snuffing out the only scoring threat Pineiro faced. Mark McLemore did the same to the Orioles Melvin Mora in a 9th inning rally with Sasaki pitching.

Bauer had allowed only two singles until one out in the seventh when Bret Boone hit a monstrous home run to straight away centerfield to give Seattle a 1-0 lead. Paniagua, Rhodes and Sasaki pitched the final two innings to preserve the win. The 1-0 victory over Baltimore extended the Mariners' streak of road series without a loss to 27.

> **Joel: Kudos to BP**
> Pineiro credited pitching coach Bryan Price after his 1-0 victory over Baltimore. After Price suggested better arm extension, the young Seattle righthander said "It felt like the ball was exploding out of my hand. It's amazing how such a little thing can cause that much difference."

Three game series vs. Tampa Bay (M's take 2)

Sports rituals go far beyond the playing field. And even the best performers are subject to the rules. Seattle rookies have been required once a year to travel home in ridiculous attire. Regardless of his stardom in Japan and .351 batting average, Ichiro was a rookie and had to follow the team mandate. On the trip home from Baltimore, Ichiro reportedly became a *Hooters* girl, wearing the white T-shirt and orange shorts of a *Hooters* waitress. *Stick to your day job, Ichiro.*

Ichiro's status as a rookie was questioned by some in baseball. *ESPN's* Joe Morgan stated "Players who have played seven or eight years in Japan should not be considered rookies. Maybe baseball needs to change the Rookie of the Year award to the Newcomer of the Year award. It was unfair for someone like C.C. Sabathia, who is a true rookie and is helping his team to win the division title." Tim Kurkjian, also of *ESPN*, disagreed, saying that Japan's league are similar to AAA baseball in North America. The 2000 AL Rookie of the Year was Kazu Sasaki, giving the indication that Japanese baseball is closer to the Major League level. Other Japanese players have begun to play on this side of the Pacific Ocean, too. Regardless, the rule wasn't likely to be changed during the season, and Ichiro deserved Rookie-of-the-Year, among many other honors.

September 3 The Mariners became the first team to clinch a playoff berth with a 3-2 victory over the Devil Rays. Another packed house at SAFECO Field witnessed the home team overcome 1st and 10th inning deficits to win in the 11th.

Jay Buhner got his first start in the field – left field – since October 15, 2000. The loyal Mariner fans greeted Bone with a standing ovation as he jogged to his new spot. He received his first challenge when Oriole second baseman Brent Abernathy hit a soft liner down the left field line. Buhner chased and went into his familiar slide, and almost crashed into the wall. The ball landed foul, but just for the effort, the fans gave Jay a long ovation.

Buhner admitted he had a tear in his eye as he strode to the batter's box for the first time. He considered retiring in March after reinjuring his foot but encouragement from his family and teammates inspired him. Coupled with his pride in accomplishment and a standing ovation from appreciative fans, the Mariner left fielder "choked up" and stepped back out of the box before resuming his first at bat. He flied out to center, but on his second at bat, Bone topped a slider that he legged out for an infield single, his first hit in 2001.

Jamie Moyer had another strong outing by giving up only one run in seven innings. Arthur Rhodes pitched a scoreless 8th, and Jeff Nelson relieved in the 9th. He was still pitching in the 10th when the Devil Rays'Ben Grieve hit a shot to dead centerfield for the go ahead run. But in the bottom of the 10th, after two were out, Mike Cameron singled, stole second and scored on Mark McLemore's single. This matter-of-fact statement belied the fact that Cameron got his hit, stolen base and run almost on sheer will. "I wasn't going to let us lose. I knew if I could get to second and Mac got a bat, he would drive me in," said the Mariners'All Star centerfielder.

Then in the 11th, John Olerud, who had come into the game in the 9th inning, led off with a single. Al Martin pinch ran for Olerud and promptly stole second. After a Carlos Guillen strike out, Ichiro got yet another infield single, sending Martin to third. Then Stan Javier seemingly on purpose hit a chopper off the plate that must have bounced 25 feet in the air. Martin could have crawled home for the winning run while the Orioles third baseman looked up hopelessly waiting for the ball to come down.

Ichiro got two hits for his 66th multiple hit game of the season, topping Alex Rodriguez'Mariner record.

September 4 Seattle's bullpen sprang a leak and the Devil Rays swam through it as the M's lost a 9th inning lead and then surrendered six runs in the 10th to lose 8-3. Freddy Garcia had pitched masterfully, going eight innings, and giving up just one run on three hits. The Mariner offense didn't get going until the 8th when Cameron hit a two run homer to take a 2-1 lead.

Garcia had thrown only 86 pitches in his eight innings, but Piniella elected to put in Kazu Sasaki to pitch the 9th. "He's out there to be the closer. He's struggled recently, and I was trying to get him some work to help him get out of it," said the manager.

Sasaki couldn't hold the lead, and gave up a run to send the game into extra innings. He got the first out in the 10th and gave the ball to Norm Charlton, who walked Ben Grieve. Then Jose Paniagua came in and got Tampa Bay's Russ Johnson to hit a grounder toward second base. Boone fielded it cleanly, but couldn't get the ball out of his glove. He touched second for the single out rather than the double play to end the inning. Paniagua then gave up five straight hits handing the victory to the Devil Rays. M's lost 8-3.

Meche on mend

Gil Meche, 23 year-old righthander on the disabled list for the season, stopped by the clubhouse and announced he would be ready for Spring Training 2002. Both Bret Boone and Aaron Sele are free agents. *ESPN's* Peter Gammons reported that one AL East GM said that with Meche and Ryan Anderson coming back from injuries, and Ryan Franklin set to become a solid starter, Boone is more valuable to the M's than Sele.

September 5 100 Wins! That was the message on the big screen at SAFECO after the Mariners' 12-6 victory in its last game with Tampa Bay for the season. Seattle became the second earliest team in major league history to win 100 games. Only the '98 Yankees were quicker, but by just one day. The win came from the offense as Edgar and Olerud drove in three runs each and Ichiro scored three runs.

Starting pitcher Aaron Sele was shelled for nine hits and six runs in 3 1/3 innings. John Halama, Arthur Rhodes and Ryan Franklin pitched 5 1/3 innings of scoreless relief. Halama earned his 10th win. The Mariner lefty became the fifth pitcher to have double digit wins.

Carlos Guillen sprained his ankle and would miss ten days. Shortstop Ramon Vazquez was called up from Tacoma, even though the Rainiers were in the AAA playoffs. In fact, four Mariner farm teams were in postseason playoffs.

Three game series vs. Baltimore (M's sweep!)

As Cal Ripken Jr. came to play at Seattle for the last time, it was time for the rest of baseball to show the Mariners respect. At 100-40, the Mariners were only the third team since 1954 to be 60 games over .500. They had lost only one of their last 19 series, and in the eleven games they needed to avoid their first three-game losing streak, they had outscored their opponents 78-34. Also, Seattle has outscored their opponents by 278 runs, and the 1998 Yankees were the only AL team to accomplish that since the 1939 Yankees. Not bad for a team without a superstar.

The Mariners were on pace to win 116 games, and tie the all time record for most wins in a season. But Manager Lou Piniella had other priorities: "Breaking the record would be nice, but we're not going to tax the team to achieve it. If the record happens, it will happen with my team getting a lot of rest." The M's needed only four more wins to surpass the Seattle wins for 1980 and 1981 combined!

September 7 It was a mismatch from the bell as the M's scored four runs in the first to give Paul Abbott a good start as he won his 15th game against three losses. Ichiro got three singles to break the AL rookies' singles mark set by Harvey Kuenn in 1953. Bret Boone homered to break Joe Gordon's 1948 record for four-baggers hit by a second baseman in a season. Ramon Vazquez, just called up, singled in his first major league at bat. Poppa Edgar Martinez quarantined the ball for Vazquez, noting the date and opponent with a *Sharpie*, before giving it to the smiling Vazquez between innings.

Abbott flirted with a no-hitter as he kept the Orioles hitless until the 6th inning, and finished with a two-hitter in eight innings. Jeff Nelson pitched a scoreless 9th. M's 10, Orioles 1.

September 8 It was Kazu Sasaki Bobblehead Day at SAFECO. Protected by 30 armed police officers, the Mariners gave away 20,000 dolls to another capacity crowd. The M's Joel Pineiro and Orioles' Rick Bauer matched again. And again Pineiro came out the winner. He pitched 7 2/3 innings of three-hit ball and gave up only an unearned run.

> Sasaki doll to Sendai Katsuo Ooe traveled from Japan for Sasaki Bobblehead Day. "He will donate the doll to the head of the area prefecture located in Sendai.
> " *Seattle Times,*
> September 9, 2001.

Ichiro collected two hits and set the Mariner mark for hits in a season, breaking the record of Alex Rodriguez. In total, Seattle got 13 hits, and won 6-1.

The Mariners topped the three million mark in attendance leading the majors in average attendance.

Just before the game, Manager Lou Piniella received a very special gift. Adrianna, Jonathan, and Andrew Royal of Bainbridge Island, ages 8, 9, and 10, had each been hospitalized with serious illnesses. All of them were avid Mariner fans, and gave their Ichiro

Bobblehead dolls to the Jamie Moyer charity bowling event. Team management heard about the generosity and asked Andrew to throw out the first pitch at the September 5th game. Andrew went out on the field in his wheelchair and made the toss, and then was given the ball.

Andrew was good luck for the Mariners who won their 100th game that night. He was on the way home after the game when he heard Piniella say he didn't have a ball from the game. Andrew told his mom to give the ball to Piniella, but the manager refused at first saying it was something that Andrew should keep. But the young man was insistent. Lou will always have a very special memory of the 100th win of 2001, thanks to three true loyal Mariner fans, **Adrianna**, **Jonathan** and **Andrew Royal**.

Tickets Wanted!

The entrepreneurial spirit struck two Mariner fans who offered to sell two seats for all 10 possible playoff games on eBay -- starting bid $6,900. Ticket brokers were offering twice the face value for lower level World Series tickets. "Tickets wanted" ads appeared in the classifieds, and one couple offered to throw in an Ichiro Bobblehead doll as an incentive. Meanwhile, Seattle announced it would add up to 500 more seats to SAFECO for the playoffs.

September 9 The M's honored Cal Ripken Jr. before the game and then completed their 13th series sweep with a 6-0 shutout of the retiring Baltimore star's team. Jamie Moyer allowed only two hits in seven innings as he improved his record to 17-5. SAFECO was like a homer-dome as Dan Wilson, Edgar Martinez and Bret Boone hit dingers. Boone drove in his 128th run breaking the AL record for RBIs by a second baseman set in 1934 by Charlie Gehringer. Rhodes and Sasaki each tuned up with an inning, and helped bring the Mariner ERA against Baltimore for the season to a microscopic 1.46.

Three game series at Anaheim
(M's take first game, then continued September 18)
September 10 Freddy Garcia was sharp again, winning his 16th game of the year against 5 losses. He gave up three hits in eight innings, and had given up only three runs in his last four starts. Five different Mariners had two hits as the team improved to 104-40. M's 5, Angels 1.

This was the M's fifth straight win, and eighth of nine in September. To break the AL record of 114 wins set by the Yankees in 1998, Seattle would have to win 11 of its last 18 games. The Mariners' magic number to clinch the AL West was at 2.

But when they went to their hotel that Monday night, September 10, 2001, little did they know that the next game they would play would be over a week away.

Chapter Twelve

SEPTEMBER 11, 2001

The phone was rudely ringing in my ear. It sat on the nightstand next to my bed and at 6:15 AM, there was no rational reason for my phone to be clamoring. I fumbled to grab it, and angrily struggled to say "hello!" into the mouthpiece.

I had stayed up unto about 3 AM the night before working on this book and was in no mood to be awakened from my slumber.

"Stan. Stan?," said the voice. I recognized it to be Mike Siegel's, this book's co-author.

"Mike. What are you doing up this early?" I responded.

"Stan, the World Trade Center - - - a plane hit it."

Then there was silence for a moment, and Mike started again. "Oh my God! There's another one!"

Suddenly, I realized something awful was happening. "I'm going to turn on the TV now, Mike. I'll call you back," I hurriedly said as the realization of what happened shocked me to an awakened state that tragic morning.

The world as we knew it changed that day. Before September 11, 2001, we lived in a world where one of our biggest complaints was about baseball players' salaries. Baseball, the Mariners' tremendous season, Barry Bonds' chase of the single-season home run record, and the pennant races of the National League became irrelevant.

We all know what happened next. I sat aghast in front of the TV set – not speaking a word, crying and angry. Every time I saw the scene replayed I couldn't help but think of my Dad. At 16 he was playing ball in the cow pastures of east Tennessee, but by 17 he was a soldier in WWII. He became a man far too young on the battlefields of Europe. Part of the greatest generation, my dad helped provide a future where war of that kind was to forever be a part of our past. I was sad for him because the sacrifices that he and his generation had made seemed like they had to be made all over again.

And every time I saw the scene replayed I was depressed for my own children, ages 21 and 17. I didn't need the President and Congress telling me that we were going to have to go to war, and that this war would last a long time. That was obvious. Because no matter how much anyone detests violence, the people who had perpetrated this grossly inhuman act had to be stopped. This war against terror will be waged by America and the 80 other countries who had their citizens die at the hands of international criminals.

Co-author Mike Siegel, who played on the streets of New York as a child, was trying to reach his brother, Victor. Mike's brother works at the Ford Foundation close to the United Nations building in Manhattan, another probable target. Victor was going in to work late that day, but never made it in. The planes crashed. Transit stopped. Victor waited at home just minutes from Ground Zero.

Mariners' pitcher John Halama, a Brooklyn native, is the son of the maintenance manager of the Merrill Lynch Building, just a block away from the World Trade Center. His father, Vasil, had gone into work that morning just like it was a normal day. Halama then became part of a frantic phone call chain with family members trying to locate his father. Finally, Vasil reached home after walking across a bridge over the East River.

Vinnie Richichi a/k/a *New York Vinnie*, the popular KIRO radio host, also from Brooklyn was awaiting word from his brother-in-law who worked in the financial district. Queens native Dave Valle, former Mariners' catcher and now a Mariners color analyst, talked with his friends who told of the grief in the streets of Manhattan. New York born Edgar Martinez found all his family OK. His uncle who works at the World Trade Center was out of town on business. Team president Chuck Armstrong, Chairman Emeritus John Ellis, and Kevin Matter, a Mariner VP were in Milwaukee for baseball meetings. With flights cancelled, the three acquired a car and drove straight through to Seattle. They even beat the team back to Seattle, which was stranded in Anaheim and couldn't get permission to fly.

I remember waking up on September 12th and wishing that the day before had been a dream. It wasn't. It was only the beginning of a nightmare.

Yet we all had to go on, Baseball was canceling games. One day's worth of cancellations was the right thing to do. To cancel more games was wrong, I thought. We had to show the rest of the world that we could go forth. There was little better than baseball to help us regain a sense of normalcy.

But I was the one who was wrong. The major league baseball players showed they were just regular people. They put down their gloves and bats. They became leaders in blood drives and wherever else they could be helpful. They spent time with their own families, too, because it was needed. This was a time that the people who made $3 million a year and the ones who made $30,000 a year were the same.

Pitcher Paul Abbott echoed the sentiment of everyone in the nation when he said that after September 11, 2001, as soon as he wakes up, he turns on the television to find out what happened the night before. Stan Javier, who was playing for the Athletics during the 1989 World Series earthquake in San Francisco, said the feelings were somewhat the same. "It was tough to focus, but now you think about what the country is going through. It's emotionally draining."

We place baseball players - all sports icons – on pedestals in American society. When they do things or say things, we place more importance on them. Yet in this instance, the normalcy of what Javier, Abbott and others had to say showed that deep inside, we as people are closer than we outwardly appear.

I went to New York just a few days after the tragedy to cover the story for several radio stations.

As a native New Yorker, I was amazed at the fact that people were friendly. Politeness was everywhere. Even the cabbies stopped blowing their horns.

For however long it lasts, New Yorkers put aside the edge, and came together as if it were one big neighborhood. - *MS*

Curt Schilling, the right-hander for the Arizona Diamondbacks, wrote an open letter about the World Trade Center and Pentagon plane crashes. It bears repeating here:

To the fans of Major League Baseball, and the victims and families of Tuesday's terrorist attacks in New York and Washington D.C.

I'd like to start off by saying that what I am writing is purely my opinion, and my family's feelings on these issues. I am not speaking for any other players in baseball, or in any other sport across our nation or around the world.

I'll begin by addressing the trivial items addressed late this week as far as our sport is concerned. The decision made by Commissioner Bud Selig on Thursday afternoon to resume games on Monday was one overwhelmingly favored by the Major League players. In our conference call on Thursday I got the impression that players, just like every other American citizen out there, didn't need baseball right now, and it was probably best said by Jerome Bettis when he stated that, "We are entertainers, and I don't think America wants to be entertained right now."

I believe that we all felt this way, and hope that the few people in this country who wanted us to play understand that we made the decision as citizens of this country, not as baseball players. To the victims and families of the tragedies inflicted on us this past week we send our hearts out to you, and our prayers that you will find some comfort, some solace in the coming weeks as this great country gets up on its feet and defends itself as the world's greatest nation, with the world's greatest people.

Like a lot of people, my thoughts Tuesday afternoon steered towards revenge, retaliation, retribution, in just how hard we could hit back.

My first cognizant thought was "Man did they pick on the wrong country." Then, after watching TV, I began to realize that not only did they pick on the wrong country, but they couldn't have picked a worse target. There is no city on this planet that more represents its nation than New York does in the United States. New York is the true definition of a melting pot. Every race, religion and color are represented in New York, and on Tuesday you saw every race, every religion, every color, come together as one nation of people fighting for one common goal -- to save lives. I can honestly tell you that I have never been as proud to be an American as I was that day, to see the men and women of this great country come together and pour their blood, sweat and tears into saving those that could be saved. They continue to do so today, and with no less effort. That in and of itself should make us proud as hell.

My wife Shonda, and our three young children stepped outside on Friday at 7 p.m., lit a candle and prayed together. We prayed that those heroic men and women of the NYPD, FDNY and the U.S. Government that sacrificed their lives in the minutes fol - lowing the first explosion at the World Trade Center are now in a safe and beautiful place.

To those families that lost loved ones in the NYPD and in the FDNY, I can only offer our sincerest thank you. Please know that athletes in this country look to your husbands and wives as they may have looked at the men of our profession when they were young, as heroes, as idols, for they are everything every man should strive to be in life and they died in a way reserved only for those who would make the ultimate sacrifice for this nation, and for the freedom we oftentimes take for granted.

Words cannot heal your wounds, not even time will heal the wounds for those who have suffered loss this week. But other than money and blood, which I hope the players in MLB will be giving of both, it is all we have to offer.

We will step on the fields of Major League Baseball on Monday night, but please know that we are not doing this as an aversion to forget what happened on Tuesday. Nothing will ever make us forget that day. But we are doing so because it is our jobs, and I honestly feel that if you do have a chance to catch a few minutes of a game, and see every sports fan in every stadium stand for that initial moment of silence, and understand when we do so that we do so for you, and for your families. And in the seventh-inning stretch when this nation sings God Bless America, we do so because we can, because in this country men and woman have died so that we can continue on as a free nation, and we will be thinking of you then also.

And it's my belief that if you watch close enough you will see players, many players in fact, trying in some small way to say thank you, and that we won't forget you or your loved ones as some of us will have messages scrawled somewhere on our hats or uniforms that you can read.

We will proudly wear the great flag of this country on our uni - forms, and it's something I hope baseball adopts forever.

The flags in this country fly at half-staff to honor those that have fallen, but the flags are the only thing going half way in this country and it's my belief that that will not change. I believe our president when he says retribution will be swift and total, as an American it's all I can go on but based on what I have seen done these past few days being done by other Americans it's more than enough.

To those out there that serve in the military, and to those with children serving in the military I offer my sincerest thanks, and our prayers are with you and yours in the days and weeks to come. We know you'll do us proud.

In closing let me say God Bless America and God Bless Americans everywhere.

Thank you,
Curt Schilling

....

The week of September 11, 2001, was the longest week of my life. My first cousin escaped from the 57th floor of the World Trade Center, but I had no relative or loved one killed. Yet an incredible sadness overtook all of our lives as if each one of us had a brother, sister, parent or close friend die tragically.

Out of the terror came heroes. Our elected leaders have led, and are leading. The fire and police departments of New York and Washington DC gained worldwide respect. People even hugged firefighters in Seattle just because we needed to. It was an expression of thanks for their lifelong devotion to people.

Co-workers in the World Trade Center and the Pentagon helped people less able make it to safety. The people of New York, not known for civility toward one another, provided a great example of coming together. Today's world has been said to be devoid of heroes. America found many heroes on September 11, 2001.

Of all the heroes on that day, and the ones since then, there were the four of United flight 93 to whom I give special note. Todd Beamer, Tom Burnett, Mark Bingham and Jeremy Glick were just regular people on a cross country flight. I'm guessing they were baseball fans. Maybe their favorite teams were White Sox or the Orioles or the Mets.

We all know what happened next. Beamer, Burnett, Bingham and Glick realized the situation. They understood they were going to die. They knew the hijackers wanted to kill as many people on the ground as possible. These four resolved to take action.

They overpowered the hijackers. The plane crashed in a field in a sparsely populated area of Pennsylvania, killing all aboard. No one alive knows the rest of the details. But we all know that through the brave acts of these four passengers, and probably through brave acts of many others on that plane, thousands of lives were saved.

Todd Beamer, Tom Burnett, Mark Bingham and Jeremy Glick – American heroes.

The day of September 11th will have tremendous significance every year. How should it be recognized? September 11, 2001 was a day of tragedy and heroes. It was a day where families needed to be together to draw strength.

Maybe September 11th should be a day when no baseball games are played, but instead we all spend time with our loved ones remembering the horrible events and remarkable courage. Perhaps a full schedule should be played and Major League baseball should donate part of the gate receipts to firefighter and police units across the nation. Possibly there should only be one game played that day . . . between the Mets and the Yankees in a field in Pennsylvania. It won't count in the standings, just in the hearts of the people.

Regardless of how we commemorate that day, everyone in the US will remember what we lost, and be thankful for the heroes among us each day. - *SE*

Chapter Thirteen

September 18 - end of
regular season

"Losing streaks are funny. If you lose at the beginning, you got off to a bad start. If you lose in the middle of the season, you're in a slump. If you lose at the end, you're choking."

      -- Gene Mauch, former manager, 1960-1982, 1985-1987

During the time that baseball games were suspended, the Mariners recalled outfielder Eugene Kingsale and pitchers Brett Tomko and Denny Stark. Tacoma's season ended when the Pacific Coast League chose to cancel further postseason play in the wake of the terrorist attacks. Tomko, who pitched a no-hitter for Tacoma earlier in the year, expressed he was looking forward to showing he was a better pitcher than when he was sent down from Seattle. But the hard-throwing righthander wouldn't get a chance to show his improvement without pitching every fifth day.

Seattle player representative and team leader Dan Wilson called a players' only meeting to discuss what they wanted to do to support those harmed in the September 11th catastrophe, and how they were feeling about returning to the field. Again, the team reflected society.

Wilson stated to the media that "working is patriotic."

A candid Jay Buhner commented "Some players say we needed to get back to the game to show we're not going to be pushed around. And I heard others say it was a time to be with families. I agree with both sides. I just don't know what it will be like to play again."

Team leader Mark McLemore echoed those sentiments: "I've heard it said it's important for us to play. But I don't think anything we do is important. I don't think sports serves a function to return to normalcy. There is no more normalcy."

Kazu Sasaki said "Even if I am on the mound when we clinch, I will not feel joy." His countryman, Ichiro Suzuki, said "We are preparing to play. I do not know if this is good or not because we may not feel the same as before."

Norm Charlton gave the reasons, perhaps unknowingly, why baseball was needed in America: "In the grand scheme of things, we're just grown men playing a game . . . we're not very important and never have been." Yet for those of us who aren't major leaguers, we needed the game. We needed something untroubled. We needed unimportant moments to give us a respite from the heavy burdens on our hearts and minds.

Lou Piniella stated: "What happened on September 11th will change life in our country. I'm not profound enough to figure out what will happen baseball-wise. . . . We'll just go out and do our jobs to the best of our ability."

And do their jobs, the Mariners did, Lou.

Three game series vs. Anaheim (M's take 2)
September 18 In his third shutout and fourth complete game of the season, Freddy Garcia surrendered only three singles as another sellout at SAFECO greeted the return of baseball. It was Garcia's 17th victory against five losses, and his 43rd against 18 losses as a Mariner since his acquisition in the Randy Johnson deal on July 31, 1998. Ichiro was 3-4, raising his average to .350. M's 4, Angels 0.

During the hiatus, third baseman David Bell strained his rib cage and outfielder Al Martin injured his elbow. Bell would be out for weeks, and Martin would not recover during the season. On the positive side, Jay Buhner, who had indicated this would be his last year, was re-evaluating. "If I have something to contribute, and the front office thinks I do, then I'll think very strongly about coming back." But Buhner added that he hadn't given the Mariners appropriate value for their investment and would make up for it "*when* I come back."

The Mariners magic number stood at 1.

September 19 Mariners clinch the division! Jamie Moyer must
have been in a contest with Freddy Garcia because for the second straight night, the Mariners pitched a shutout. This time, the starter wasn't allowed to go the distance, but the result was the same. Moyer improved his record to 18-5, giving up only three hits in six innings

for the M's 106th win of the season. The win also clinched the home-field advantage for the first two rounds of the playoffs. Since the M's were so good on the road, this factor may be considered insignificant. M's 5, Angels 0.

The previous six games were Seattle's best of the season, outscoring their opponents 36-3 during that stretch. Over Moyer's previous 12 starts, he was 9-0 with a 1.38 ERA.

But the most memorable part of the game was the celebration. There wasn't a wild scene at home plate with all the players in a pile. There wasn't a bottle of champagne in each player's hands. There was the team of committed professionals kneeling around the mound in a circle in a moment of silence for the victims of the tragedy . . . a fitting celebration at the right time by the classiest of champions.

Another job for McLemore

Somehow I knew that at the most meaningful moment of the season, there would be Mark McLemore. After the win clinching the division title, McLemore hoisted a large American flag above his head as he walked around the field waving to the appreciative crowd. But McLemore's gesture was more than that. The emotions of the time were still with the firefighters in New York clinging to hope that they would find someone alive under the rubble. Mark McLemore's display of the flag in that title celebration seemed to speak for every person. It was a salute from baseball to the real heroes of the world. In this wondrous season, now filled with overwhelming sorrow, Mark McLemore helped make us all proud again. – *SE*

September 20 Seattle had a game scheduled against Anaheim, but the team "took the day off" instead. Oh there were players on the field in Mariner uniforms, but it was a typical late-in-the-season line-up when there isn't a pennant race. Ichiro, McLemore, Olerud, and Bell didn't start. Javier played right field until Eugene Kingsale came in. Buhner played left field. Gipson played third base. Pat Borders, just acquired, caught.

Aaron Sele was on the mound for Seattle, and gave up six hits, five walks and three runs in seven innings. He wasn't the loser, though. John Halama and Norm Charlton each gave up a run as the Mariners seven game winning streak was broken. Halama's string of 17 1/3 scoreless innings ended with the run he permitted in the 9th before Charlton entered. Angels won 6-3.

At a charity auction held by Mariner wives to benefit terrorist relief efforts, an Ichiro autographed bat brought $7,000! Arthur Rhodes auctioned a pair of earrings (not THE earrings) for over $1,000. The Mariner wives raised nearly $40,000 over these past two games for the benefit of victims in the September 11th attacks.

Three game series at Oakland (A's sweep ☹)

Mariner fans were tight. Seattle had traveled to Oakland, the major league's best team after the All Star break. The Mariners' year-long streak of not losing a series on the road was on the line. The fans didn't want any team, especially the A's, breaking that streak.

But manager Lou Piniella had other thoughts. "We're going to get ready for Cleveland. My biggest job now is to get the bullpen sharp. And that will take steady, consistent work." He added that Jose Paniagua needed work and that Joel Pineiro would get a look out of the bullpen since he would not be a starter in the postseason.

Piniella admitted: "We'll put a lineup out there that is competitive, but I'm going to tinker a bit just to see what it looks like." With injuries to Boone (jammed heel), Bell (sore ribs) and Martin (elbow) and with Buhner still getting up to speed, whether the Mariners could win enough in the 15 games left to set the AL record for wins in a season was not in Piniella's sites.

September 21 It was the regular Mariner lineup with the exception of Ramon Vazquez at second in place of Bret Boone. Of course, Mark McLemore didn't have a regular position. So he played third base for David Bell.

Afirst inning home run by Oakland's Jason Giambi off Seattle's Paul Abbott gave the 30,000 A's fans something to cheer about. Giambi would have a perfect day: 2-2 with two walks. Abbott, who struggled to get his curveball over the plate, pitched five innings, and then Franklin, Tomko and Paniagua each got in an inning of work. Only Franklin, who gave up two runs on two hits and three walks, was scored upon.

Oakland's Cory Lidle stymied the Mariners' offense though, which managed only eight random singles. Mike Cameron hit a 9th inning homer, reaching the 100 RBI plateau for the first time in his career. A's won 5-1.

September 22 For the first time all season the Mariners lost three games in a row. The 11-2 loss at Oakland assured Seattle of their first series loss on the road. Joel Pineiro got the surprise start for the Mariners and wished he had stayed in the bullpen. The A's pounded out seven hits and five runs (only two earned) in just two innings. Denny Stark relieved Pineiro and added to the problem. Pineiro and Stark, the two Seattle rookie pitchers, were behind 9-0 after just five innings. Charlton, Nelson and Paniagua all worked, but only Paniagua came through without giving up a run.

September 23 Oakland's Mark Mulder won his 20th game of the season as the A's swept Seattle, and extended the M's losing streak to four. Mariner fans were strangely silent at watering holes around the city as it seemed the A's had proven their point. Seattle may just not be the best team in baseball, despite their incredible 106-44 record.

Freddy Garcia became generous all of a sudden, giving up three home runs and five runs in six innings. It was a feast or famine game for Seattle's ace. Though he gave up the runs, and walked four batters, he also struck out seven. Rhodes and Sasaki both worked an inning, with Sasaki giving up two hits and two runs. A's won 7-5.

Piniella, responding to questions about the Mariners losing streak, stated: "We were flat and didn't play well all weekend. We got enough hits, we just didn't hit with men in scoring position. But, our job is to get ready for the postseason and that's exactly what we are going to do."

OK, Lou, but it still makes me nervous to get swept at Oakland. - SE

Three game series at Texas (M's sweep!)
An ugly rumor was spreading: Pat Gillick was leaving Seattle to save the Red Sox from despair. Boston, a once proud franchise, was in such utter chaos that it would make sense for the new owners to steal baseball's hottest executive. Gillick categorically denied the rumor.

Meanwhile, Manager Lou Piniella stated he wanted Jay Buhner as part of the 25 member playoff roster. Buhner's bat was becoming stronger and more consistent. Plus, Piniella wanted Bone's leadership on the field as well as in the clubhouse.

September 24 Jamie Moyer had two starts left and a record of 18-5. He wasn't going to get to pitch many innings, but his performance in this game against Texas was enough to give him his 19th win this season and 150th win of his career. It was Moyer's tenth straight win, which tied Paul Abbott's club record set earlier in the year.

The run support that was lacking in the Oakland series reappeared. The M's had 13 hits, including three from Bret Boone, and two each from Ichiro Suzuki, Mike Cameron and John Olerud. M's won 9-3.

September 25 At this point in the season, it must have been hard for teams not in a pennant race to play hard. The Rangers were 70-80 going into this game, and Seattle pounced on Texas with four runs in the second. Whatever spark Texas may have had in this game was snuffed out.

It was a rout. The Mariners won 13-2 behind 16 hits and homers by Guillen, Olerud and Martin. Boone drove in four runs as Seattle played 15 position players. Aaron Sele pitched seven strong innings, surrendering only one earned run. He went over 200 innings pitched for the fourth straight season.

The Mariners uncharacteristically made four errors in the game, and had committed six errors in the first two games with Texas.

The win was Seattle's 56th on the road (against 22 losses) beating the 1971 Oakland Athletics' American League record for wins on the road. Piniella admitted that a contributing factor to the Mariners' uncanny abilities away from SAFECO was the fact that his team hit with more power on the road. So much of the early season belief about the Mariners was that the team was built for SAFECO Field, but the record of road wins leads to the unmistakable conclusion that the M's were built simply to win.

Ranger fans investigated
Late in the September 25th game with Texas, center-fielder Mark McLemore stopped the game and summoned the umpires. McLemore was pointing to the stands and the umpire called for security guards. Then there was a scrambling among the fans in the area. Stadium security removed two people and alerted police. The game resumed.

McLemore, who lives in the Dallas area, later revealed he had received threats, which he would have overlooked had it not been for the fact that the hecklers knew his address. "That threatened my family and that was too much to let go," he said.

Arlington police were investigating.

September 26 It was another one of those "get ready for the play-offs" games, where five Mariner pitchers took the mound, and most of the team's position players took the field. On the strength of a five-run 5th inning, led by Bret Boone's two-run single and Stan Javier's two-run double, the Mariners defeated Texas 7-5.

Paul Abbott improved his record to 16-4 in an unimpressive five innings, giving up four runs, and six hits, including two home runs. Pineiro, Nelson, Rhodes and Sasaki each pitched an inning.

The win completed the Mariners' 15th series sweep of the season. Alex Rodriguez broke the Texas franchise (going back to the Washington Senators) record for home runs with his 49th. On a team of hitters, A-Rod was the best. Even though his team was one of the worst in the American League, Alex had an MVP season.

Three game series vs. Oakland (M's take 2)
While the frenzied fans eagerly awaited the Oakland Athletics to come to Seattle, Manager Lou Piniella admitted he was worried about the M's fielding. Pitching and defense had been the theme all year long. In fact, Seattle had the American League's fewest errors but had committed seven errors in the past nine games. "We're not a strike-out pitching team. So defense is key to the success of our pitching staff," said Piniella. "There's been a little loss in focus and we have to get that back before the playoffs."

Speaking of the playoffs, there were 15,000 tickets available to the general public for games 1 and 2 of the American League Division Series. All available playoff tickets for the ALDS were sold in 53 minutes and no one was hurt or arrested.

September 28 Another jam packed crowd intoxicated with Mariner mania flooded SAFECO Field and was treated to a Seattle win over the visiting A's. Freddy Garcia pitched well, except for one inning. This one inning mental lapse had become a pattern, hopefully not one to be extended into the postseason. Garcia threw five innings of scoreless baseball, but in the 6th, Oakland scored three runs on a walk and three hits. Charlton, Rhodes and Sasaki each pitched scoreless innings.

In the meantime, Ichiro started the game right for the Mariners by singling, and taking third on Javier's double. Cameron received an intentional pass to load the bases following a Boone strikeout. Then, a fielder's choice and Jason Giambi error permitted two runs to give the Mariners the lead. The Mariners missed an opportunity to put Oakland starter Mark Mulder out of the game. With the bases loaded and only one out, Seattle failed to get a timely hit. That would not bode well when playing good hitting teams, such as Cleveland, Oakland or the Yankees.

Seattle scored three more runs in the 3rd inning on four hits. Ichiro lead off with an infield single. His hustle down the first base line caused Athletic shortstop Miguel Tejada to throw the ball to right field, giving Ichiro second base. This was the kind of pressure Ichiro put on defenses all season long. A Javier sacrifice put Ichiro on third with only one out. This style of play, which the critics panned early in the season as "small ball," had been a lethal weapon in the Mariners' arsenal. Even if Seattle didn't get the big inning, like in the Kingdome days, the continual pressure wore on opposing starting pitchers. That necessitated the opposing team to use their bullpens more often against the M's, depleting their staffs. It is no wonder the Mariners won so many series during the season.

The Mariner lineup didn't include four injured regulars. Guillen (ill), McLemore (sore knee), Bell (sore ribs) and Martinez (stiff neck) missed the game. Regardless, the A's 20 game winner, Mark Mulder, was the loser, lasting six innings, giving up nine hits, three walks and four earned runs. M's won 5-3.

The Mariners 53rd sellout helped break their all time attendance record at 3,234,909, with six home games remaining. But that wasn't the big news. In the September 28 edition of the morning *Seattle Times*, there was a well-written piece by Jose Miguel Romero about Carlos Guillen. The article clearly took several days in the making. Romero discussed how Guillen overcame his "oft-injured" label in the 2000 season.

Romero's piece contained two very interesting quotes. "I think we can be set (at shortstop) for the next few years if we can keep him healthy," Lou Piniella, and "It feels good not to be injured. I suffered a little but now I feel healthy," Carlos Guillen. *[Seattle Times, Carlos Guillen: An everyday kind of guy* by Jose Miguel Romero, September 28, 2001]

Just before the game that night, and only hours after the printing of the article talking about how valuable he was to the Mariners, Carlos Guillen was diagnosed with tuberculosis. Doctors believed Guillen had contracted the disease in his native Venezuela where TB was at nearly at an epidemic level. He may have had TB all season long, and in retrospect, Guillen's teammates indicated that the young shortstop had been listless and appeared physically drained for some time. The close contact among those on the team meant that each Mariner would have to be checked for TB. No one else, fortunately, had the disease. Though early indications were that Guillen would only miss a week of baseball, he was out until the American League Championship Series, and even then was only a part-time player.

September 29 Jamie Moyer's remarkable ten game winning streak was broken but he would still have one more chance for 20 wins. Ichiro broke a 90-year old record when his 4th inning single was his 234th hit, making him the rookie with the most hits. Shoeless Joe Jackson had set that mark with Cleveland in 1911. Edgar had four RBIs in the game to reach 115 for the season.

On the down side, Oakland came back to take the second game of the series led by Miguel Tejada's first SAFECO cycle. A's won 8-4.

Edgar Martinez reportedly participated in a pre-game home run hitting contest with himself. A Japanese TV game show gave Edgar a chance to win some cash, and had $15,000 in his pocket on three home runs. One more pitch – for $20,000 or nothing – was made. Edgar popped out, leaving $20,000 in $100 bills on home plate.

After the game, Jose Paniagua apologized for his outburst the previous day. He had been particularly critical of Mariner doctors concerning Carlos Guillen. Many of his words were expletive-deleteds, and he indicated that too many people in his homeland, the Dominican Republic, had died from TB because they couldn't afford medicine to fight a disease which people in America had beaten long ago. He vowed to be a regular visitor to his friend, Carlos Guillen, who was in the hospital.

One more thing – another game at SAFECO, another sellout. That's 54 sellouts in 76 games.

September 30 Seattle and Oakland had played 18 games between each other. This game would decide who won the season series. Meaningless? Yes and no.

It was meaningless in the sense that both teams had already clinched playoff berths. Both teams were merely getting players ready for the postseason. But it wasn't meaningless because both teams were trying to establish momentum as the playoffs began. And, one of these two teams would establish momentum over the other. Besides, to the rabid Seattle fans, the game was VERY important.

Seattle starter Aaron Sele was nasty! That means something good, mom, not bad. Sele threw some wicked curveballs in holding the potent Athletic offense to one single in the first six innings, and surrendered his only run of the game in the 7th on doubles by Jason Giambi and Jermaine Dye. Jeff Nelson pitched a strong 8th, but Arthur Rhodes gave up four hits and two runs in the 9th for his worst performance in months.

At the plate, the Mariners were pretty nasty, too. Ace Oakland pitcher Tim Hudson was able to feel up close and personal how the Mariners felt about him as he yielded ten hits in just 6 1/3 innings. Ichiro got his eighth homer and John Olerud smacked his 20th as the Mariners tied the third winningest season in history. The 6-3 win was Seattle's 111th, tying the 1954 Cleveland Indians. The series win gave the M's a remarkable 42-6-4 series record throughout the season. M's won 6-3.

Carlos Guillen spent his 26th birthday in Northwest Hospital, as the team boarded the plane for Anaheim.

Continuation of three game series at Anaheim, suspended from September 11 (M's complete sweep!)

After the Oakland series at SAFECO, there really wasn't anything to do in the season except compile records and get people healthy for the playoffs. David Bell had lingering rib injuries, and anyone who has ever had sore ribs knows that it hurts just to breathe. Hitting a 95-mile-an-hour fastball with hurt ribs or diving to your right to grab a one hopper was out of the question. Mark McLemore who played (fill in the blank for a position) during the regular season, but would play shortstop for Guillen in the postseason, had a bum knee. A shortstop with a gimpy leg would have a hard time going into the hole to nab a Roberto Alomar grounder. And, left-handed hitting Al Martin had an injured elbow that kept him from throwing. The Mariners already had someone in the lineup who could hit but not field (Edgar). But they needed that left-handed bat.

So, the beginning of October which was still the regular season because of the September 11 tragedy, posed the same difficult challenge for Manager Lou Piniella he had a month ago: getting the team prepared for the postseason.

October 2 Float like a butterfly, sting like a bee! That was the new mantra of the Mariners' own Edgar Martinez in the game against Anaheim. And it would be his last game for a few days, too.

The game was out of hand – way out of hand. The Mariners were scoring at will. The Angels had long since put their halos to sleep in the 6th when the minister-like Edgar Martinez stepped to the plate. A pitch came inside to him, much too inside for Edgar's liking. It struck him on the arm and deflected up to his face. As he lay in the batter's box, Mariner fans were aghast with the prospect that the player who had defined his position was dreadfully injured. But all of a sudden, like Superman shaking off kryptonite, Edgar bounced up to his feet and charged the mound. The 38-year old hadn't won too many races in the past decade, but he beat everybody to the pitcher's hill, 60'6" away from home plate and started flailing away at Anaheim pitcher Lou Pote. Players from both teams subdued hostilities, and Edgar was escorted to an early exit. Pote went back to the mound.

In the 8th, young Seattle righthander Joel Pineiro made some friends on the Mariner bench. Anaheim's Troy Glaus stepped into the box and Pineiro promptly put a fastball in his ribs. Just as promptly the home plate umpire tossed Pineiro.

It's an old baseball maxim: You hit my guy, I hit yours (a/k/a an "eye for an eye, a tooth for a tooth"). But a look at the circumstance showed that Seattle lost the battle, even though they won the war. They lost one of their best hitters, and they lost a pitcher. Ironically, the guy who started it all, Anaheim's Lou Pote, didn't lose anything. *Go figure!*

Ultimately, the American League suspended Edgar for two games and Pineiro for three. Neither suspension was appealed and both players seemed to wear the penalties like badges of honor.

After the game, Manager Lou Piniella stated, with a bit of a tongue in his cheek: "I've never seen Edgar so upset in all my years with him. But everyone is fine now." Mike Cameron, the soft-spoken Georgian, couldn't hide a smile, though: "Man! I ain't never seen Edgar like that. Did you see how fast he ran to the mound?"

Ichiro had the night off. So Stan Javier, took the leadoff spot and got four hits. The light hitting Charles Gipson got three hits. By the sixth inning, the Mariners had five players on the field who weren't even on the roster on May 1: Pineiro, Pat Borders at catcher, Ramon Vazquez at shortstop, Ed Sprague at third and Eugene Kingsale in left.

Paul Abbott got his 17th win with an unimpressive five innings, five-hit, six-walk, three-run game. But a win is a win, and it was the M's 112th. M's 14, Angles 5.

October 3 The Mariners completed the sweep with a 4-3 win but Freddy Garcia didn't pitch like an ace. Once again, Freddy struggled in one inning – this time the first – as the first three Angels singled, two of whom scored. Garcia righted himself and ended with six innings pitched, giving up six hits, three runs, walking one and striking out seven. Garcia got a no-decision in the game which prevented him from becoming the first pitcher since the Tigers' Denny McLain in 1968 to go 6 wins, 0 losses against one team in a season.

Ichiro was 4-5, and broke the record for singles (188) in a season set by Wade Boggs in 1985. Bret Boone singled in the winning run in the 8th, for the Mariners 113th victory. Norm Charlton got the win, and Kazu Sasaki his 44th save.

Four game series vs. Texas (M's take 3)

The Mariners had 113 wins. They needed just one more to tie the American League record for wins in a season set by the 1998 Yankees. They would need to win all four to break the all time record for season wins by the 1906 Chicago Cubs. *You remember those Cubs, right?* Mordecai "Three Fingers" Brown was the lead pitcher and their double play combination was immortalized in verse:

> *Baseball's Sad Lexicon*
> These are the saddest of possible words:
> "Tinker to Evers to Chance."
> Trio of bear cubs, and fleeter than birds,
> Tinker and Evers and Chance.
> Ruthlessly pricking our gonfalon bubble,
> Making a Giant hit into a double--
> Words that are heavy with nothing but trouble:
> "Tinker to Evers to Chance."
>
> -- Franklin Pierce Adams

There were plenty of distractions to keep the Mariners from getting as mentally sharp as possible for the playoffs. But Manager Lou Piniella was determined to avoid those distractions. He would lean heavily on Mark McLemore. He would have to because his regular shortstop was not available. At 36-years old, this was McLemore's best season. His career high in steals and batting average took place largely when Mac batted second. Hitting in the #2 slot does not do well for one's average if the leadoff hitter is above average. With Ichiro as Seattle's leadoff man, McLemore would have to find any way he could to get Ichiro to second base. Many of those ways meant a negative to Mac's batting average, but that didn't faze Piniella as he prepared his final thoughts for the first postseason assignment. "I have all the confidence in the world with McLemore at shortstop, or just about anyplace else on the field. He's proved that," said the manager. "And wherever he plays, he hits."

McLemore and David Bell returned for the first game against the visiting Rangers. Of course, Carlos Guillen did not. He underwent a procedure to insert an artificial clot to control minor bleeding. Guillen's illness meant that the Mariners'plan to carry three catchers in the postseason was dimmed. That also meant that Ramon Vazquez, who didn't join the team until after September 1, would likely make the playoff roster.

October 4 Win # 114! Seattle's Jeff Nelson became the only player in the history of baseball to play on two teams to win 114 games or more in a single season. "I hope people realize what we just did. A few years ago nobody outside the Northwest would have heard anything about this team without Ken Griffey, Jr. Now it's won 114 games and who knows how many more?" said Nelson.

This win was never in doubt. Scoring twelve runs in the first four innings, Seattle outmanned the Rangers. McLemore, playing his first game since September 26th, celebrated his 37th birthday with three hits. In fact, every Seattle starter had reached base before the 3rd inning was completed. Al Martin was the DH and went 3-4. Tom Lampkin hit two doubles and drove in four runs. Ichiro got a hit, making him the third major leaguer since 1930 to reach 240 hits in a season. And Jay Buhner hit his first home run in 2001!

Bret Tomko pitched well, surrendering four hits and one run in five innings. One of the hits he gave up was a home run to Alex Rodriguez. It was A-Rod's 52nd home run and 200th hit of the season. By the end of this game, Alex had 135 RBIs and was batting .323. This guy can play!

John Halama and Jose Paniagua finished the game with a combined four scoreless innings. M's won 16-1.

October 5 Win # 115! There's no need to discuss the 1998 New York Yankees anymore. The team that holds the American League record for most wins in a season is the 2001 Seattle Mariners. Until our record is broken, all other teams will now be compared to the Mariners.

The game was typical Mariner fashion, too. Jamie Moyer was on the mound, and recorded his 20th win, making him the oldest (38) in major league history to win 20 games for the first time. Moyer was . . . well . . . Moyer. He pitched seven innings, gave up four hits, didn't walk anybody, and allowed only two runs. The lefthander who makes opposing hitters want to bring a tennis racket to the plate, threw only 93 pitches, in another efficient, get-everybody-involved game.

The M's scored first, as they seemingly always did when Moyer pitched. The team was 86-8 when scoring first.

Rhodes and Sasaki each pitched one hitless inning as they tuned up for Cleveland.

Olerud and Boone hit homers, and Boone moved into a tie for the league lead for RBIs. Ichiro singled, tying him with Babe Herman (1930) and Heinie Manush (1928) for 10th in hits in a single season. M's won 6-2.

In the postgame press conference, an emotional Piniella stated that his 2001 Mariners were a "once-in-lifetime bunch of guys."

> **Moyer is money**
> From a fan's standpoint, it is a joy to watch Jamie pitch. He works fast. He throws strikes. He makes the hitters swing the bat and gives the fielders opportunities to make plays. There's an enthusiasm about him that belies his stoic nature. He scares me, though, because his pitches look fat. But it's so fun to watch power hitters take mighty swings against a Moyer changeup only to top the ball for a ground out to shortstop. If it came down to one game – winner take all - I'd want Moyer on the mound for me. – *SE*

There was good news off the field, too. Carlos Guillen was released from the hospital. His hope was to be in uniform for the Cleveland series, even if he wasn't activated.

In anticipation of coming home, even though he's with the Indians, Seattle resident Omar Vizquel tossed the first salvo in the postseason propaganda battle. "I guarantee you that if the sun is hitting the earring in a certain way, I'll ask the umpires to have him take them out again," said Little O. *Bring it on, Omar!*

October 6 Win # 116! The Mariners tied the record. This wasn't just any record. The record the Mariners' tied was older than Joe Dimaggio's 56-game hitting streak in 1941. It was even older than Pete Alexander's 1916 record for shutouts in a season. It was a record that less than 1/10 of 1 percent of the people alive today have even the remotest chance of remembering. The 2001 Seattle Mariners tied the 1906 Chicago Cubs for most wins in a season.

To make matters even more unusual, the M's shut out the Rangers for the first time any team had shut them out this year. Even stranger, Seattle used five pitchers in a 1-0 game!

Denny Stark got the Rangers out 1-2-3 in the first. The Mariners were facing Doug Davis, who ended the season 11-10 - - pretty good for a team that was 73-89. Davis got Stan Javier to ground out to third and Mike Cameron to send a lazy fly to right. Then Bret Boone came up. The AL RBI leader found a 2-1 fastball over the outside part of the plate and belted a towering fly ball to deep center field. Texas centerfielder Ricky Ledee went back to the track, looked up and saw Boone's blast fly away for the 1-0 lead. That would be the only run scored in the game.

Stark pitched three innings, giving up only one hit. Paul Abbott pitched the 4th and 5th innings, also giving up just one hit. Then Joel Pineiro, in his first appearance after his suspension, pitched two perfect innings, striking out four batters. Jeff Nelson and Kazuhiro Sasaki finished with perfect innings to preserve the 1-0 victory. The shutout was the Mariners' 14th, another category in which the M's lead the league.

Doug Davis for Texas pitched his best game of the year, losing 1-0 in a complete game four hitter.

The 58th sellout at SAFECO witnessed one of the best games of the season. At a time when the Rangers should have been playing out the string, they were hustling out ground balls, led by Alex Rodriguez. If Texas ever gets pitching, they will be a team to fear. Until then, though, Seattle will welcome Texas with open arms and eager bats.

October 7 At 116-45, the Mariners entered the game at 71 games over .500. In and of itself that was a tremendous statistic. Before the 2001 season, the most a Seattle team had ever been over .500 was 22. The Seattle chapter of the Baseball Writers of America didn't wait for the last game to give out its Mariner MVP award. Refusing to tackle the dilemma, the Seattle BWA named Ichiro and Boone co-MVPs. Mariner pitcher of the year? Again, the Seattle BWA named co-winners – Garcia and Moyer. The Unsung Hero Award was easy; McLemore.

The Mariners had set many records during the season, but there was one yet to set: the most wins by any team in a season. Seattle had one chance to make the 1906 Chicago Cubs second best.

> **High on Mariners**
> "When spring training was over, if you had told me we would win 116 games, I would have thought you'd been smoking something."
> – Manager Lou Piniella

Another capacity crowd on the final night of the regular season gave the Mariners a home attendance of 3,507,507, the highest in the majors in 2001. The SAFECO sellout was the 59th of the season.

Piniella chose to get pitchers ready for the playoffs. Aaron Sele started and was supposed to go no more than 100 pitches. He didn't last that long. After five innings, he had permitted three runs on eight hits, but left with the game tied at three. The Rangers' Rafael Palmeiro hit his 47th homer in the 3rd off Sele. It was his 10th four-bagger against Seattle this year.

Ichiro led off the Mariners' first with a double, giving him 135 games in which he had a hit. That tied the major league record with Rogers Hornsby (1922), Chuck Klein (1930), Wade Boggs (1985) and Derek Jeter (1999). Dan Wilson and Jay Buhner homered for the other Mariner runs.

After Sele left the game, Piniella chose the pitch-by-committee method again. Charlton, Paniagua and Rhodes each pitched scoreless innings. Jeff Nelson came in to pitch the 9th, and started well. After he got the first two out, the next two Rangers got on base via a single, then a walk. Rafael Palmeiro, who has owned Seattle all year, singled to right driving in the winning run. Rangers 4, M's 3.

The M's didn't win the 117th, and there was a tinge of disappointment among Mariner faces. Perhaps the disappointment should have been in Nelson's slump that started in August. Or the disappointment could have been that the Mariners only had a total of 17 hits in their last three games . . . and this was against Texas Ranger pitching. Regardless, Seattle's place in regular season history was firmly sewn, but the playoffs started a new season where regular records meant nothing.

September to regular season end Magical Moments
(20 wins - 7 losses . . . Season 116-46)
1. 100 wins! (9/5)
2. M's honor Cal Ripken with permanent plaque at SAFECO (9/9)
3. M's clinch AL West - McLemore hoists flag (9/19)
4. Ichiro breaks singles record (10/3)
5. Moyer wins 20th (10/5)
6. 116 wins!! (10/6)

Chapter Fourteen

The 2001 Postseason

"...It is a haunted game in which every player is measured against the ghosts of all who have gone before. Most of all, it is about time and timelessness, speed and grace, failure and loss, imperishable hope-- and coming home."
-- Ken Burns, Baseball

After 116 wins and leading the league in hitting, pitching and defense, many in Seattle thought the Indians of 2001 would be even easier than the White Sox of 2000. The American League Division Series was going to be a blow-out and Cleveland would be lucky to even be competitive in any game. Fortunately, Manager Lou Piniella knew better.

Only someone forgot to tell the Indian players that they had no chance. In fact, knowledgeable baseball fans knew that the playoffs were different. The five game series to get to the championship contained many unknown quantities. All it took was a great game from a good pitcher, and a so-so game from a good pitcher, and the entire dynamic of the end of the season could easily change.

American League Division Series 2001
Game 1, October 9 at Seattle

Cleveland's Bartolo Colon has had the potential to be one of the game's best pitchers for several years. He's listed at 6'0" but he's a lot closer to 5'9", and he looks like he weighs every bit of 225 lbs. He really looks much more like a fullback than a pitcher. But in the game against Seattle, he looked like Bob Gibson.

Colon had some help from SAFECO Field. The game started at 1:20 PM, and a clear blue sky was made even more intense by uncharac- teristically bright Pacific Northwest sunshine. The shadows crept over the stadium from behind home plate and created a very difficult line of sight between the mound and the batter's box.

With two hard throwers starting (Freddy Garcia was on the mound for Seattle), it would be not be a pleasant afternoon for hitters.

Regardless of the weather, though, Colon was nearly unhittable. He brought a 14-12 record with a 4.09 ERA, and had surrendered career highs in hits, runs and home runs. But on this day, his pitches looked like aspirin tablets – very fast aspirin tablets. Colon struck out ten Mariners in eight innings, gave up only six hits and no runs. Only one Mariner reached third base and that was on a throwing error. His pitches were clocked as high as 98 mph in the 1st inning and by the 8th, he had even sped up to 99! Those pitches would have been nearly impossible to hit if there were no shadows at all.

Ichiro touched Colon for three hits, but otherwise Seattle's offense was anemic.

Freddy Garcia pitched three innings of great baseball. He was in total command – just like Colon – until the 4th inning. Garcia, 18-6 during the regular season and the league leader in ERA, did have one shortfall this year. He seemed to lose focus for one inning a game. Game 1 of the 2001 ALDS validated the criticism of Garcia.

> In light of recent events, all the players were required to undergo security checks before entering the clubhouses. The guard didn't recognize veteran Cleveland pitcher, Dave Burba. When asked his name and position, Burba replied "I'm a pitcher, but sometimes I've been just a thrower."

In Cleveland's half of the 4th, the first six batters reached base. Three of them scored. The way Colon was pitching, those runs were all that was needed. Even though Garcia found himself again in the 5th, by the 6th he was done, and the Indians had a 4-0 lead. Mariner hitters were unable to solve Colon, and the game was as good as over. Paniagua pitched the 8th and gave up a home run to Ellis Burks, and John Halama pitched a scoreless 9th.

Arecord crowd of 48,033 attended. Indians won 5-0.

Game 2, October 11, at Seattle

The schedule was unusual in that this was the second straight game at SAFECO, but the teams had a day off in between games. Like the first game, two similar pitchers were vying for the win. Seattle's 38-year old Jamie Moyer, the master of deception, and Cleveland's 38-year old Chuck Finley, former fireballer, were on the hill.

Moyer was a craftsman. It was as if the baseball was a yo-yo and Jamie pulled the string. The ball darted in, out, around and down – avoiding the sweet part of Indian bats like there was some type of science fiction force field protecting horsehide from touching wood.

There was something else about Jamie Moyer games. It's been uncanny throughout the year. When Jamie pitches, the Mariners score early. Chuck Finley found that out the hard way. It had been 15 years since Finley had pitched in the postseason. Despite having won nearly 200 games and thrown over 3,000 innings, the aging Indian lefthander had pitched only two postseason innings, and had never won a game in playoff baseball during his entire illustrious career.

Finley threw 14 pitches in the 1st inning that made his 15 year wait for another postseason shot extremely painful. Ichiro led off with a walk. Mike Cameron took an 0-2 pitch over the bullpen in left for a two run homer. Bret Boone followed with a single, and Edgar crushed a first pitch fastball far over the fence in center for another two-run homer.

It was a good thing that the M's scored early because they managed only three more hits after the 1st inning, one a David Bell dinger.

> "The first inning wasn't what I envisioned it to be like."
> – Chuck Finley,
> October 11, 2001

In the top half of the 7th, Cleveland's Ellis Burks and Jim Thome singled to lead off the inning. Manager Lou Piniella replaced Moyer with setup man Jeff Nelson. The Mariner with the most playoff experience, Nelson had a poor second half of the season. But, again, it was playoff time and Nelson stepped it up.

He walked Travis Fryman to load the bases with nobody out, but then got on track. A ground-out double play brought in the only run the Indians would score. Then Einar Diaz hit a soft liner to center for the final out.

Arthur Rhodes pitched a flawless 8th, and Kazu Sasaki gave up a harmless single in the 9th to close out the victory. Just like in the 116-win regular season, Nelson, Rhodes and Sasaki closed down the opposition. M's won 5-1 to even the series at one win a piece.

> "That first one I could have swung at twice and still missed it."
> – Jim Thome, who struck out twice against Moyer
> [*Seattle Times*, October 12, 2001]

Another sellout crowd (48,052) witnessed a name to watch: Danys Baez. The Indians'reliever is an Indian star of the future, and perhaps that future is the 2002 season. Baez, a 24-year old Cuban rookie, hit 101 on the radar in the 9th inning.

Even in the postseason there are off-the-field events. In this instance there was a bullpen incident that wouldn't have attracted much attention if it weren't for whom was involved: John Rocker.

Relief pitchers at SAFECO Field are behind left field and separated from the fans by a wire fence. A raucous crowd seized the opportunity provided by the porous fence to hurl insults at the thin-skinned Rocker. The frustrated Indians'reliever took only so much, and then threw a cup of water on the fans.

The story was a quick sensation as a result of Rocker's past and his latest escapades. Several of the Seattle media, including the Seattle Times' Larry Stone, however, were more forgiving. ". . . no one deserves to be verbally pummeled the way Rocker apparently was by the rowdies who hang out near the bullpen. Rocker may be a boor, but the statute of limitations on his infractions has expired. Cut the guy a break." [*Seattle Times*, October 13, 2001]

Stone was right, but didn't go far enough. The Seattle organization must take some responsibility for protecting players from ridiculous behavior. Interestingly, management issued warnings to the fans about harassing A-Rod. In Texas, unruly fans were ejected when they recited Mark McLemore's address. Seattle has created an open invitation with its bullpen array for abuse by fans. Seattle's front office management must stop this absurd behavior from ever happening again.

Game 3, October 13, at Cleveland

Going into the first game of the ALDS at Cleveland, Mariners' starting pitcher Aaron Sele was looking for run support. But he was seeking a turnaround in his career against the Indians. He had a 5-7 record before taking the mound at Jacobs Field, but it didn't take long to show his record wasn't on the upswing in this outing.

And for the first time all season, the Seattle Mariners looked like a team whose season was at the end.

Rookie southpaw C.C. Sabathia, 17-5 with a 4.39 ERA, was the pitcher for Cleveland, and quickly got behind. Ichiro led off the game with a single to left, took third on Cameron's double. Boone struck out, but Edgar was intentionally walked, loading the bases. Sabathia wasn't in a groove, though, and gave Olerud a pass, forcing in a run. But the M's couldn't make any more of the rally, as Jay Buhner, starting in left field, and catcher Dan Wilson both popped out.

That was pretty much the offensive highlight of the day for the M's, and Cleveland proceeded to unleash their hitting power. The Indians scored two runs on three hits in the 1st. Then two more Indian runners crossed home in the 2nd on Omar Vizquel's triple. Lou Piniella had seen enough of Sele, and started the 3rd inning with Paul Abbott on the mound. Juan Gonzalez greeted Abbott on the first pitch with a long home run to left field. The Juan-gone homer was the first of four runs in the inning. Cleveland led 8-1 after three innings.

The onslaught continued. Abbott gave up eight runs in three innings. After two scoreless innings from John Halama, Jose Paniagua entered the game to mop-up. But, Cleveland used Paniagua as a scrub brush and tallied five more runs in the inning.

> "It was embarrassing."
> – Mike Cameron
> October 13, 2001

Cleveland won 17-2 in one of the most lopsided postseason games in history. Sabathia, who pitched six innings, became the second youngest pitcher to win a division game. Only Fernando Valenzuela for the Dodgers in 1981 was younger.

The Mariners' pitching was pathetic in Game 3, but the hitting continued a dangerous trend. Including the last three games of the regular season against Texas, Seattle was averaging six hits a game in their previous six games. The M's team batting average – at .288 in the regular season - was hovering 100 points lower over those six games. Had Sele and Abbott combined to give up just three runs, the Mariners would still have lost.

With Game 4 at Cleveland looming in the wings, the Mariners had to win, or their historic season would be over.

Game 4, October 14, at Cleveland

The first postseason do-or-die game for the Mariners was at hand. The game was at enemy territory and there would be a capacity crowd of 45,025 screaming Indian fans spurring on the home team.

It was a rematch of game 1 pitchers – Garcia vs. Colon, but before the game started there was a 2:20 rain delay adding even more tension for the anxious Seattle fans.

Both Garcia and Colon looked sharp early, even though Gonzalez touched Freddy for a solo homer in the 2nd. It was probably the only bad pitch he threw when he was on the hill.

> *Players and rain delays*
> The long wait to start could have made it tougher on the team with the most to lose – Seattle. It wasn't tough for Ichiro. He had brought his pillow from home, propped it up on a training table, and had a little snooze time.

In the meantime, Bartolo Colon was heaving aspirins again, but there seemed to be a quiet confidence, an almost karma-like aura around the Seattle players that let everyone know the M's were going to get to Colon. It wasn't until the 7th inning, and Indian manager Charlie Manuel went with Colon as long as he could, but the Mariners seemed in control after the top of the 7th.

It was vintage 2001 Seattle baseball. John Olerud started the inning with a tremendous at-bat. Colon got ahead at 1-2 in the count, but then if the ball was close, the Puget Sound native fouled it off. Then Colon missed on a few pitches, and Olerud seemed to break the Indian pitcher's concentration as he worked a leadoff walk. A Stan Javier single and Mike Cameron walk loaded the bases. Al Martin pinch-hit for Dan Wilson, and hit a sharp grounder to first. The slightly drawn-in Jim Thome, Cleveland first-sacker, dove and

> MLB Editor, Pat Gallagher, called Aaron Sele the "number 1 key" to the Mariners winning in the post-season. "The Mariners need Sele to get the post-season monkey off his back. Game Three in Cleveland would serve as an opportune time for the 31-year-old hurler and could serve as a momentum builder for the rest of the playoffs, assuming the M's advance." [*Keys in the Mariners – Indians series*, MLB.com, October 8, 2001]

snagged the ball, quickly picked himself up, and threw home for the force out.

A double play got Cleveland out of the inning, and Seattle would squander another opportunity. Former Indian David Bell muscled a fly to left, deep enough to score Javier from third, tying the score. With two outs and two on, in a tie game, Colon would have to face the leading hitter in the league, and a player who was batting over .500 in the season series – Ichiro Suzuki.

Ichiro wasted no time and bounced a seeing-eye single to shallow right scoring another run. Mark McLemore followed suit, singling in yet another run. Colon was done, and the M's had a 3-1 lead.

In the bottom of the 7th, Juan Gonzalez hit one again, but it stayed in the park for a double. After a Thome ground-out, Jeff Nelson came in and threw some wicked sliders. His breaking pitch for the third strike against Ellis Burks was so tough it was uncatchable, and went to the screen. Burks landed on first base, in an unusual passed ball-strike out. Travis Fryman hit into a fielder's choice, scoring Gonzalez. Arthur Rhodes entered for the final out of the inning.

Aone-run lead in the 8th should have given Mariner faithfuls' confidence, but Cleveland's hitters were so prolific, that an extra run couldn't hurt. Seattle complied. In the 8th, Cameron doubled in a run, and in the 9th Martinez homered to score himself and Ichiro, who had hit his third single of the game.

Going into the bottom of the 9th, Juan Gonzalez was leading off again, but Rhodes struck him out looking. Then Kazu Sasaki relieved, and easily disposed of Jim Thome and Ellis Burks, to force a game 5. M's won 6-2.

Game 5, October 15, at Cleveland

There couldn't have been a better circumstance for the Mariners. They were at home and Jamie Moyer was on the mound. That spells W-I-N for the M's.

Moyer was a craftsman again. In six innings of pitching, he gave up three hits and walked one, allowing one run in the process. Moyer was so magic that he struck out the side in the 4th – all of them looking. The ones he kayoed were Juan Gonzalez, Jim Thome and Ellis Burks. Among them, they hit 112 homers and drove in 338 runs during the season. But they were putty in Jamie Moyer's hands.

> "We were going to have a long plane ride back to Seattle. I thought Cleveland might as well have a long ride too." Lou Piniella, after the Game 4 victory

There were 47,867 Mariner fans at SAFECO who all knew that since Moyer was pitching, the Seattle offense would be potent. Chuck Finley started for Cleveland, and in the 2nd inning, loaded the bases with two walks and a hit batsman. Finley then got Dan Wilson and David Bell to strike out, and switch-hitting Mark McLemore came to the plate with two outs, bases still loaded. McLemore batted .169 in the regular season against lefthanders. But never doubt Mark McLemore. He hit a single in the gap in left center scoring two runs to put the M's ahead.

In the Indians 3rd, Moyer gave up a run on the only three hits he would permit. Yet, the inning ended when a frustrated Roberto Alomar grounded into a double play. That is the mark of an at-bat against Jamie Moyer – "frustration."

It became a typical Seattle game from there. Moyer left after six innings, and in came Jeff Nelson. He was superb. Nelson pitched 1 2/3 innings, striking out four. Arthur Rhodes got the lefthanded hitting Kenny Lofton to pop out to short center in the 8th, and Kazu Sasaki set down Vizquel, Alomar and Gonzalez in the 9th – *uno, dos, tres*. It was a quiet ending to a volatile series for the Mariners.

By the way, Ichiro was 3-4 in the game, bringing his series average to .600. M's won 3-1.

Bring on the Yankees!

American League Championship Series

Fans who had braved another all-night vigil for tickets were just part of the Mariner pandemonium as the dreaded Yankees came to town. College students got extra study time in line (or so they would like their mothers to believe). Employees took vacation for the sleepover outside the ticket booth. And neighbors even held a block watch meeting as their dogs devoured pizza, all while in line for Mariner tickets. It only took one hour to completely sell out the 26,000 seats available for the first two games at SAFECO.

There was a friendly bet between the two cities. Seattle Mayor Paul Schell wagered a Seattle vacation, apples and salmon, while New York mayor Rudy Giuliani staked a Times Square vacation, dinner, theater tickets and assorted local foods. Everyone and everything was set. Let the games begin!

Game 1, October 17 at Seattle

"We're going to do what we've done all year. It's worked. Why change it?" – Lou Piniella, 10-16-01, when commenting on the upcoming series with the Yankees.

The series with the Yankees was more like one long game. But there was something more than baseball on the diamond. After September 11, 2001, there was a different spirit that permeated the Yankees. The Yankees were something positive for a city where so much catastrophe had been wrought. All of America – and in fact baseball fans everywhere wanted something good to happen for the city of New York. Unfortunately for the Mariners, the Yankees were that "something good."

> Sunday was supposed to be Yankees Day at the Tokyo Dome. The American national anthem was supposed to be played by a U.S. military band. Public address announcements were supposed to be made in English. One fan was even supposed to win a round-trip airline ticket to New York. Out of respect to those who lost their lives in last Tuesday's terrorist attacks in New York and Washington, D.C., the Nippon Ham Fighters canceled the festivities on Thursday. But the game against the Chiba Lotte Marines was held as scheduled.
> – *Japan Times*, September 17, 2001

The Mariners activated Carlos Guillen for the ALCS. Only a few short weeks before, Guillen had surgery to assist in his recovery from TB. He hadn't played in a game in 19 days, but he had gained back most of the weight he lost from the illness. It was unknown how much of his strength he had regained, though, from months of becoming weaker from TB.

So it was surprising when Guillen's name appeared in the starting lineup in Game 1 hitting in the important # 2 slot. He was 0-3 with a strike out, and made a miscue in the 4th inning that cost the Mariners at least one run. The Yankees' Jorge Posada hit a line drive into the right field corner. Ichiro hustled over to get the ball while Posada, head down, rounded first on his way to second base. Ichiro's rocket arm laced the ball into second base several feet ahead of Posada's slide. But Guillen was out of position and Posada was able to slide around the missed tag.

The 47,644 in attendance vehemently booed the umpire's call, but television replays showed the correct call had been made. The next batter, Paul O'Neill, then ripped a two-run homer into right field to give the visitors a 3-0 lead.

Throughout the month of September and in the extended regular season in October, Mariner manager Lou Piniella repeatedly emphasized that his goal was to get the team ready for the playoffs. Each Mariner would get enough rest to heal minor wounds, but would play enough to maintain timing.

That's why it was also surprising to see Jay Buhner in left field instead of Mark McLemore or Stan Javier. McLemore and Javier were both switch-hitters who each had a solid season for the Mariners. Both were excellent outfielders. While McLemore hadn't hit well against lefthanders, he, like Javier, was a clutch performer.

Buhner had only 45 at-bats during the regular season and only three at-bats in the Cleveland series. He was stinging the ball at times, but didn't appear to have the feel of the game just yet. This was especially worrisome since each player was asked to "pick up his game a level" that is necessary in postseason play.

Andy Pettitte was on the mound for New York, and made Mariner hitters look terrible. Not only did the Mariners not get a hit until the 5th inning, but most Mariner batters were unable to even come close to a hit. An Edgar Martinez single and Mark Cameron double had

Mariners on second and third with nobody out. At the time, the score was 3-0 Yankees, and there was hope among the Mariner faithful that it was rally time. John Olerud hit a grounder to the right side for an out, enabling Edgar to score. Then, Buhner and Dan Wilson struck out swinging, and stranded Cameron in scoring position.

In the meantime, Aaron Sele had control problems. Not only was he walking people (three in six innings), but he was constantly behind hitters in the count. Throughout the season Sele was very stingy with free passes. But this wasn't the Sele who averaged 17 wins in each of the previous four years. This was the Sele of the playoffs, who had never won a postseason game. Against average teams, Sele's efforts could have been a win. But this was the Yankees and this was the playoffs. Giving up seven hits, three walks and three runs in six innings couldn't provide a win on this day. Sele's postseason winless streak continued.

Even if Sele had pitched well, the Mariners only had four hits, and that won't win many games.

The 9th inning was adventuresome for both teams. In the Yankees' half, Alfonso Soriano hit a deep fly to left field off Mariners' reliever Jose Paniagua. Soriano looked up and quickly went into his home run trot. But the ball hit the scoreboard, and the Yankee rookie ended with a single. He eventually scored, but was later seen on the listening end of little chat with Manager Joe Torre in the dugout.

The Mariners did something in their half that few teams do – score a run on Yankee reliever Mariano Rivera. Ichiro hit a one-out double to left, and scored on two wild pitches. It wasn't enough. Yankees won 4-2.

Game 2, October 18 at Seattle

Mike Mussina, probably the best Yankee starter at the time, took the mound for the Yankees, faced by the Mariners' Freddy Garcia. The lineup was back to normal, with McLemore at shortstop and Javier in left, but it didn't make any difference. The Mariners still only managed six hits, and scored their two runs on Javier's two-run homer over the centerfield fence in the 4th inning.

The Mariners' best scoring opportunity was in the 1st inning. Ichiro led off with a single, and after a McLemore flyout, Boone singled to put two runners on base. One of the game's best hitters, Edgar

Martinez came to the plate. He hit a sharp grounder to third, and the Yankees easily had an inning-ending double play.

The M's had another chance in the 3rd when Ichiro led off with a slicing drive to center that Bernie Williams should have caught. Instead, Ichiro landed on second base, the recipient of a two-base error. But McLemore, Boone and Martinez couldn't get him home.

Working on three days rest for only the second time in his career, Seattle's Freddy Garcia continued his pattern of pitching from the regular season – one bad inning. A walk and three hits brought in three Yankee runs in the 2nd. Otherwise, Garcia was solid, giving up just those three runs in 7 1/3 innings. Arthur Rhodes and Jeff Nelson held the Yankees thereafter, but since very few Mariners were even hitting their weights, New York's three runs in the 2nd were as good as 100. Yankees won 3-2.

After the game, the Mariner press conference was poignant. Manager Lou Piniella was adamant. Pounding on the table, he made it clear: "Before you ask any questions, I've got one thing to say. We're coming back to Seattle to play game 6. We've beaten this team [Yankees] five out of six times and we're going to do it again. Print it!"

With that statement, Lou took the pressure off his players. He kept the media out of the player's faces. He made the headlines for his players, who had just lost two straight at home. Afterward, Piniella would say that he didn't mean to manipulate the New York media, but that he was speaking from his heart.

Thank goodness for Lou's heart! The players gained confidence from their manager. "As soon as I heard what Lou told the writers about this series coming back to Seattle for game 6 . . . it is something I like to hear. I know when Lou says something like that, he means it." [*Bret Boone Playoff Diary*, October 18, 2001, MLB.com.] Mark McLemore said it another way. "That's great. He didn't have to say that. We're confident we can do our jobs." But Edgar Martinez said it most succinctly: "When Lou speaks, we all listen."

Going to New York for the next three games, down 0-2, was not a situation the Mariners would ever have believed they would encounter. As Lou had said many times, "In order to beat the Yankees, we must get to their starting pitching." In games 1 and 2, the only hitting you heard from the M's was from their backsides landing on the bench when they sat after making another out.

Game 3, October 20 at New York

It was just a matter of time. It didn't even matter that Mariner pitcher Jamie Moyer permitted a Bernie Williams' two-run homer in the 1st inning. There was just a feel about the game that Seattle would break out of its slump.

Playoff legend Orlando "El Duque" Hernandez was pitching for New York, and it was in the 5th inning that Seattle's hitters finally appeared. Two singles and a walk loaded the bases, and with two outs, Bret Boone came to the plate. The Mariner MVPcandidate was hitting .143 in the 2001 postseason coming into the game, and the M's needed his RBI bat badly. Boone took a 2-1 pitch and hit a flare over the shortstop into left field. The Yankees' Chuck Knoblauch raced in and dove for the ball but came up short. Boone had a single and the Mariners had two runs. It was the first time in the series that Seattle had even tied the Yankees.

In the 6th, John Olerud led off with a homer – another great Olerud at bat where he fouled off several pitches until he found one to his liking. Stan Javier singled, Mike Cameron walked. By then, El Duque was done.

Mike Stanton relieved for New York and threw Dan Wilson's sacrifice bunt into left field. Javier scored, and Cameron and Wilson wound up on second and third. Ichiro came to the plate, ready to extend the Mariners'lead, but Yankee manager Joe Torre ordered an intentional pass. The bases were loaded and Mark McLemore took his place in the righthanded batter's box. The popular "I'll play anywhere as long as I get to hit" McLemore slammed the first Stanton pitch deep in to the gap into left center for a triple scoring all three runners. Bret Boone then hit a blast over the centerfield fence, to give Seattle a 9-2 lead.

Moyer pitched through the 7th, giving up a total of four hits and two runs. The only time there was even a scare was in the 3rd when the Yankees' Soriano hit what should have been a home run. But leftfielder Stan Javier leaped up, extending his glove over the fence, and snatched it away from a fan who had his glove ready to make the catch. Javier gave a glance back at the fan who was sure he had a souvenir as if to say "maybe next time."

Jose Paniagua came in to pitch the 8th for the Mariners. Seattle fans were surprised because Paniagua had been the least effective Mariner on the mound all year. Visions of losing the big lead to the potent Yankee hitters weren't calmed when the Yankees scored a run on three hits and had two men on base when Bernie Williams came to bat. But Williams hit a sharp grounder to Bret Boone, who neatly snagged the ball, tossed to McLemore at second who then fired to first for the inning ending double play. John Halama pitched a perfect 9th. M's won 14-3 on 15 hits.

> Buhner pinch hit for Boone in the 9th inning of Game 3, and hit a rocket out in the park in center field. It was only the second home run to ever reach the centerfield bleachers in the postseason since Yankee Stadium was remodeled decades ago. Reggie Jackson was the first.

Game 4, October 21 at New York

This was the game that broke the Mariners' backs. New York came back to tie in the 8th and win 3-1 in the 9th against the Mariners' two best relievers. Even though after the loss, Seattle was down three games to one, the series was over in the hearts and minds of many Mariner fans, who held but a glimmer of hope. The players spouted all the usual clichés after the loss. "We can't dwell on it. We've got to come out and play [Game 5]," Mike Cameron. "We play one game at a time," Mark McLemore. "It may have sucked something out of us tonight, but tomorrow we'll be fine," Bret Boone.

Skipper Lou Piniella didn't give one of the worn-out quips. Instead he was brutally honest: "This puts us in a precarious position."

From a baseball fan's standpoint it was a great game. Roger Clemens started for New York and Paul Abbott for Seattle. Clemens is a certain, first-ballot hall-of-famer. Abbott is a journeyman. Clemens has won five Cy Young awards. Abbott doesn't even have five complete games. But Paul Abbott proved he had the heart of a lion.

Neither pitcher was sharp inside the strike zone, but both were unhittable. Clemens pitched five innings, giving up only one hit and no runs. He walked four batters, though, and never seemed to be in control of his pitches.

Abbott lasted five innings of no-hit baseball, walking eight but not giving up a run. Some might say that because Abbott walked so many, he didn't pitch well. That wasn't true. As the Atlanta Braves' pitching staff has shown for ten straight years, walking a batter isn't necessarily a bad thing. Paul Abbott proved it wasn't because he wouldn't permit the powerful Yankee hitters anything good to hit. "I wasn't going to throw something down the middle and let them hit it. I wasn't going to give in," said Abbott.

So after five innings of scoreless baseball, both managers let their bullpens take over. Since Seattle had a deeper relief staff, the game favored the Mariners.

Mario Mendoza came in for the Yankees in the 6th and got Boone, Martinez and Olerud out -- 1-2-3. Norm Charlton entered in the 6th for the Mariners and gave up a deep fly ball to Bernie Williams. But Cameron chased it down for the first out. Tino Martinez doubled, and the Mariners walked Posada to set up the double play. Torre sent the righthanded hitting Shane Spencer to bat for Paul O'Neill. Piniella countered by bringing in Jeff Nelson to pitch, clearly showing that even though the game was just in the 6th inning, both managers were treating it as if each inning was the last.

Nelson was extraordinary! He walked Spencer but coaxed Scott Brosius to ground into a double play, preserving the tie.

In the Mariners' 7th, Tom Lampkin worked Mendoza for a two-out walk, but David Bell hit a liner that Mendoza threw up his glove and caught.

In the bottom of the 7th, Nelson was even more superb. He threw wicked pitch after wicked pitch to Soriano, who kept getting just enough of the ball to hit fouls. But then he couldn't catch up to a Nelson blazer and struck out. After a Chuck Knoblauch ground out, Derek Jeter went back to the bench the same way Soriano did, sending the Yankees out to the field.

In the top half of the 8th, Ichiro led off with a grounder to Jeter, who hurried his throw to beat the racing Mariner rightfielder for the first out. Mark McLemore hit a sharp liner to Soriano who leaped to catch it for the second out. Then Bret Boone snapped his popeye-like forearms around a Mendoza fastball and sent a high fly ball to left field. Chuck Knoblauch could only stare up into the sky as the ball sailed over the fence to give the Mariners the lead 1-0.

With just six outs to go and the best bullpen in baseball, it looked like Seattle was going to tie the series.

The first three scheduled hitters for the Yankees were lefthanded. So Piniella brought in Arthur Rhodes to shut them down. David Justice led off, and visions of the 2000 ALCS when Justice hit THE home run off Rhodes danced silently in fans'heads. Not this time, though. Justice struck out with his bat on his shoulder.

Bernie Williams came to the plate, and the count got to 3-1. This was a hitter's count, and Rhodes didn't need to give Williams anything he could drive. But the Mariner lefthander was sharp, getting a swinging strike and then getting a foul ball. The count was 3-2. Nobody was on base. Rhodes looked for the sign from catcher Tom Lampkin. He didn't like what was called, and shook off Lampkin. The sign came again and Rhodes shook him off yet one more time. Or was Rhodes playing a head game with the Yankees' lifetime .305 hitter?

Rhodes stared at Lampkin, who put down 1 finger, patted the catcher's mitt and held up the target. Rhodes wound and threw. Williams swung, and hit a high fly ball to right center field. Ichiro ran back to the wall. Cameron came running over, but neither could get a glove on it. It was too far over the fence.

After the game Rhodes said that Williams hit a good pitch, high and tight, but close to the strike zone. Actually, Rhodes'pitch was a fastball down the middle of the plate. A good major league hitter will take that pitch downtown any day. This was the playoffs and the situation was crucial. *As I watched what was happening between Rhodes and Lampkin I said out loud "I hope he's not shaking off the breaking pitch." [SE]*

Even if Rhodes had thrown a curve in the dirt for ball four, it would have been better than throwing a fat pitch. He had been so good all year. Rhodes'season was one of the best ever for a reliever. His 8-0 record, 1.72 ERA, 83 strikeouts and 46 hits in 68 innings was remarkable. But instead of Justice in 2000, it was Williams in 2001.

The game entered the 9th with a 1-1 tie, and Seattle fans knew that the Yankees had grabbed the upper hand. The home team always has the advantage in a tie game because they get the last at-bat.

Mariano Rivera pitched the 9th for the Yankees. He threw three pitches and got the Mariners out. Some say that Mariner batters were too anxious and should have taken some of Rivera's pitches. That is nonsense. Rivera walked one person every eight innings in the 2001 regular season. He is known to throw first-pitch strikes. In fact, normally, the best chance a batter has against Rivera is on the first pitch. Regardless of when he throws the pitch, though, the Yankees' incredible 32-year old Panamanian reliever is nearly impossible to hit.

In the bottom of 9th, Piniella chose to go with his closer of all year – Kazuhiro Sasaki. The Mariners' 33-year old Japanese reliever had a year that rivaled Rivera's. His splitter was hard to hit but hard to control. His fastball reached the 90's. In the year 2000 Sasaki had given up ten home runs in 62 innings. In 2001 he had improved that to giving up only six homers in 66 innings.

But this was the playoffs.

Spencer ground out to David Bell at third to lead off the bottom of the 9th but Brosius followed with a single. The next batter was rookie Alfonso Soriano. He had been a free swinger most of the season, but was improving. During the regular season he walked only once every 21 times at the plate. It didn't have to be over the plate for Soriano to try to hit it, which caused him to strike out six times as much as he walked.

Sasaki stood on the mound, took a deep breath and threw the first pitch as 56,375 Yankee fans waited. Ball one. The next pitch made Soriano another Yankee hero. Sasaki threw a fastball on the outside part of the plate. Soriano guessed right, went with the pitch, and hit it over the fence in right field.

The game was over. The Mariners' bullpen, the best of any in the 2001 season, had failed. And New York had beaten the best of that great bullpen. Yankees 3, Mariners 1.

"I had a homer hit off me and we lost the same series to Yankees, so I feel more frustration than satisfaction about my season," Sasaki told reporters at Narita Airport.

When asked about his solid performance in the All-Star series, Sasaki, commented, "There were a lot of things that went well, but I don't really remember. In the end, it happened that I had that homer hit off me in the league championship, so disappointment is what I feel the most," said a dejected Sasaki.

Sasaki said he was preparing a quick turnaround and would work on increasing his power for next season.

"After I rest for about a week, I'd like to work out as much as possible and increase my strength. I need to elevate to a World Series level."
- *Japan Times,* October 27, 2001

Game 5, October 22 at New York

The Mariners had one more game to play. They could have come back from a three games to one deficit, but not after the previous game. So, Game 5 of the ALCS was the final game of the season for this historic team.

In a rematch of game 1, Aaron Sele and Andy Pettitte were on the mound. Some questioned whether Sele should start, saying that Garcia could come back on three days rest, or that Joel Pineiro would be better than Sele, who had pitched in five postseason games and had an 0-5 record. But Piniella expressed confidence in his players, reiterating that the M's were going to keep to what they had done all season.

Then Lou benched McLemore and Javier, putting Guillen at shortstop, and played Buhner in right field. Ichiro played left field for the first time all season.

Later, Piniella would say that he felt putting Buhner in right and Ichiro in left made a better fielding outfield for the Mariners in the expansive Yankee Stadium. He added: "Look, Jay and I have been together for nine years, and if you're going to expect loyalty from the players you have to give loyalty. If this was going to be Jay's last game, I wanted it to be in right field."

Game 5 – win or out for the Mariners. It was a disaster. Sele threw hanging curves which the Yankees cheerily pelted. Seattle's fielders looked dazed and confused. After Sele, John Halama found initial success, only to load the bases in the 6th so that Pineiro could come in and allow all three Yankee runners score. Finally, Jose Paniagua came in for an inning so that he could give up a three-run homer to Tino Martinez that may still be going. Yankees 12, Mariners 3.

> **ESPN and KJR's John Clayton, known for his football knowledge, made an interesting observation about the ALCS. "The Yankees are a team made to win games by a score of 2-1. The Mariners are made to win 4-3." Clayton is right. New York's $30 million starting pitching staff was too good for the Mariners to beat. . . . this year.**

For the second straight year, the Yankees had eliminated the Mariners in the American League Championship Series.

The Mariners' season of 2001 ended on a down note. Only one team in the postseason gets to win its last game. The Mariners won 120 games and lost 52 in 2001 – including the regular season and the playoffs. All those wins really did provide the thrill of victory. The Seattle Mariners of 2001 set a new standard for victories and impacted the game in so many ways: new Japanese superstar, "small ball" and loyalty to players and the team were just a few of the memories to cherish.

The loss to the Yankees in the ALCS, unfortunately, showed us that the agony of defeat is real, too. We fans wanted to help Ichiro jump 25 feet in the air to catch Bernie Williams home run. We felt the frustration of not getting on base, or seeing a pitch from the M's get slammed for a hit. We comiserated with Mike Cameron and Dan Wilson as they sat on the bench following Game 5 with TV cameras showing their deep disappointment.

But nothing can replace the historic accomplishments and sheer fun of the 2001 season. As much joy as it was for the players, it was bliss for the fans to bask in the glow of a group who played as a team.

Even though this season is over, we can hardly wait for Spring Training. For baseball fans in Seattle and for Mariner fans around the world, the 2002 season can't get here fast enough.

Chapter Fifteen

Where do we go from here?

"You spend a good piece of your life gripping a baseball and in the end it turns out that it was the other way around all the time."
- Jim Bouton Ball Four

At the trading deadline of the 2000 season, Mariner GM Pat Gillick was looking for a hitter. He came up with Al Martin. Since that time, the M's have continually been in search of another bat. That need could not have been any more obvious than in the 2001 postseason.

But to get quality, the Mariners must give quality. For several years, Seattle has coveted some of the young arms in its farm system. Perhaps now is the time to test those arms, either for the major league club or for another team. If those young pitchers are as good as Seattle management thinks, they will bring the hitters needed in trades.

Ironically, following one of the best seasons any team ever had in the history of the game the Seattle baseball organization has many difficult questions. The first question relates to its prize general manager, Pat Gillick. As this is being written, Gillick has indicated he "is looking forward to the next baseball season," but he won't commit to that season being in Seattle. He's been an integral cog in building the team, and the only place higher to go is to the World Series. Anything less than that will have the natives restless.

In the meantime, several clubs have expressed an interest in acquiring Gillick's services to build their teams.

Whoever is general manager has a tough job. As fans, we're interested. We may even have a voice. The fans must speak about what we learned from the 2001 season, and how the Mariners can improve. As the off-season arrives, the M's have nine free agents.

There <u>is</u> going to be substantial change in the personnel on this team.

The Mariners were the oldest team in baseball in 2001. That is largely an irrelevant fact, though, because so many of the older players were part-time, such as Al Martin, Ed Sprague, Stan Javier and Pat Borders. Actually, having an older team can be optimal because older players are content to fill needed roles.

The skill of the field manager is crucial to having those older players work well with younger talent. Lou Piniella did a masterful job throughout the season. Did he make mistakes? Sure, and we as fans are quick to point them out. Although we don't have to bear the responsibility for our demands, we do pay for the tickets. That gives us the right to fair criticism and there's not a manager around who doesn't get questioned.

One thing is clear: No fan, baseball expert or even player expected the Mariners to win 116 games in 2001. Just because it was done, doesn't mean that the M's will do it again in 2002, or ever again. The last time it was done was before World War I. But the M's must improve in certain positions. Otherwise, the World Series will be a dream, rather than a reality.

Before we consider a future course of action, we must consider the goal. Wallace Mathews, New York sports columnist, commented that the Yankees' victory marked the death-knell of the regular season. Comparing baseball to the NHL, NFL and the NBA, Mathews said that the major league's regular season is now similar to an "undercard fight." He added:

> *"From April to September, the Seattle Mariners weren't just good, they were dominant. ... By reducing the importance of regular season games you reduce the integrity of your league. What's the point of going all out, every game, if you still need to run a gauntlet of teams just to reaffirm your status as the best? . . . The Mariners, who were outplayed, pure and simple, by the Yankees, don't deserve to be mourned. But the integrity of baseball's regular season certainly does." [New York Post, October 23, 2001.]*

In fact, the Yankees have nearly $30 million in their four starting pitchers. Several teams don't have that much money in their entire payroll. This disparity has been discussed many times over in the press, and team owners publicly wring their hands over the "lesser franchises." But until the lords of baseball determine that major league revenues should be shared, it will take a tremendous amount of money to buy a world series championship.

The interesting points that Mathews raised, though, don't account for the fact that the Mariners didn't hit well in the postseason, or that several Mariner pitchers were hammered by the same Yankee hitters that had been putty in their hands only a few months before.

So, like the title of the chapter, **where do we go from here**?

The Mariners have nine free agents: David Bell, Bret Boone, Pat Borders, Jay Buhner, Norm Charlton, Al Martin, Mark McLemore, Aaron Sele, and Ed Sprague. Several of these players were key to the success of the 2001 Mariners and could play similar roles in 2002.

But before we consider the impact of Seattle's free agents on the Mariner lineup, we must review position by position to see where we are. That starts with pitching.

Pitching

Starting Pitching/Long Relief
During the 2001 season, Gillick sought a # 1 starter. Freddy Garcia proved he is well on his way to becoming one of the best pitchers in the league. He needs to take a step up next season and avoid that one bad inning. But look for Freddy to take his place among the elite on the mound in 2002.

Gillick already indicated that the starting four were **Garcia** (age 25), **Moyer** (38), **Abbott** (34) and **Pineiro** (23). Where does that leave Aaron **Sele** (31)? He was 15-5 last year, and has averaged 16 wins and over 200 innings a year for the last five years. But he has to become more reliable in big games. It's one thing to be 0-7 in post-season play and pitch well, like Randy Johnson did before his success in the 2001 posteason. But Sele, at 0-6 in postseason play has pitched poorly in each of those games. He is simply not affordable at $7.5 million. The hard call is that at age 31 Sele may be coming into his best years as a pitcher. More than likely, he will not own a Mariner uniform in 2002.

That leaves Moyer, who proved himself time after time. He will be 39 in the 2002 season. Roger Clemens is 39 too. Moyer will baffle opposing hitters again and win at least 15 games for Seattle next season. The "junk" he throws will extend his career.

Paul Abbott had many unimpressive outings in 2001, but his stock had to rise with his gutty performance in Game 4 of the American League Championship Series against Clemens. If you go strictly on wins-losses, Abbot got paid $1.7 million to go 17-4, and Sele got paid $7.5 to go 15-5. Keep Abbott, especially because he can pitch in long relief.

Joel Pineiro is ready to take his place as a starter in the rotation. He could form a nucleus with Freddy Garcia that would anchor Seattle's starting pitching for years to come.

Many people are down on John **Halama** (29), and should be . . . when he gets the ball up. But when he pitches down in the strike zone, changes speeds and uses his changeup, he's effective. Keep Halama, and make him become Jamie Moyer's shadow. Have him available for spot starting and long relief. Lefthanders are in short supply. Then give him just one more year to make it. If he's traded, the M's have to find a lefthander somewhere.

For the past several years, Mariner fans have been salivating over Gil **Meche** (23) and Ryan **Anderson** (22). Meche has a 12-8 career record with Seattle, and has tremendous potential, but his injury makes him an unknown. He has the arm to be a 200-game winner, but nobody knows. If he makes the major league club, he will need to pitch. Pencil him in as the fifth starter and hope he gets there.

Ryan Anderson is the Randy Johnson look alike with a blazing fast-ball, little control and injured. Sound familiar? He needs one year of pitching where he can work on his mechanics and get himself ready for the major leagues, assuming he can recover from his injury. Keep him at AAA in 2002 and he'll be ready to be a Mariner starter in 2003. What if he surprises everyone and is ready in 2002 because he's worked so hard in the offseason? That's a pleasant problem Mariner management would love to have.

Denny **Stark** (27) was the Pacific Coast League pitcher of the year in 2001. Stark needs the opportunity to pitch every fifth day. He won't get that in Seattle. Perhaps he could be a long reliever, but he is a player who should be used to trade for a hitter.

Ryan **Franklin** (28) had a good year for the M's. Unfortunately for him, he had options left. So he got to be the player who bounced back and forth between Seattle and Tacoma. He throws hard, has good control and could be a winner somewhere else. He's in the same boat with Denny Stark, but Franklin proved his affinity for long relief in 2001. He's valuable in a trade, but a keeper unless a good offer is made.

Bret **Tomko** (28) is in an even worse situation than Stark or Franklin. Tomko needs to pitch every fifth day. He has been an opening day starter in the major leagues. He simply hasn't had a chance to succeed with Seattle. He won't get it in 2002 and it would be best for him to help him find another place to pitch.

Relief Pitching
The pride of the team in 2001, the bullpen core should remain the same in 2002. There is no reason to suspect lesser performances from any of the three key pitchers. In fact they're likely to improve.

Kazu **Sasaki** (33) completed his second year showing he is clearly one of the best closers in the game. But he also showed he's vulnerable to the long ball, especially when he hasn't pitched in several days. He's vowed to work hard to make himself better in the offseason. Bet on it.

Jeff **Nelson** (35) is signed through 2003, and even though he had some lulls in 2001, showed what it's like to pitch in the playoffs. Though he's older than most relief pitchers, he keeps himself in great shape. He does need to work on his control, though. Relievers don't have the luxury of wasting walks, and his breaking pitch became something that batters let go by for a ball too often. He throws in the mid 90's, and it's pretty well known that Bryan Price would like to see him throw more fastballs. Look for another great year out of Nelson in 2002.

Arthur Lee **Rhodes** (32) is reaching the pinnacle of his career. Like Nelson, he's signed through 2003, and he should have another great year next season. But he has to know that he can't throw his fastball by every hitter in every situation. Sometimes a breaking pitch will do just fine. This is a way he will break his playoff jinx.

Norm **Charlton** (38) was a complete surprise for the Mariners in 2001. He served a great role by getting the tough lefthanded hitter out and pitching an occasional inning. Having Norm Charlton is a must if the closing relief staff (Nelson, Rhodes and Sasaki) can be good finishers. That's a given. He's a free agent, loyal to Piniella, and as long as The Sheriff can pitch like he did in 2001, the M's should keep him.

Many times over the past several years, Jose **Paniagua** (28) has been termed the Mariners'closer of future. He's proven just the opposite, though. He's actually gotten worse over the past several years, and was relegated to mop-up duties near the end of the season. He will likely be with another team in 2002.

Position Players

Catchers

Dan **Wilson** (32) and Tom **Lampkin** (37) are both signed for 2002. While they're older for catchers, Piniella used them in such a way as to preserve their knees in 2001. Neither is a great hitter, but Wilson came on strong after a slow start. Lampkin had a down year at the plate, but it's difficult to gain timing with such limited playing time. But the Mariners need more offense out of the catching position. It's not a problem position for 2002, but soon will be. Should the M's go after another catcher now? That's a question that will be asked quickly if neither Wilson nor Lampkin have a good start next season.

Chris **Widger** (30) was hurt all season. He's an unknown. Former World Series MVP Pat **Borders** (38) is a free agent, and the type of player who would be good for the organization, but can be picked up any time during the year – if needed.

1B – The Mariners are set for several years with John **Olerud** (33). He is one of the best glovemen in the game. He's good for a .300 batting average and 90 RBIs. His bat slows late in the season. There is a remote possibility of a change for him. Jason Giambi is a free agent and has indicated a preference to stay on the west coast. If the Mariners were to land Giambi, Olerud could move to leftfield. He has volunteered to do that several times over the past two years to enable Edgar Martinez to be in the lineup against the National League. You would prefer Olerud's glove and first base, but if Giambi were to come to Seattle, Olerud's glove would work very well in left field. If that doesn't happen, Backup first baseman, Ed **Sprague** (34) is a free agent and not likely to be retained.

2B – Bret **Boone** (32) is a free agent. He had probably the best year of any second baseman in the history of the game. Reportedly, he wants a five year deal worth about $10 million/year. At 32, it will be difficult for any team to justify spending that much money on a 36 and 37 year-old infielder. Yes, he was a career .255 hitter going into the 2001 season, but his previous two years showed steady improvement. Since we're spending someone else's money, the Mariners should pull the trigger if Boone will take $10 million/year for three years.

If Seattle can't re-sign Boone, perhaps Mark **McLemore** will be back, or the unproven Ramon **Vazquez** will step up. Willie **Bloomquist**, from AA, probably isn't ready yet.

> "One great thing about baseball is that there is always a tomorrow. My teammates enable me to have a tomorrow."
>
> - Bret Boone
> October 16, 2001,
> MLB.com

SS- Carlos **Guillen** (26) is eligible for arbitration. Some believe he will be the Mariners shortstop for a decade. Others aren't convinced because Guillen is injury prone. Either Vazquez or the young Antonio **Perez** may be the shortstop of the future, but neither is proven. Keep Guillen and pray he stays healthy.

The 2B and SS positions are key to the 2002 season. Unless Boone is re-signed, and Guillen is reliable for an entire season, the M's have only several raw rookies from the farm system to play the positions. It would be unrealistic to expect World Series numbers from new players in the middle of the infield AND the pitchers they support.

3B – David **Bell** (29) is a free agent. He played a Gold Glove third base, but is a .260 hitter. Because he's so good in the field, the Mariners should try hard to keep him. It will surprise some how much interest there will be in Bell over the winter, but as more organizations understand that pitching and defense has replaced the home run in making a good team, players like Bell will become more valuable.

If not Bell, the Mariners are said to be interested in Scott Rolen of Philadelphia. Supposedly he wants out of Philly. He's 26, an excellent fielder, and a .285 hitter. He would be a great addition to the Mariner infield.

RF – What can anybody say? We are all looking forward so much to watching **Ichiro** (28) play for years in right field, that he is a main reason why we can't wait for the 2002 season to begin.

CF – Mike **Cameron** (28) has been better than just about anyone thought he would be after his acquisition from Cincinnati in the Griffey deal. He is a tremendous outfielder and hits with power. But his power numbers don't justify all those strike outs. If he can improve his hitting for next year, he could have a break-out season in 2002.

LF – This was a committee assignment in 2001. Al **Martin** is a free agent and never fulfilled his potential. He's gone. Stan **Javier** has retired. Juan Gonzalez is on the market. He's 32, a power hitter, an adequate outfielder and will cost a bundle. He's exactly what the Mariners need. Can Seattle afford to pay Boone and Gonzalez? Another way to ask that question is: If the Mariners make it to the playoffs in 2002, can we all watch our team crumble again under the force of anybody else's pitching staff?

The answer is that the M's <u>must</u> be an active participant in the Gonzalez sweepstakes.

Mark McLemore (37) would like to be named the full time left fielder. Then, as a free agent, he would stay in Seattle. But can the Mariners guarantee LF to McLemore? He's simply too valuable because he can play so many positions and maintain his hitting. McLemore is 37 but in excellent shape. He's great in the clubhouse and was one of the main reasons why Seattle had such strong team chemistry in 2001. He is an asset to try to retain.

Charles **Gipson** (29) needs a chance to play. He's a great fielder and baserunner, but he's never proven he can hit even his weight. The Mariners proved in the playoffs they needed another hitter, and Charles Gipson couldn't help. Seattle should work with him during the offseason to improve his hitting. If he does, then he's a force in the LF hunt. If he can't show the potential to be a .280 hitter by next year, then he should be allowed the opportunity to develop his talents elsewhere.

Eugene **Kingsale** (25) is a Charles Gipson type waiting in the wings. He's almost as fast and a better hitter. Scott Podsednik (25) debuted in 2001 with a bases loaded double and could compete for an outfield spot in 2002.

Jay **Buhner** (37) is a source of disagreement. Some say let him retire. He's served the Mariners well, and would be a tremendous addition to the organization in some capacity. Others say that he had so little playing time in 2001 due to his injury that he didn't have his timing when he finally was cleared to play. Ultimately, Jay and his body will make that decision.

DH

Edgar **Martinez** (38) is the best to ever play the position. While it may be considered utter heresy to say anything remotely negative about Edgar, there are some realities that must be addressed. He will be paid $10 million in 2002 to hit – and only hit. He has so many injuries that his use will be limited. Unless he hits a screaming line drive, which he often does, anything on the ground is an out, and often a double play. Can Edgar get himself in better shape in 2002 to avoid injuries? Would Edgar be willing to restructure his contract to make it easier to sign Juan Gonzalez?

The DH is the easiest position to fill on a major league roster. Seattle has had a luxury of having the best. Edgar, himself, knows he can provide more to the team than he did in 2001. Most of that involves his own ability to prepare his body better for a long season.

General Manager

Not every move Pat Gillick has made is great, but just about anyone would want his batting average. His professionalism and foresight is a huge asset to Seattle, but his home is in Toronto. It may be difficult to keep him. As of this writing, it's unknown whether Gillick will return in 2002. We should all hope so. If for no other reason, he should want to return to get the hitter he's been looking for since he got here. Besides, Seattle is the only place you can watch Ichiro play 162 games a year.

Where do we go from here? We go to the World Series!

Rob Neyer, sports columnist, posed a question whether the Mariners were a dynasty in the making. *[ESPN.com, October 8, 2001]* A decade ago, Seattle fans believed that a 4th place finish was good. Now, we fans expect the playoffs. The bar has been raised forever as to Seattle baseball. That's the price management pays for being good.

The turnaround started with Lou Piniella. It continued with Howard Lincoln and has reached its highest point with Pat Gillick.

Seattle hasn't achieved the top yet, but is readily recognized as one of the best organizations in baseball. It will be challenging to maintain that level in the front office and improve the team on the field. The promise of better hitting must be fulfilled. From the major league roster all the way down to the rookie leagues, the Mariners have solid pitching. If better hitting is somehow acquired, the Mariners really are a dynasty in the making.

But before the word "dynasty" can be attached to the M's, there must first be a World Series ring. If the 2000 season was preparation for 2001, then this magical, just-completed 116-win season, was preparation for the World Series in 2002. It will be done on the backs of Freddy Garcia and Jamie Moyer, with relief from Nelson-Rhodes-Sasaki. Ichiro will lead off with an infield single. Mike Cameron will cure his swing-and-miss ills and double Ichiro home. Then Edgar will powder the pitch to the wall, driving home Cammy.

We're ready for Opening Day. **Where does the line for World Series tickets form?**

That is where we go from here.

2001 Mariner Hitting Statistics

Name	GP	ab	r	h	2B	3B	hr	rbi	bb	so	sb	obp	avg
Borders	5	6	1	3	0	0	0	0	0	1	0	.500	.500
Suzuki	157	692	127	242	34	8	8	69	30	53	56	.381	.350
Kingsale	10	15	4	5	0	0	0	2	2	2	2	.444	.333
Boone	158	623	118	206	37	3	37	141	40	110	5	.372	.331
Martinez	132	470	80	144	40	1	23	116	93	90	4	.423	.306
Olerud	159	572	91	173	32	1	21	95	94	70	3	.401	.302
Sprague	45	94	9	28	7	0	2	16	11	18	0	.374	.298
Javier	89	281	44	82	14	1	4	33	36	47	11	.375	.292
McLemore	125	409	78	117	20	3	5	57	67	78	39	.384	.286
Cameron	150	540	99	144	30	5	25	110	69	155	34	.353	.267
Wilson	123	377	44	100	20	1	10	42	20	69	3	.305	.265
Bell	135	470	62	122	28	1	15	64	28	59	2	.303	.260
Guillen	90	308	48	80	18	0	5	53	31	62	4	.333	.259
Abbott	2	4	0	1	0	0	0	0	0	1	0	.250	.250
Martin	100	283	41	68	15	2	7	42	37	59	9	.330	.240
Vazquez	17	35	5	8	0	0	0	4	0	3	0	.222	.229
Lampkin	79	204	28	46	10	0	5	22	18	41	1	.309	.225
Buhner	19	45	4	10	2	0	2	5	8	9	0	.340	.222
Gipson	94	64	16	14	2	2	0	5	4	20	1	.282	.219
Sanders	9	17	1	3	2	0	0	2	2	3	0	.263	.176
Sele	3	6	2	1	0	0	0	1	2	0	0	.282	.167
Podsednik	5	6	1	1	0	1	0	3	0	1	0	.167	.167
Garcia	2	7	0	1	0	0	0	0	0	4	0	.143	.143
Moyer	1	1	0	0	0	0	0	0	0	0	0	.000	.000
Charlton	1	1	0	0	0	0	0	0	0	1	0	.000	.000
Rhodes	3	1	0	0	0	0	0	0	0	0	0	.000	.000
Nelson	3	0	0	0	0	0	0	0	0	0	0	.000	.000
Paniagua	3	0	0	0	0	0	0	0	0	0	0	.000	.000
Halama	1	1	0	0	0	0	0	0	0	0	0	.000	.000
Franklin	1	1	0	0	0	0	0	0	0	0	0	.000	.000
Sasaki	2	0	0	0	0	0	0	0	0	0	0	.000	.000
Fuentes	3	0	0	0	0	0	0	0	0	0	0	.000	.000
Totals	162	5680	927	1637	310	38	169	881	614	989	174	.360	.288

2001 Mariner Pitching Statistics

Name	GP	GS	W	L	S	CG	IP	H	R	ER	HR	BB	K	ERA
Rhodes	71	0	8	0	3	0	68.0	46	14	13	5	12	83	1.72
Pineiro	17	11	6	2	0	0	75.1	50	24	17	2	21	56	2.03
Nelson	69	0	4	3	4	0	65.1	30	21	20	3	44	88	2.76
Charlton	44	0	4	2	1	0	47.2	36	19	16	4	11	48	3.02
Garcia	34	34	18	6	0	4	238.2	199	88	81	16	69	163	3.05
Sasaki	69	0	0	4	45	0	66.2	48	24	24	6	11	62	3.24
Moyer	33	33	20	6	0	1	209.2	187	84	80	24	44	119	3.43
Franklin	38	0	5	1	0	0	78.1	76	32	31	12	24	60	3.56
Sele	34	33	15	5	0	2	215	216	93	86	25	51	114	3.60
Abbott	28	27	17	4	0	1	163	145	79	77	21	87	118	4.25
Paniagua	60	0	4	3	3	0	66	59	35	32	7	38	46	4.36
Fuentes	10	0	1	1	0	0	11.2	6	6	6	2	8	10	4.63
Halama	31	17	10	7	0	0	110.1	132	69	58	18	26	50	4.73
Tomko	11	4	3	1	0	0	34.2	42	24	20	9	15	22	5.19
Stark	4	3	1	1	0	0	14.2	21	15	15	5	4	12	9.20
Totals	162	162	116	46	56	8	1465	1293	627	576	160	465	1051	3.54

Hitting legend: GP - Games Played; ab - at bats; r-runs; h-hits; 2B-doubles; 3B-triples; hr-home runs; bb-walks; so-strikeouts; sb-stolen bases; obp-on base percentage; avg-batting average

Pitching legend: GP - Games Played; GS - Game started; W-wins; L-losses; S-saves; CG-complete games;IP-innings pitched; h-hits; r-runs; er-earned runs; hr-home runs; bb-walks; k-strikeouts; ERA-earned run average

Mariner Autograph Section

Paul Abbott _____

David Bell _____

Bret Boone _____

Pat Borders _____

Jay Buhner _____

Mike Cameron _____

Norm Charlton _____

Ryan Franklin _____

Brian Fuentes _____

Freddy Garcia _____

Charles Gipson _____

Carlos Guillen _____

John Halama _____

Stan Javier _____

Eugene Kingsale _____

Tom Lampkin _____

Al Martin _____

Edgar Martinez _____

Mark McLemore _____

Jamie Moyer _____

Jeff Nelson _____

John Olerud _____

Jose Paniagua _____

Joel Pineiro _____

Scott Podsednik _____

Arthur Rhodes _____

Anthony Sanders _____

Kazu Sasaki _____

Aaron Sele _____

Ed Sprague _____

Denny Stark _____

Ichiro Suzuki _____

Brett Tomko _____

Ramon Vazquez _____

Dan Wilson _____

About the Authors

Stan Emert grew up in the southeastern part of the United States as an Atlanta Braves fan. "The Braves weren't too good, then, but were a fun team to watch. Rico Carty played left field and turned every fly ball into an adventure. But could he hit!"

A business development and strategic marketing consultant, Emert formerly practiced law in the eastern US. He also serves as an assistant basketball coach at Lakeside High School in Seattle.

Mike Siegel is a nationally known talk show host who has worked primarily in current events. He grew up in the New York area as a Brooklyn Dodgers fan. "My heart was broken when the Dodgers moved to Los Angeles until 1995. Then the Seattle Mariners won me for life!"

Siegel has hosted programs in Seattle and other major U.S. markets, as well as several nationally syndicated programs.